REBELLION

ESSAYS 1980-1991

MINNIE BRUCE PRATT

Other books by the author:

Crime Against Nature
We Say We Love Each Other
Yours in Struggle (co-author)
The Sound of One Fork

REBELLION
ESSAYS 1980-1991

MINNIE BRUCE PRATT

Firebrand
Books
Ithaca, New York

Several of these essays have appeared in earlier versions in the following books and periodicals: *The American Voice, Bridges, Feminary, Frontiers, Gay Community News, InVersions: Writing by Dykes, Queers and Lesbians* (Press Gang-Canada), and *Yours in Struggle: Three Feminist Perspectives on Anti-Semitism and Racism* (Firebrand Books/Long Haul).

Book and cover design by Betsy Bayley
Typesetting by Bets Ltd.

Printed in the United States on acid-free paper by McNaughton & Gunn

Library of Congress Cataloging-in-Publication Data

Pratt, Minnie Bruce.
    Rebellion : essays, 1980–1991 / Minnie Bruce Pratt.
      p.   cm.
    Includes bibliographical references.
    ISBN 1–56341–007–9 (cloth). — ISBN 1–56341–006–0 (paper)
    I. Title.
  PS3566.R35R4   1991
811'.54—dc20   91–35238
                                                      CIP

Acknowledgments

Many people have helped me think through and write this work, and I acknowledge them, with thanks, in the essays that follow. Here I thank, with special gratitude, Joan E. Biren (JEB) whose vision of living as a lesbian artist inspired me to attempt this in my own life, and who has given me invaluable political analysis, brilliant editorial comments, and a loving, challenging relationship for the last ten years. My deep appreciation also to my editor and publisher, Nancy K. Bereano, for her continued confidence in, and support of, my work; her belief in the power of words helps keep me writing. Thank you to Biddy Martin whose encouragement helped me begin this book. I could not have finished this work without the much-needed computer counseling of Laura Nichols and Linda Martin, and without other helpful technical assistance and support from Nanette Gartrell and Dee Mosbacher, Michael Martin, and Joyce Kornblatt—heartfelt thanks to all of them.

This book was supported in part by a grant from the National Endowment for the Arts.

Contents

Rebellion 9

Identity: Skin Blood Heart 27

"I Plead Guilty to Being a Lesbian" 83

My Mother's Question 111

When the Words Open 125

The Friends of My Secret Self 139

Books in the Closet, in the Attic,
    Boxes, Secrets 151

Money and the Shape of Things 167

Watching the Door 187

The Maps in My Bible 191

Poetry in Time of War 227

Rebellion

May 26th, 1861—They look for a fight at Nor-folk. Beauregard is there. I think if I were a man I'd be there too.

June 27th, 1861—This Spotswood is a miniature world. The war topic is not so much avoided. . . . A Richmond lady told me under her breath that Mrs. Davis had sent a baby's dress to her friend Mrs. Montgomery Blair in Washington and Mrs. Blair had responded: "Even if the men kill one another, we will abide friends to the bitter end, the grave."

> Mary Boykin Chesnut,
> *A Diary from Dixie*

Every spring in Mrs. Alice Meigs' class we wrote an essay for the UDC contest; that was in the late 1950s when I was in the seventh, eighth, and ninth grades in Bibb County, Alabama. UDC was the United Daughters of the Confederacy; the local chapter was named after William Pratt, a great-uncle of mine who served as a colonel in The War Between the States (which we *never* called the Civil War because we believed in the rule of the States, not in the Union). Most of the older women I knew were Daughters—Mrs. Sarah Williams, for

This essay was first published in "Being Disobedient," a special issue of *Feminary: a Feminist Journal for the South, Emphasizing the Lesbian Vision*, vol. 11, no. 1–2 (1980).

instance, and her unmarried sister, Miss Bessie Bagby. They went to my church and lived in the house on the curve at the top of town hill, with a green parrot on the porch that screamed at me when I walked by. The Daughters got together once a month at someone's house to talk and knit or tat, sometimes to hear the war letters of a cousin or grandfather, and to eat cheese straws and drink punch afterwards, almost like Presbyterian sewing circle, except that was at night and they had Bible lessons instead.

The Daughters sponsored the Essay Contest and celebrated Confederate Memorial Day every spring in school assembly. One year they presented a medal to my cousin, Alsey Pratt, Jr. I don't know why they gave him the medal. Maybe it was because he was a doctor and a Pratt and hadn't left but had come back home to practice medicine. Despite, or perhaps because of, the fact that he knew people so well he could diagnose any disease in town just by looking you in the eye, he took to drink and drugs; his office burned down; he had a car wreck on the way to Tuscaloosa and became bedridden. He started reading the Koran just before he died, and we thought he had turned into a heathen as well as a degenerate. We prayed for him at church. A one-man lost cause. But the UDC ladies kept putting wreaths at the foot of the stone soldier in front of the courthouse on the square. Its inscription still reads:

> To Our Confederate Heroes
>
> These were the men who by the simple manhood of
>   their lives
> By their strict adherence to the principles of right
> By their sublime courage and unspeakable sacrifices
> Have preserved for us through the gloom of defeat
> A priceless heritage of honor.
> When the call came they left all for the front
> And for four years without recompense or reward
> They fought bravely for local self government
> And the rights of the state.
> Many of whom gave all, and all of whom gave much.

I wanted to be a hero too. I could have joined the Children of the Confederacy—Em and Claude Hornsby did, but then their mother was from Montgomery. Anyway, I would still have been a child. So I read books like *Four Years With Marse Robert* and wrote essays on Stonewall Jackson and on the Confederate Navy. And on the Heroines of the Confederacy.

I was a very good child, but I speculated about being a rebel. I was obedient at school, got perfect grades, went to church three times a week, and read the Bible every day. When I got older, I hardly ever dated, never talked back to my mother or father, never came home late. No one would have called me willful. But I imagined what it was like to fight with Jackson, to go on a forced march with him in the Valley, or on a charge in the Wilderness, his stern, lean face bent over Little Sorrel, a dusty campaign cap pulled down over his piercing grey eyes, intensely concentrating his will on the given task. (He was a Presbyterian too.) He never gave up on what he wanted. He had a memorandum book in which he penned the rules of his life: "Disregard public opinion when it interferes with your duty. . . . Be truthful in all things. . . . You can be what you want to be. . . . Govern yourself." He had a wife, but she was an interrupter and sickly, always complaining. He, on the other hand, ate standing up to improve his digestion and maintain his alertness. I wanted to be like Jackson.

Growing up, I lived with a father who regularly became disgusted with himself and drunk. He was a brilliant man who believed devoutly that the Catholic-Communist-Jewish conspiracy was trying to overthrow segregation. He worked as a sort of clerk (even now I'm not sure what he did) in a local sawmill owned by Brady Belcher. Meanwhile, I took tenth-grade American history, in which we never got beyond the Spanish-American War, because we rushed through the American Revolution and spent most of the year on The War. We learned, again, that this war was not over slavery but over states' rights.

I heard, but paid little attention to, stories told by my grandmother Ora about her childhood during the Reconstruction, except for the parts about the Choctaws coming to trade their baskets for flour and sugar. She was raised by her mother, MaMa Carr, who was widowed and took care of her husband's father. While MaMa cooked, he would lean against the mantelpiece and tell his story about lying down one night at bivouac in Petersburg, Virginia, only to wake up the next morning covered with snow. MaMa raised a handful of children by keeping a boardinghouse in Pushmataha, Alabama, for drummers, the traveling salesmen who rode through on their way to Meridian. There was no money. Every woman in our family knows that MaMa Carr could make the most elegant dessert out of nothing but day-old biscuits, milk, sugar, and cinnamon.

May 6th, 1862—To wear the color of slaves is the worst. The misery of poverty is alike everywhere; many a person can be beaten with many stripes, by his own family, his father or mother, his schoolmaster, his superior officer by land or sea, his master if he is an apprentice, her husband if she be a woman, everybody who chooses, if she be a child. Wherever there is a cry of pain, I am on the side of the one who cries.

I did not understand, until years after I had left home, that the heroes I worshipped for their individual willful pursuit of honor and right were men who were doing this for *their* rights, for the rights of white men; that it was very true that The War had been fought for states' rights, but that this was the same as fighting it for slavery, since at issue was the right of the white men who ran the Southern states to maintain their rule over Black men and women, and white women, too; that some were kind, thoughtful, gallant, even principled men in their way, but they still were not going to give up power and control of their "rights." I did not see until years later that while I admired those dead heroes, the living men around me were miserable; that the heroes had fought not for change but for the right to keep things the way they were; that, in fact, every war I knew of that had ever been fought was between two sets of men, each wanting to run things their way. I fantasized about the Great Rebellion because I wanted some vicarious motion, change, control of my life, but this was a delusive daydream, one that white people of the old Confederacy had been caught in since before The War, the daydream, the romance of rebellion, the breaking out of the nightmare of slavery, race hatred, economic differences, sex differences. This was a romance because the act of rebellion satisfied the need for change while the values which were defended, those of white male supremacy, remained the same.

I was fascinated by Jackson and Lee and Stuart because I was confined in my life as a white woman, as a girl; they fulfilled my great need to move, to rebel, to change, without my having to change at all; their obsession with will attracted me because I was allowed a will only in regard to those "below" me, Black men and women, and later, children. I was not encouraged to consider using my will against those white men who determined how things were. Such use of the will was never discussed in my home: the will that was valued was the will of the dead heroes, the will for things to remain the same. I realized years later that my mother and grandmothers and great-grandmothers had been heroines, in one way, and had used their will to grit their teeth and endure, to walk through the ruins, blood, and mess left by men.

I understood finally that this heroic will to endure is still not the same as the will to change, the true rebellion.

November 8th, 1861—There was a striking picture upstairs. A perfect beauty is an uncommon sight and here was one; nobody denies that. It is her profession, and yet she can't bear to go out and show herself. She is as beautiful as flesh and blood ever gets to be, and she is always exquisitely dressed. Today it was soft mull muslin, all fluffy and fluted and covered with Valenciennes lace. She said she did not expect to ask anyone into her room and she did not mean to leave it. She was in a terrible fret. The trimming they had brought her from Camden to finish her baby's fine frock did not suit her taste at all. We had a few minutes' polite conversation on immaterial subjects, and I left her as I found her, in a rage of disappointment about the trimming.

July 3, 1862—When the six girls troop in, I wonder if a handsomer group was ever collected in one room. If it were not for this horrid war, how nice it would be here. We might lead such a pleasant life. This is the most perfectly appointed establishment, such beautiful grounds, such flowers, and fruits.

When I was growing up I would go once a week to my Uncle Francis' house to visit Andrea and Hattie. He was my father's brother; they were the sisters of his wife. They had some mysterious disease of the nervous system, and Andrea had been confined to a wheelchair since her middle teens, Hattie a little later. They were in their fifties when I knew them. Hattie only came for a visit for a few months during the year; she was plumper than Andrea, more merry, and spent a lot of time doing crossword puzzles. Andrea was very thin, and she spoke so softly that I had difficulty understanding her. Her feet fascinated me; they rested, slightly swollen and white, in low-cut black shoes. I tried to understand that she couldn't move them.

They lived in an L-shaped room built onto the small main house and never left it except for journeys to the kitchen for meals or to the living room for a brief visiting hour with Aunt Mary in the afternoon. Uncle Francis would wheel them in, and they had the highest praise for his gentleness and patience. No other men came into their room. When I went there, it was quiet; there was no sound, except perhaps for the scratch of Hattie's pencil and the bees in the yellow roses climbing on the porch screen.

Andrea would catechize me on my week. Had I done any housework? Yes. What? Vacuuming, dusting. Had I dusted under everything? Had I lifted each object and dusted under it? Well, no. She pointed out that although this dusting might look right to another's eye, *I* would know that there was still dust there. She was quite alarmed when, as I approached my teens, I started to ride my bicycle to the small town across the river bridge, where there was a public library. She asked me at each visit if I had been careful. She found it very upsetting that I went by way of the traveled road (the only way over the bridge) with trucks passing by. She asked if I was not nervous about the noise, the trucks, if I looked carefully. I didn't understand why she felt my trips to the library were dangerous, the same way I didn't understand why, about this time, my mother began to insist that I wear shoes when I went up to town (*shoes* in the summer), or why she began to say my cousin and I were too old to ramble around by ourselves. This made no sense to me at all.

I enjoyed standing on the bridge at 8:00 A.M. on a June morning, the sun beginning to burn hotly down my neck, to watch the turtles sunning on dead logs jammed up against the shore. There were old ones as big as platters, on down to small turtles the size of my hand. Every once in a while a turtle that had gotten hot enough would push itself off into the water; I was too high to hear the plop, but I knew how cool the water was. I wanted to jump off the bridge into the water but I never admitted this to myself. It was too improbable. As I got older, I became uncomfortably aware of how exposed I felt leaning against the rail, watching the turtles; I wore shorts, and the log trucks driven by sawmill men passed within a foot of me. Sometimes the men yelled strange unintelligible remarks at me.

By the time I got to the library, found my books, and started back home, it was usually very hot, in the nineties at ten o'clock in the morning. Even if I got some water at the library, I was thirsty before half the way was done. I would stop at the Dairy Queen next to the Southern Belle Motel to get water, because they had an outside fountain so I didn't have to ask anyone for it. Actually, they had two outside fountains, one marked *White* and the other marked *Colored*. I had gone my entire life to segregated schools (I was then about thirteen) and had been raised by a Black woman who always sat in another room while we ate the food she cooked. I had never crossed the color line knowingly, certainly did not think of it as a barrier that should be breached, only thought of it as one of the natural boundaries of my life, like the river bridge or the steep hill I had to push my bike up to get home. But one library trip, when I stopped to get water, without thinking about it at all, I went to the *Colored* water fountain (one of the rusty porcelain kind with a metal spring handle) and took a quick but deliberate drink. I did not tell anyone I had done this, and put it out of my mind almost as soon as I got home. But I know that right after I had taken this drink I was puzzled that there was no change, nothing was different around me. The water had just tasted like water.

July 24th, 1864—Mrs. Kirkland discomfits the natural village curiosity. She will see no one, literally; not even her father. . . . Kirkland died the 19th. . . . The Judge says it is all nonsense, her refusing to come downstairs; but he refuses to go up to her room, so they have not met. He is devoted to her children, and his wife brings him full accounts of his daughter. She goes upstairs, dear old soul.

November 25th, 1864—Becky Wallace dilated upon the doctor's horror of our actual condition. He "wished she was dead and that his daughter had never been born." Mrs. W. was calm and serene; she would take refuge in the insane asylum of which her father is the head. She knew no Yankees would venture there, and it was bomb proof. She added: "But Mr. Petigru says all South Carolina is an insane asylum. That will not save us from fire and sword."

I joined a sorority when I went off to college. This was the University of Alabama at Tuscaloosa, in 1964, a couple of years after Wallace had "stood in the schoolhouse door," and the federal government had desegregated it anyway. But this and the civil rights marches and the violence seemed to me to be happening in another country; they had nothing to do with me.

My sorority initiation, which was based on the Eleusinian mysteries, was the first religious experience I ever had. I was led, after a secret password, into the darkened den, which had been cleared of furniture, the TV draped, and was filled instead with women in white, in a circle, each holding a candle. Into a great stillness one of the hierophants read the ceremony, while I was led around the circle, in a pattern that duplicated the descent into Hades by Kore/Persephone and her rebirth. At one point during the chanting I had to lie on the floor and be covered by a green cloth. This was my death and burial. When the cloth was lifted, I was welcomed solemnly into the sisterhood. I felt some power or energy tremble inside me, and was happy.

What we did together as sisters, in addition to the ceremonies and individual friendships that we developed, was to compete with other sororities for the highest grades, the most beauties, the most wins in women's sports, and the most girls pinned or engaged to KA's (or SAE's). In the fall we added new members through rush: a woman interested in joining visited each sorority in a scheduled round of parties, then was invited back if the sorority was interested in her. To get ready for rush we had to learn to recognize girls we already knew we wanted, because of their families or grades or looks. All of us, forty or so, would sit in the dining room with a slide projector, shouting out names as high school graduation pictures flashed up on the wall: "Hitsy Parnell!" (She was really Wilhemina.) "Carol Self!"

The first day of parties was ice-water teas, called so because of the brutal September weather, ninety-five degrees and we were all in girdles and stockings. The rushees streamed through a house every fifteen minutes all day with only time for a glass of cold water, while we went through "rotation," our system for passing the girls around, *always* being cordial to each one, but, of course, able to talk so much more easily to our favorites because we knew their faces, their hometowns, hobbies, and grade-point averages. There were sixteen sororities on campus then, two of which were for Jewish women, who always came through rush on ice-water tea day, but then never came back. They were not issued invitations; the question was never raised in the dining room when we discussed who we wanted to see again. Since I had been brought up in a family where the Catholic-Communist-Jewish conspiracy was a fact of life, I found this perfectly natural. But in my junior year, the first Black woman came through rush. This was a shock. We were gathered into the dining room and told by our advisors that the Black woman would be in the house on ice-water tea day, that we were to be very nice to her since she did not know what she was doing and was merely being used by other people. I found out later that after she came through the line, where we all shook her hand, and smiled, and said hello and her name (looking at her name tag, since her face was not one we had flashed on our screen), she was taken out of rotation by two other junior women, at the instruction of our alumni advisor. They talked at the courtyard window for the fifteen minutes of the party. I never learned what they talked about. I don't remember her name. She, of course, was not asked back.

During this time, I worked on the college literary magazine, which was otherwise staffed by men, all admirers of the poetry of Allen Tate, John Crowe Ransom, Robert Penn Warren. In their essays and their poetry, the Fugitives embalmed the past of the South, making a strange macabre glory out of defeat. I read Tate's "Ode to the Confederate Dead":

> *You know the unimportant shrift of death*
> *And praise the vision*
> *And praise the arrogant circumstance*
> *Of those who fall*
> *Rank upon rank, hurried beyond decision—*

and believed it still. Here were the heroes, dead in the last century, the last people who were able to act. And that was what poets of the South, who were all male poets, wrote about: the men who were dead heroes. I went to literary parties, and listened to men talk about the Fugitives, and got a thrill when I heard them sing:

> *Oh, I'm a good old Rebel,*
> *Now that's just what I am;*
> *For this "fair land of freedom!"*
> *I do not give a damn.*
> *I'm glad I fit against it,*
> *I only wish we'd won.*
> *And I don't want no pardon*
> *For anything I've done.*

Even though I had never done anything unpardonable in my life.

I was still very good, very quiet. I was dating one of the men on the literary magazine, but I never went with him to his apartment. Visiting a man, whether you were a woman over or under twenty-one, was grounds for getting kicked out of school, as was drinking if you were under twenty-one. Some of the other women in the sorority defied the rules. Mary Ann Stone, for instance, swore constantly and loudly. (She was from Texas.) She also left bloody tampons on the floor of her room, which the maid had to clean up. Once she and her current boyfriend stole the sacred robes from the basement, where we usually held ceremonies, put them on, and rode by on his motorcycle, shouting and flapping, as we all stood and sang outside after supper. I did not like Mary Ann Stone; she was too loud and drank too much, probably peach brandy, and she sneaked out at night, after the house was closed, to be with her boyfriends.

One night in the spring of my sophomore year I set my alarm for four in the morning. I was in love, the pear trees were blossoming in the Baptist cemetery, and I wanted to get up and see the sun rise, walk out to the Quadrangle, and watch it rise through the lines of oaks just fringing out in green. Earlier in the spring the man I was dating had taken me to the top of the Art building at twilight, had shown me how to climb the rough board stairs to the coppered roof. We sat and watched the sunset, peach and magenta over the oak trees, still bare-branched, and the lamps coming out like lightning bugs below. So I had set my alarm for 4:00 A.M. to see the sun come up, alone. When the clock went off in the thick spring blackness, I got up, dressed, and hurried downstairs. Only when I reached the double, carved front doors did I realize, did I remember, that if I opened the doors, an alarm would go off. We were locked in every night, and we knew it was to keep us in (away from men). But I had never wanted to stay out all night with a man, and had never realized that the doors could keep me from going out alone, to do something I wanted to do *alone.* I stood there for a long time with my hand on the door, but I knew that if I walked out the alarm would go off, the campus police would come, red lights flashing, and I would have to run on the back ways to get to the Quadrangle without getting caught, and even then, I would be out alone in its expanse, no one else around at that time of the morning (which had been the point, after all.) They would easily see me, and what would I say? *"I just wanted to see the sun rise, alone"?* They would never believe me.

I went back upstairs and sat on my bed and watched the brick walls of the Zeta house across the way get pinker and pinker in the growing light. In the winter I married the man I was dating, one of the two poets on the magazine. (I was the third, but neither they nor I believed that). I stopped writing when I married, but my feeling far, far down, floating and never thought and never said was, *"Now I can go outside when I want to."*

March 3rd, 1861—I have seen a Negro woman sold upon the block at auction. I was walking. The woman on the block overtopped the crowd. I felt faint, seasick. The creature looked so like my good little Nancy. She was a bright mulatto with a pleasant face. She was magnificently gotten up in silks and satin. . . . I dare say the poor thing knew who would buy her. My very soul sickened. It was too dreadful. I tried to reason. "You know how women sell themselves and are sold in marriage, from queens downwards, eh? You know what the Bible says about slavery, and marriage. Poor women, poor slaves."

April 19th, 1865—One year ago, we left Richmond. The Confederacy has double-quicked down hill since then. Burned towns, deserted plantations, sacked villages! / "You seem resolute to look the worst in the face," said General Chesnut wearily. / "Yes, poverty, no future, no hope." / "But no slaves, thank God," cried Sally.

When I went home this spring, my mother and father, who are now in their seventies and eighties, had a Black man come by to mow their lawn. They, very sincerely, "think the world of him"; his name is Henry James. While he was mowing the lawn, my mother took a pitcher of ice-water and a glass out to him. He came to the door once to get a match for a cigarette. He never came in the house. It was not discussed; it was not thought of. There were no words exchanged; it was just done.

And I saw again what I had been taught all my life: who to let in and who to keep out. Until not so very long ago, I did not know that I was being kept in also, and thought of a house only as shelter. I did not even think of what I and my mother and other women were doing when we agreed, silently, unconsciously, to wear shoes of a certain style in certain places, to walk only in certain places at certain times, to accept without much question what was going on outside our home, the doings of white men, to accept Jewish women or Black women into our homes only in certain rooms under certain limited circumstances.

These limits of manners and custom seemed natural to me; and if I felt twinges of dissatisfaction, the only women that I saw break these boundaries seemed to me to rebel like men, with drinking, cursing, dirt, random sex. This disgusted me. They did not seem to like other women, or themselves much, and I did, having been raised by older parents in a rural area where the Victorian segregation of the sexes was still maintained, and where a separate women's culture was still real. If I were to rebel, I had to be able to do so and keep my self-respect and my love of women. Feminist and lesbian theory finally gave me an analysis to understand when and why women got kept in or kept out, and why I should rebel against this *because* of self-respect.

But after a time in the movement I began to see some disturbing similarities to my sorority, in my behavior and that of my feminist sisters. It's true that we wore more denim, and talked about racism and classism and sexism, but somehow, still, there were certain people, like the women who worked in the local chicken processing plant, who were never in the room when we held our meetings.

It was about this time that I began an effort to remember the streets and stores in the town where I grew up, the places where I could and couldn't walk alone, the doors that were for me, and the doors that were for Black men and women. I began to try to remember the limits that were as charged as electric fences, and even now are so hard to remember, since I didn't touch them *then*. I began to try to see what limits I accept now, without thinking, and try deliberately to touch them. I always know when I do: there is the pain, the shock, the disapproval, and the alarm of the others around me.

March 1st, 1861—Went to pay my respects to Mrs. Jefferson Davis. She met me with open arms. We did not allude to anything by which we were surrounded. We eschewed politics and our changed relations.

March 22nd, 1861—There was tragedy on the way home from Montgomery; a mad woman taken from her husband and children. Of course she was mad, or she would not have given her grief words in that public place. Her keepers were along. What she said was rational enough, pathetic, at times heartrending. It excited me so I quietly took opium. It enables me to retain every particle of mind or sense or brains I have, and so quiets my nerves that I can calmly reason and take rational views of things otherwise maddening.

My grandmother Ora and great-aunt Janie and my aunts Lethean, Evie, and Ora Gilder, and my mother Virginia could and can talk. They tell stories about any small event that floats by through their days: the best place to find Jerusalem artichokes, the night Evie dreamed she was a carrot, the day the Ellison sisters used the binoculars. But the hidden depths of their lives, and the lives of the people who live down in the Quarters or in Four Points by the sawmill: they do not make stories of these happenings. Under the rippling surface of their stories is a deep, deep silence, deeper than the deepest part of Schultz Creek, where we went to swim in the summer, and colder than any part of its spring-fed stream. I knew that at the bottom of this depth were things as sharp as the limestone ridges in the creek, which would slice my hand or foot if I touched them unwarily. At the bottom of the silence were things too dangerous to talk about. But Mama just said that she didn't like to gossip.

When I was fifteen and learning to drive our green '54 Chevy, my mother let me practice by taking her out in the county on her visits to her clients. (She was then working for the Department of Pensions and Security, the Alabama welfare agency.) We would go down the rutted back roads, where even the elderberries in the low places were red with dust in the summer, over to Primitive Ridge, or Smith Hill in West Blocton. She wouldn't let me come inside while she visited people, and never did say much about them, but I could tell that there were some she didn't worry about, like Mattie, who "had the spirit" and was likely to start talking in tongues at any minute. Mattie crocheted for extra money; her living room was decorated with pink-and-white doilies.

Then there were those Mama agonized over, like the young woman who was the mother of four at seventeen. She was slightly retarded but was trying to teach herself to read; my mother would take her the *Ladies' Home Journal* and *Redbook* every month. And there was the woman with ten children who wanted no more. My mother had arranged for her to get birth control pills, but something had gone wrong and she had become pregnant. I sat in the car the day of the visit my mother learned this; I could see my mother on the sagging porch with the woman, who was crying. Under the porch where it was cooler was a bunch of children; there were a lot of flies, and dirt, and crying. When my mother came back she had a familiar stony look and said, "I don't see how it will ever change."

Once we went to Marvel, which had been a booming coal town in the twenties, when my mother lived there as a young girl while her father worked as a security man for the coal company. By the time of our visit it was almost deserted. Mama showed me where the company store had been. I remember that I sat and read the Book of John while she visited that day, trying to convince myself that the words "I am the Way, the Truth, and the Light" held some promise of things being different. I remember thinking, *I can't grow up and do this like my mother; I will feel the pain too much.*

The summers before my freshman and sophomore college years I worked at Cahaba Manufacturing Company to earn money for tuition; we made women's and children's sportswear. I worked on the jacket assembly line setting grippers. I figured I must have put on half a million grippers that summer. At lunch break some of the women often went outside to eat under the picnic shelter and get some sun, no matter how hot it was, since the plant was windowless. I usually went out, too, but sat alone at a table apart from the others reading *The Peloponnesian Wars* or *Tom Jones* or some other book that would be a course requirement for me in the fall, carefully removing myself from the women who were going to do this work for the rest of their lives.

Still, I sat close enough to hear them talk, and it was there that

I first heard gossip of the sort that my mother disdained, stories of the private actions that did not match the public morality. Thelma Perkins and Martha Colburn had a long conversation one lunchtime about a man who was married but having an affair with a woman twenty years younger, who also worked at our plant. He and his wife were Presbyterians and went to my church; I had wondered why his wife, a tall, thin, austere woman with her hair pulled back in a bun, had stopped coming. She had left town and him, an unheard-of action. As for the man, he was the Young Adults teacher in our Sunday School. I had heard him quaver through the scripture lesson many times, and as I listened to Thelma and Martha speculate, I realized that *all that time* he had been breaking the Seventh Commandment.

I saw, with a shock, for the first but not the last time, that the good lives people said they wanted were not the lives they led. Sitting in the heat, with this crowd of women, all of us linty with cotton dust, I saw stretch out around me a landscape that I did not know, filled with people leading lives that I had not imagined, lives which were not in pursuit of goodness and justice. I forgot this moment very quickly, but I remembered it later, when I began to practice memory.

October 11th, 1861—We went in the afternoon to the Negro church on the plantation. . . . Jim Nelson, the driver, the stateliest darky I ever saw, tall and straight as a tree, with a fine face, and not so very black but a full-blooded African, was asked to lead in prayer. He became wildly excited, on his knees, facing us with his eyes shut. He clapped his hands at the end of every sentence, and his voice rose to the pitch of a shrill shriek, yet was strangely clear and musical, occasionally in a plaintive minor key that went to your heart. Sometimes it rang out like a trumpet. I wept bitterly. It was all sound however, and emotional pathos. There was literally nothing in what he said. The words had no meaning. It was the devotional passion of voice and manner which was so magnetic. . . . It was a little too exciting for me. I would very much have liked to shout too.

I have often asked my mother about events in her past, and had her say that she really didn't remember how she felt about them, that this or that was "just something that had to be done." I used to think that the silence which still surrounds the emotional lives of her and her sisters was deliberate, a deliberate withholding from me of their secrets and knowledge as women. But now I think that this loss of memory is a result of the silence, of the never talking, never thinking about what may lie under the surface, the awful truths. It is a result of years and years spent trying to do what was right in silence and isolation, as my mother did, within a system which she thought could not be changed. Because for my parents' generation, and for much of mine, and even for some still living in the South, there was no need to talk of what lay all around. To talk, to gossip, to complain, to raise your voice, to shout about what was happening to you or around you was useless; it was not reasonable; it was *foolish*, if not crazy, since the social order, the nature of people was set, doomed, and no amount of shouting would alter creation.

It was not a possibility that talking about something would release a passion for change and thus bring about change. Instead, there was in the silence a fear that to let out the pain and anger would bring chaos, anarchy. Inequality between men and women, rich and poor, Black and white, was ordained; there was the curse of Ham in the Bible, and of Adam and Eve, too.

Since order was based on inequality, there was nothing to be done but keep your manners, lower your voice, and go through life to your death with intense grace, like J.E.B. Stuart riding to his doom in his last cavalry charge with plumes in his hat and a smile on his face. For genteel white men and women, manners and fairness to others, especially those "lower" than yourself, was important, since other people were not responsible for their position. I can remember walking with my father when I was four or five, downtown by the town square. He always raised his hat with extreme courtesy when meeting a Black woman he knew. He inquired quickly about her family, in sentences so rapid that they often weren't completed, and sometimes interrupted himself in his haste to fulfill the ceremony, so that frequently he did not hear her answers. For it did not matter what anyone said, or did, since death was the only real change. Mary Boykin Chesnut said in 1864, "No, I will not stop and think, when there is only death to think of." To embroider the surface of doom with style and manners was the only way to keep your reason.

Long after I began to question parts of the preordination of my life, I kept, without knowing it, the feeling that change was not only useless, but dangerous, since with it chaos would come, and insanity, the release of terrible pain. And I lived a life of interior silence until my late twenties, a life, I think, very much like my mother's; there are whole months of my married life that I cannot remember. When, through my love for another woman, I released the passion in me for the first time, I began to see that to live was to create, not to die. I became like the sorority woman at school who we all thought was crazy when she broke the rules by openly going to civil rights marches in Tuscaloosa and moving in with her boyfriend, to live with him in the daytime, instead of just sneaking out to sleep with him at night. I found out exactly how manners, doing what is "reasonable," can be used to cage us and keep us from shouting for changes, as I argued with my husband who told me to leave the house until I could behave in a "civil manner," and then hit me when I would not keep quiet. For a while I valued this incident for the insight it gave me into how men control women's words and actions by violence. Lately it has taken on for me an added significance, as an example of how when we speak, say certain things, certain words, we rebel; we put ourselves outside manners and civilization; we step over a boundary into the forbidden.

I learned to do this first as a lesbian and a feminist. I lost the part of manners that kept me from action when I refused to be discreet about my love for other women, and my husband got custody of our two boys; that's when my grandmother, then ninety-six, wrote, "I pray for you every night. Do you think you should go see a psychiatrist?"

And I have learned there are other ways to cross the boundary. After the February 2nd anti-Klan march in Greensboro, I wore my bright-yellow *Stop the Klan* button around Fayetteville. And at Seven-Elevens and at garage sales, white men would stop me and look at it and smile and say, ever so politely, "Why, I belong to the Klan" (whether they actually did or not was, of course, irrelevant) and then become verbally abusive when I refused to accept this as a joke. I had crossed their line between white and Black; I had, to them, repudiated whiteness and joined with the others.

I had never had this sort of reaction to any women's buttons I had worn, but I realized that they had literally not been radical enough— they had been *Pass the ERA* buttons. If I had worn a button that read *Support Lesbian Mothers*, I'm sure the abuse would have been intense, because I would have absolutely broken through a boundary set around my life as a woman.

I am trying to teach myself to cross these boundaries, many of which I have lived within my whole life and have never seen. I practice seeing the limits and then crossing them, if I am brave enough at the moment.

I remember Mary Boykin Chesnut, her strengths and her weaknesses, in order to live like her, in order to live differently from her:

> *June 9th, 1862—I am so ill. Mrs. Ben Taylor said to Dr.*
> *Trezevant: "Surely she is too ill to be going about. She*
> *ought to be in bed." / "She is very feeble, very nervous as*
> *you say; but then she is living on nervous excitement. If*
> *you shut her up she would die at once." / A prostration*
> *of the heart is what I have. Sometimes it beats so feebly I*
> *am sure it has stopped altogether. Then they say I have*
> *fainted, but I never lose consciousness.*

I remember Lillian Smith who said:

> *. . .the most dangerous demagogues are those that crouch*
> *in our own minds, whispering lies at a time when we so*
> *desperately need to hear the poet's deep truths. . .*

who said:

> *Teach us to listen to sounds larger than our own heart beat;*
> *that endure longer than our own weeping in the dark.*

I begin to understand that a white woman of the South can live and
write, but not of the dead heroes. She can live and write a new kind
of honor, the daily, conscious actions of women in true rebellion.

Notes

The quotations from Mary Boykin Chesnut's *Diary* are from the Ben Ames
Williams' edition of that work. The Lillian Smith quotations are from her col-
lection of writings, *The Winner Names the Age,* edited by Michelle Cliff (New
York: W.W. Norton, 1978).

Identity: Skin Blood Heart

I live in a part of Washington, D.C., that white suburbanites called "the jungle" during the uprising of the sixties—perhaps still do, for all I know. When I walk the two-and-a-half blocks to H Street, N.E., to stop in at the bank, to leave my boots off at the shoe-repair-and-lock shop, I am most usually the only white person in sight. I've seen two other whites, women, in the year I've lived here. (This does not count white folks in cars, passing through. In official language, H Street, N.E. is known as the "H Street Corridor," as in something to be passed through quickly, going from your place on the way to elsewhere.)

When I walk three blocks in a slightly

This essay was first developed as a speech given at the plenary session, "Racism and Anti-Semitism in the Women's Movement," at the 1983 National Women's Studies Association conference in Columbus, Ohio.

27

different direction, down Maryland Avenue, to go to my lover's house, I pass yards of Black folks: the yard of the lady who keeps children, with its blue-and-red windmill, its roses of Sharon; the yard of the man who delivers vegetables, with its stacked slatted crates; the yard of the people next to the Righteous Branch Commandment Church of God (Seventh Day), with its tomatoes in the summer, its collards in the fall. In the summer, folks sit out on their porches or steps or sidewalks. When I walk by, if I lift my head and look toward them and speak, "Hey," they may speak, say, "Hey" or "How you doin'?" or perhaps just nod. In the spring I was afraid to smile when I spoke, because that might be too familiar, but by the end of summer I had walked back and forth so often, *I* was familiar, so sometimes we shared comments about the mean weather.

I am comforted by any of these speakings for, to tell you the truth, they make me feel at home. I am living far from where I was born; it has been twenty years since I have lived in that place where folks, Black and white, spoke to each other when they met on the street or in the road. So when two Black men dispute country matters, calling across the corners of 8th Street—"Hey, Roland, did you ever see a hog catch a rat?"—"I seen a hog catch a *snake*."—"How about a rat? Ever see one catch a *rat?*"—I am grateful to be living within sound of their voices, to hear a joking that reminds me, with a startled pain, of my father, putting on his tales for his friends, the white men gathered at the drugstore in the mornings.

The pain, of course, is the other side of this speaking, and the sorrow, when I have only to turn two corners to go back in the basement door of my building, to meet Mr. Boone, the janitor, who doesn't raise his eyes to mine, or his head, when we speak. He is a dark red-brown man from the Yemassee in South Carolina—that swampy land of Indian resistance and armed communities of fugitive slaves, that marshy land at the headwaters of the Combahee, once site of enormous rice plantations and location of Harriet Tubman's successful military action that freed many slaves. When we meet in the hall or on the elevator, even though I may have just heard him speaking in his own voice to another man, he "yes-ma'ams" me in a sing-song; I hear my voice replying in the horrid cheerful accents of a white lady. And I hate my white womanhood that drags between us the long bitter history of our region.

I think how I just want to feel at home, where people know me. Instead I remember, when I meet Mr. Boone, that home was a place of forced subservience, and I know that my wish is that of an adult wanting to stay a child: to be known by others, but to know nothing, to feel no responsibility. Instead I recognize, when I walk out in my neighborhood, that each speaking-to another person has become fraught, for me, with the history of race and sex and class. As I walk I have a constant interior discussion with myself, questioning how I acknowledge the presence of another, what I know or don't know about them, and what how they acknowledge me means. It is an exhausting process, this moving from the experience of the "unknowing majority" (as Maya Angelou has called it) into consciousness. It would be a lie to say this process is comforting.

I meet a white man on Maryland Avenue at ten at night, for instance. He doesn't *look* gay, and he's younger and bigger than me. Just because he's wearing a three-piece suit doesn't mean he won't try something. What's he doing walking here, anyway? One of the new gentry taking over? Maybe that's what the Black neighbors think about me. If I speak, he'll probably assume it's about sex, not about being neighborly. I don't feel neighborly toward him, anyway. If he speaks to me, is that about sex? Or does he still think skin means kin? Or maybe he was raised someplace where someone could say, "I know your mama," if he didn't behave. But he's probably not going to think about her when he does whatever he does *here:* better be careful.

In the space of three blocks, on one evening, I can debate whether the young Black woman didn't speak because she was tired, urban-raised, or hates white women; and ask myself why I wouldn't speak to the young professional white woman on her way to work in the morning, but I do at night (and she doesn't speak at all). Is this about who I think I may need for physical safety?

And I make myself speak to a young Black man; if I don't, it will be the old racial-sexual fear. Damn the past. When I speak directly I usually get a respectful answer. Is that the response violently extorted by history, the taboo on white women? Last week the group of Black men on 10th Street started in on "Can I have some?" when Joan and I walked by. Was that because they were three? We were white? We were lesbian? Or because we didn't speak? What about this man? He is a man. And I would speak to him in the *day*time.

After I speak and he speaks, I think of how my small store of manners, the way I was taught to be "respectful" of others, my middle-class, white-woman, rural Southern Christian manners, gave me no ideas on a past Sunday afternoon, in the northwest part of the city, on how to speak to the Latinos and Latinas socializing on the sidewalks there.

And I think of how I'm walking to visit my Jewish lover. When we walk around the neighborhood together, we look like two white women, except the ladies in my building say we look like sisters, because we're close and they can see we love each other. But I'm blonde and blue-eyed, she dark-haired and brown-eyed; we don't look a bit like sisters. If the white people and the Black people we meet knew she was Jewish as well as white, how would their speaking alter?

I reckon the rigid boundaries set around my experience, how I have been "protected," by the amount of effort it takes me to walk these few blocks being as conscious as I can of myself in relation to history, to race, to culture, to gender. In this city where I am no longer of the majority by color or culture, I tell myself every day: In this *world* you aren't the majority race or culture, and never were, whatever you were raised to think; and are you getting ready to be *in* this world?

And I answer myself back: I'm trying to learn how to live, to have the speaking-to extend beyond the moment's word, to act so as to change the unjust circumstances that keep us from being able to speak to each other; I'm trying to get a little closer to the longed-for but unrealized world, where we each are able to live, but not by trying to make someone less than us, not by someone else's blood or pain. Yes, that's what I'm trying to do with my living now.

I take the moments when I speak and am spoken to, the exchange with dignity, respect, perhaps pleasure, as fragments of that world; but often the moment slips, the illusion of acceptance vanishes into the chasm of the world-as-it-is that opens up between me and another. Yesterday when I said, "Hey," smiling to the white-headed white woman coming with difficulty down the walk, she spat at me, shout-singing, "How much is that doggy in the window?"—her disdain for the uselessness and childishness of my manners in a world where she labored down the sidewalk. Why should she give me the approval of her smile?

The stark truth spoken in public, the terror of what is said about my place on the other side of the chasm between me and another, makes me want to pretend I didn't hear, to cover the truth up. The answer, like the impulse, comes from home: where great-great-aunt Rannie stripped naked before company, against the remonstrance of her scandalized niece. "*Ran*-nie, you're nekkid as a jaybird!" "Yes," said Rannie, calmly, "and the jaybird is a pretty bird." Rannie reminds me to listen for the beauty in the stark truth that someone tells me, that which seems brutal and may terrify me. This listening is one way of finding out how to get to the new place where we all can live and speak to each other for more than a fragile moment.

If you and I met today, reader, on Maryland Avenue, would we speak? I don't know what barriers of gender, color, culture, sexuality, might rise between us when we saw each other. Nor do I know what may come between us as I talk in these pages about the barriers that we struggle with every day, issues of morality like anti-Semitism and racism.

Here my friend Dorothy has protested: "Morality! I'd call it ethics." She hates the word, it having been used against her often. It's true. Her Baptists, and my Presbyterians, not to mention others we could name, have turned the word on us too much. But, Dorothy, *ethics* sounds like classical Greece to me. What if I say, not *morality* but—

I'm trying to talk about struggling against racism and anti-Semitism as issues of how to live, the right-and-wrong of it, about how to respect others and myself. It is very hard for me to know *how* to speak of this struggle because the culture I was born and raised in has taught me certain ways of being that reduce the process of change to ought-to, that reduce the issue of how to live to ought-to.

I was taught to be a *judge* of moral responsibility and of punishment only in relation to *my* ethical system; was taught to be a *martyr*, to take all the responsibility for change, and the glory, and expect others to do nothing; was taught to be a *peacemaker*, to mediate, negotiate between opposing sides because *I* knew the right way; was taught to be a *preacher*, to point out wrongs and tell others what to do. Nowadays, I struggle not to speak with the tones or gestures or notions of these roles when I raise, out loud, with other women, those interior questions that I have asked myself, about my understanding of anti-Semitism and racism.

Sometimes after I have spoken of these issues, women who are like me come up to me and say:

They feel so ashamed, I spoke and they didn't, they would never be able to act so bravely, I might be able to do it but not them, ever. Or they say how can I be so self-righteous, hurt and punish others, divide women, how can I think I am better than others. Sometimes they say they are glad I have pointed out the racism or anti-Semitism, they hadn't noticed, and didn't know how or what to do about these problems.

Sometimes they say they are glad I spoke, since these problems are important, but they realy don't see how any of this affects them personally. Or they may say they are so tired of hearing about these issues, and they don't see how any of this affects them personally. Or they say they are so tired of talk, why don't we just *do* something. Or who do I think I am, to speak for them as white or gentile, their experience has been different. Sometimes they say, painfully, that they have had experiences in their own lives parallel to the ones I recount, but have not been able to speak to anyone about this.

I know that, sometimes, when women make these remarks to me it is because *I* was not clear about my own struggles, fears, mistakes, responsibility, complicity, plans for actions; or because I have failed in my struggle with the old ways of being and am acting them out in my style, manner, tone, ideas. Sometimes, I believe, the remarks are made because women are handing their power and responsibility over to me, because of their own upbringing or assumptions that place me in a certain role in relation to them; and because they are not feeling their own various powers—bravery, creativity, knowledge, and ability to change.

I am struggling now to speak, but not out of any role of ought-to; I ask that you try not to place me in that role. I am trying to speak from my heart, out of need, as a woman who loves other women passionately, and wants us to be able to be together as friends in this unjust world; and as a woman who lives in relative security in the United States, and who is trying to figure out my responsibility in wider struggles against injustice.

I am speaking my small piece of truth, as best I can. My friend Barbara Deming has reminded me: We each have only a piece of the truth. So here it is: I'm putting it down for you to see if our fragments match anywhere, if our pieces, together, make another larger piece of the truth that can be part of the map we are making together to show us the way to get to the longed-for world.

Where does the need come from, the inner push to walk into change, if we are women who, by skin color, ethnicity, birth culture, are in a position of material advantage where we gain at the expense of others, of other women? A place where *we* can have a degree of safety, comfort, familiarity, just by staying put. Where is our *need* to change what we were born into? What do we have to gain?

When I try to think of this, I think of my father. When I was about eight years old, he took me up the front marble steps of the courthouse in my town. He took me inside, up the worn wooden steps, stooped under the feet of folks who had gone up and down to be judged, or to gawk at others being judged, up past the courtroom where my grandfather had leaned back in his chair and judged for over forty years, up to the attic, to some narrow steps that went to the roof, to the clock tower with a walled ledge.

What I would have seen from the top, on the streets down below around the courthouse square: the Methodist church, the grey lime-stone building with the county Health Department, Board of Education, Welfare Department (my mother worked there), the yellow brick Baptist church, the Gulf station, the pool hall (no women allowed), Cleveland's grocery, Ward's shoestore. Then all in a line, connected: the bank, the post office, Dr. Nicholson's office (one door for whites, one for Blacks). Then separate: the Presbyterian church, the newspaper office, the yellow brick jail, same brick as the Baptist church and as the courthouse.

What I could not have seen from the top: the sawmill, or Four Points where the white mill folks lived, or the houses of Blacks in Veneer Mill Quarters.

This is what I would and would not have seen, or so I think: for I never got to the top. When he told me to go up the steps in front of him, I tried to, crawling on hands and knees, but I was terribly afraid. I couldn't, or wouldn't, do it. He let me crawl down; he was disgusted with me, I thought. I think now that he wanted to show me a place he had climbed to as a boy, a view that had been his father's and his, and would be mine. But I was not him: I had not learned to take that height, that being set apart as my own, a white girl, not a boy.

Yet I was shaped by my relation to those buildings and to the people in the buildings, by ideas of who should be working in the Board of Education, of who should be in the bank handling money, of who should have the guns and the keys to the jail, of who should be *in* the jail; and I was shaped by what I didn't see, or didn't notice, on those streets.

Not the way your town was laid out, you say? True, perhaps, but each of us carries around those growing-up places, the institutions, a sort of backdrop, a stage set. So often we act out the present against a backdrop of the past, within a frame of perception that is so familiar, so safe, that it is terrifying to risk changing it even when we know our perceptions are distorted, limited, constricted by that old view.

So this is one gain for me as I change: I learn a way of looking at the world that is more accurate, complex, multilayered, multidimensioned, more truthful. To see the world of overlapping circles, like movement on the mill pond after a fish has jumped, instead of the courthouse square with me at the middle, even if I am on the ground.

I feel the *need* to look differently because I've learned that what is presented to me as an accurate view of the world is frequently a lie: so that to look through an anthology of women's studies that has little or no work by women of color is to be up on that ledge above the town and be thinking that I see the town, without realizing how many lives have been pushed out of sight, beside unpaved roads.

I'm learning that what I think that I *know* is an accurate view of the world is frequently a lie: as when I was in a discussion about the Women's Pentagon Action with several women, four of us Christian-raised, one Jewish, my lover Joan, a photographer. Describing the march through Arlington Cemetery, one of the four mentioned the rows of crosses. I had marched for a long time through that cemetery; I nodded to myself, visualized rows of crosses. No, said Joan, they were *headstones,* with crosses or Stars of David engraved above the names. We four Christians objected; we all had seen crosses. But Joan had photographs she had taken of the march through the cemetery, laid them on the table. We saw rows and rows and rows of rectangular gravestones, and in the foreground, clearly visible, one inscribed with a name and a Star of David.

So I gain truth when I expand my constricted eye, an eye that has only let in what I have been taught to see. But there have been other constrictions: the clutch of fear around my heart when I must deal with the *fact* of folks who exist, with their own lives, in other places besides the narrow circle I was raised in. I have learned that my fear is kin to a terror that has been in my birth culture for years, for centuries—the terror of a people who have set themselves apart and *above,* who have wronged others and feel they are about to be found out and punished.

It is the terror that has been expressed in lies about dirty Jews who kill for blood, sly Arab hordes who murder, brutal Indians who massacre, animal Blacks who rise in rebellion in the middle of the night and slaughter. It is the terror that has *caused* the slaughter of all those peoples. It is the terror that was my father, with his stack of John Birch newspapers, his belief in a Catholic-Communist-Jewish-Black conspiracy. It is the desperate terror, the knowledge that something is *wrong,* which tries to end fear by attack.

When I am trying to understand myself in relation to folks different from me, when there are discussions, conflicts about anti-Semitism and racism among women, criticisms, criticism of *me,* and I get afraid; when, for instance, in a group discussion about race and class, I say I feel we have talked too much about race, not enough about class, and a woman of color asks me in anger and pain if I don't think her skin has *something* to do with class, and I get afraid; when, for instance, I say carelessly to my Jewish lover that there were no Jews where I grew up, and she begins to ask me, How do I *know*? Do I hear what I'm saying? and I get afraid; when I feel my racing heart, breath, the tightening of my skin around me, literally defenses to protect my narrow circle, I try to say to myself:

Yes, that fear is there, but I will try to be at the edge between my fear and the outside, on the edge at my skin, listening, asking what new thing will I hear, will I see, will I let myself feel, beyond the fear. I try to say: To acknowledge the complexity of another's existence is not to deny my own. When I acknowledge what my people, what those who are like me, have done to people with less power and less safety in the world, I can make a place for things to be different, a place where I can feel grief, sorrow, not to be sorry *for* others, but to mourn, to expand my circle of self, follow my need to loosen the constrictions of fear, be a break in the cycle of fear and attack. When I can do this, that is a second gain.

To be caught within the narrow circle of the self is not just a fearful thing, it is a *lonely* thing. When I could not climb the steps that day with my father, it marked the last time I can remember us doing something together, just the two of us; thereafter I knew on some level that my place was with women, not with him, not with men; later I knew more clearly that I did not want his view of the world. I have felt this more and more strongly since my coming out as a lesbian. Yet so much has separated me from other women, ways in which my culture set me apart by race, by ethnicity, by class.

I understood abruptly one day how lonely this made me when a friend, a Black woman, spoke to me casually in our shared office; and I heard how she said my name, the drawn-out accent: so much like how my name is said at home. Yet I knew enough of her history and mine to know how much separated us: the chasm of murders, rapes, lynchings, the years of daily humiliations done by my people to hers. I went and stood in the hallway and cried, thinking of how she said my name like home, and how divided our lives were.

It is a pain I come to over and over again, the more I understand the ways in which I have been kept from other women, and how I keep myself from them. The pain, when, for instance, I realize how *habitually* I think of my culture, my ethics, my morality, as the culmination of history, as the logical extension of what has gone before; the kind of thinking represented by my use, in the past, of the word *Judeo-*

Christian, as if Jewish history and lives have existed only to culminate in Christian culture, the kind of thinking that the U.S. government is using now to promote Armageddon in the Middle East; the kind of thinking that I did until recently about Indian lives and culture in my region, as if Indian peoples have existed only in museums, and only since white folks came to this continent; the kind of thinking that separates me from women in cultures different from mine, makes their experience less central, less important than mine.

It is painful to keep understanding this separation within myself and in the world. Sometimes this pain feels only like despair. Yet I have felt it also to be another kind of pain, where the need to be with other women can be the breaking through the shell around me, a coming through into a new place, where, with understanding and change, the loneliness won't be necessary. And when this happens, then I feel a third gain.

How do we begin to change, and then keep going, and act on this in the world? How do we *want* to be different from what we have been? Sometimes folks ask how I got started, and I must admit that I did not begin by reasoning out the gains; this came later and helped me keep going.

But I began when I jumped from my edge and outside myself, into radical change, for love—simply love—for myself and for other women. I acted on that love by becoming a lesbian, falling in love with and becoming sexual with a particular woman; and this love led me directly, but by a complicated way, to work against racism and anti-Semitism.

It is another kind of breaking through to even write this, to put these words before you. I anticipate the critical voices that say, "Your sexuality is irrelevant to the serious issues of anti-Semitism and racism"; that say, "You are being psychologizing, individualistic"; the voices that say, "You should want to work on these issues because that is the right thing to do, for justice, for general principles." I anticipate the other, perhaps subvocal, words: "Disgusting." "Perverted." "Sinful." "Unnatural." "Not fit to live."

I hear these voices sounding now because I have heard them before: from folks on the street, from political co-workers, from women at my job, from the man I was married to, from my mother. They are the judging, condemning voices that despise me, that see me as dangerous, that put me in danger, because of *how I love:* because of my intimate, necessary, hopeful love, for which I have been punished and been made to suffer bitterly, *when I have disclosed it.*

I could conceal this love from you. I could hide this part of myself as some light-skinned, European-looking folks in this country have hidden parts of themselves that kept them from fitting in, assimilating, being safe in white Christian culture: hidden their religion, or the poverty or working class of their people; or their ethnicity, any connection to "undesirable" people, to Jews, or Mediterranean or Middle Eastern peoples, or Native Indians, or Asian peoples, or to any people of color.

I could pass in this way, by hiding part of myself. I fit neatly into the narrow limits of what is seen as "normal" in this country. Like most lesbians, I don't fit the stereotype of what a lesbian looks like. Unless my hair is cut quite short and unless I am wearing the comfortable, sturdy clothes and shoes that are called "masculine," I look quite stereotypically "American"—like a woman in a toothpaste ad.

But in this writing, I cannot hide myself, because it is how I love that has brought me to change. I have learned what it is to lose a position of safety, to be despised for *who I am.* For being a lesbian, I have lost my children, those I loved almost as myself, and I have had my pride, as Barbara Deming says, "assaulted in its depth...since one's sexuality is so at the heart...at the heart of one."[1] It was my joy at loving another woman, the risks I took by doing so, the changes this brought me to, and the losses, that broke through the bubble of skin and class privilege around me. I do not want what Barbara Deming has called "liberation by analogy." I do not want to fight someone else's fight because, for whatever reason, I don't acknowledge and fight my *own* oppression.[2] So I speak here of how I came to my own fight, through the oppression I suffered as a lesbian and a woman; and how I came to an understanding of my connection to the struggles of other women and people different from myself.

In the fall of 1974, I moved with my husband and children to an eastern North Carolina town whose center was not a courthouse, but a market house, with an open first story of four arched brick walls, a closed brick second story, a circle of streets around it. I heard more about the market house at a dinner that welcomed my husband to his new job. In a private club overlooking the central circle, the well-to-do folks at the table, all white, chatted about history, the things sold in the past at the market house, the fruits and vegetables, the auctioned tobacco. "But not slaves," they said.

The Black man who was serving set down the dish, and broke

through the anonymity of his red jacket. No, he said, there *had been* slaves there: men, women, children sold away from their mothers. Going to the window, he looked down on the streets and gave two minutes of facts and dates; then he finished serving, and left. The white folks smiled indulgently and changed the subject. I recognized their look, from home. I was shocked that he had dared speak to them, yet somehow felt he had done so many times before, and I knew, without letting myself know, that as he spoke there stood behind him the house slaves who had risked whipping or worse when they challenged with their words the white folks' killing ignorance.

What he told me was plain enough: This town was a place where some people had been used as livestock, chattel, slaves, cattle, capital, by other people; and this use had been justified by the physical fact of a different skin color and by the cultural fact of different ways of living. White men and their families had considered Black people to be animals with no right to their children or to a home of their own, and white people still did not admit that they had done any wrong, nor that there had *been* any wrong, in *their* town. What this man was saying was clear: Be warned; they have not changed.

By the end of dinner, I had forgotten his words. They were about the past, seemed to have nothing to do with me. Yet, after almost ten years in university towns, I was returning to the landscape of my childhood, changed into a city with buying and selling at its heart, the country club its social center rather than the church (but Blacks and Jews still not welcome), a town with a conspicuous police presence, the U.S. Army's second largest home base, with combat veterans who had trained to the chant, "Here is my prick, here is my gun, one is for killing, the other for fun."

Every day I drove around the market house, carrying my two boys between home and grammar school and day care. To me the building was an impediment to the flow of traffic, awkward, anachronistic; or sometimes in the early spring light it seemed quaint. I had no knowledge and no feeling of the sweat and blood of people's lives that had been mortared into its bricks, nor of their independent joy apart from that place.

What I *was* feeling was that I would spend the rest of my life going round and round in a pattern that I knew by heart: being a wife, a mother of two boys, a teacher of the writings of white men, dead men. I drove around the market house four times a day, traveling on the surface of my own life: circular, repetitive, like a game at the county fair, the one with yellow plastic ducks clacking after each other on a track, until they fall abruptly off the edge, into inevitable meaningless disappearance; unless, with a smack, one or two or three vanish from the middle, shot down by a smiling man with a gun.

For the first time in my life I was living in a place where I was conscious of being afraid because I was a *woman*. No one knew me by my family: there were no kindnesses because someone knew my mama or my pa, and no one was going to be nice to me because of my grandfather. I was only another woman, someone's wife, unless I was alone; then, walking down Hay Street to the library, I could be propositioned as a prostitute, or, driving at night on the Boulevard, threatened as a cunt. At home when I complained about the smiling innuendo of a gas station attendant, my husband said I should be complimented: this in a town where *R & R* stood for *Rape and Recreation*.

Not such a surprising realization: to understand that women are used as sexual pets, or are violently misused, are considered sexual prey. But, there it was: for the first time I felt myself to be, not theoretically, but physically and permanently, in the class of people labeled *woman:* and felt that group to be relatively powerless and at the mercy of another class, *men*.

I was not at all accustomed to thinking of myself as belonging to an *oppressed* group. The last time I had understood myself to belong to a specific class of people was when I was a teenager. At the height of Black civil rights demonstrations in Alabama, and brutality by white police and citizens, I received a request from a German penpal for my views on what was going on, and wrote what I remember now as an eloquent justification of white supremacy. I did not reflect on what repetition of Nazi history, what cries of Aryan superiority were called up by my words. Sliding aside the polite lie that "Here we just treat everyone as individuals," I justified how we were treating folks—us, the superior class, me in the group *white*.

By the time I was midway through college, I had slipped into being unselfconscious of myself as white; this happened as I became liberal. This meant that I looked on with my philosophy class as a few students demonstrated while Gov. Lurleen Wallace (serving in place of her segregationist husband) reviewed the ROTC troops, the students getting trained to defend Alabama from "outsiders"; all the white boys saluted under the white dogwoods flowering on the Quad, while we debated the usefulness of protest. Two years later, on the night of Dr. King's death by assassination, I drove with my husband and a friend into Birmingham, curfewed after a day of violence, drove in to look around the empty downtown streets in the spring rain, looking for I don't know what; and not finding it, went to the Tutwiler for drinks, not thinking of ourselves as white, of course, nor in any way out of place on the streets that night, because we were intellectuals, and not bigoted, not at all like James Earl Ray or any white person who did violence for racist reasons.

I slipped from thinking of myself as white, to thinking of myself as *married,* without much regard for other categories in the meantime, except for a few startling moments. I felt *gentile* (though I didn't know the word) when a Jewish man I was dating called it off because I was "too much like a girl he might marry." I was baffled by this: I thought of Jewishness as a state of being defined by Christianity, a category changeable by conversion or association with Christians; I couldn't understand why this was something he didn't seem to want to do.

Going through the negotiations to marry a Catholic-raised man, I had some longer moments of feeling *Protestant.* As debates went on between my husband-to-be and the priest who was counseling us under the new guidelines of Vatican II, I puzzled over the need for an intricate resolution between *them,* two men, about what kind of birth control I would, or would not, use.

After the wedding, I was relieved to think I was simply myself: a nonreligious, thinking person, who happened to be married. But sometimes my life as a *woman* bulged outside the safe bounds of *wife,* as when I was shaken and terrified with two unplanned pregnancies. Walking to my graduate school classes at the university in North Carolina, I put the width of the sidewalk between me and the woman sitting at the literature table in front of the library. The pamphlets and the two-cent newsletters—*Research Triangle Women's Liberation Newsletter,* August 11, 1969—were loose on the cardboard table and were not safely *in* the library.[3] At the other edge of the sidewalk, I tried to separate myself from the new ideas about what it meant to be a woman. I rushed away slowly through the humid air, weighted by my unborn second child, who sat like a four-month-old rock in my stomach.

During the last months of my pregnancy, I shared a class with Elizabeth, the woman from the literature table. She analyzed men and power, fathers and sons in Shakespeare's *Henry IV;* the other students thought she was crazy; I was afraid she was. One evening, as I carried my enormous heavy belly from the seminar table to my car, she told me that she thought I was brave to stay in school, unlike so many other married women with children, and she wished me well. I thought of how the men in my department had begun to joke that they would get stuck with me in the elevator and I'd go into labor. That evening I cried the ten miles home. She had spoken to me as a *woman*, and I'd been so lonely, without knowing it: her speaking to me changed how I thought of myself and my life.

The ideas of women's liberation came rushing toward me, arrived at the university town through the writings of feminist and lesbian-feminist groups, like The Furies of Washington, D.C.; and through individual women, like Sara Evans Boyte, who taught off-campus classes in women's history—women who had heard the ideas from New Haven, by way of Chicago, by way of white women who had worked in the civil rights movement in the South, who had learned the principles of liberation in the homes and at the sides of Black women, young and old, who were the political organizers in their communities.[4]

When I found myself living as a wife in the market town, where the circle of my life was becoming more and more narrow, I felt like I was being brick-walled in; then the ideas that I'd learned from Elizabeth and the other women became personal to me. I began to feel the restrictions around me as a woman, through the pressure of neighbors and country-club social friends about how I should act as a woman, through the extremity of the violence reported daily in the news: "Fourteen-year-old girl taken from car at county fair, raped at gun-point." But I still moved unthinkingly through the town as a white person born to the culture, unaware of how much this fact pushed away from me the daily limits placed on other women by men.

For being a woman was the constriction that I felt. I was in a place like home, but grown-up; I didn't want to be there, curfewed by night, watched by day, by some of the twenty-five thousand more men than women in the town. I felt surrounded. I wanted to go some place where I could just *be*; I was homesick with nowhere to go.

The place that I missed sometimes seemed like a memory of childhood, though it was not a childish place. It was a place of mutuality, companionship, creativity, sensuousness, easiness in the body, curiosity in what new things might be making in the world, a place of hope, safety, and love.

Like a memory of July: The slash of morning sun on my face as I walked with my cousin Anne down to the gravel pit, through the maze of small canyons with clay walls. The place where I put my face against the clay, the sweat of cool water in the heat, the flesh of the earth. We would stay all day there, get cleanly dirty, dig clay, shape pots, retreat to the cool, then out in the heat again in a place we knew was ancient because of the fossil rocks we found, ancient and serenely a home.

It was a place I had been to with my father, who took me and my mother to the woods. Not to hunt (for he was not a hunter), but to walk, he with a double-bladed ax that he raised to trim dead branches, in silence except to name the trees (black-jack oak, sweet bay) and to say how to step (high over logs where copperheads liked to rest cool). His silence that may have been his prayer to the trees that he counted as dead board feet on weekdays at the sawmill (but he is dead now, and I will never know what went on in his mind). His silence that taught me to listen to the life rushing through the veins of the animal world.

The place that I missed was a place I had been in recently, just before my move to the market town, when, with a few other women, I had begun the talking about the forbidden that was called *consciousness-raising:* making a place where I had said the words *masturbation, orgasm,* out loud for the first time. In the startled silence of the other women, I felt that I had abruptly created a new world out of the stuffy plastic apartment where we were meeting.

In the market town I began to try, steadily, to make a place like the memory, yet that would last longer than a morning or an evening. It was to be a place where I could live without painful and deadly violence, without domination: a place where I could live free, *liberated,* with other women. I began doing some political work, organized another consciousness-raising group. Then I fell in love with a woman, after she told the group a secret about herself. I thought I had come again to the place of intense curiosity, powerful creativity. It was March, it was April, wisteria, dogwood, pink tulip magnolia. But I began to dream my husband was trying to kill me, that I was crossing a river with my children, women on the other side, but no welcome for me with my boys.

The place I wanted to reach was not a childish place, but my understanding of it was childish. I had not admitted that the safety of much of my childhood was because Laura Cates, Black and a servant, was responsible for me; that I had the walks with my father in woods that were "ours" because my people, only three generations back, had driven out the Creeks who had lived there; that I was allowed to have my children and one evening a month with women friends because I was a wife who always came home at night to her husband. Raised to believe that I could be where I wanted and have what I wanted and be who I wanted, as a grown woman I thought I could simply claim my desire, even if this was the making of a new place to live with other women. I had no understanding of the limits that I lived within; nor of how much my memory and my experience of a safe space was based on places that had been secured for me by omission, exclusion, or violence; nor that my continued safety meant submitting to those very limits.

I should have remembered, from my childhood, Viola Liuzzo, who was trying to reach the place by another way, shot down in Lowndes County, Alabama, while driving demonstrators back to their homes during the Selma-to-Montgomery march. Her death was justified by Klan leader Robert Shelton on the grounds that "She had five children by four different husbands...her husband hadn't seen her in two, three months...she was living with two nigger men in Selma...she was a *fat* slob with crud...all over her body...she was bra-less."[5] Liuzzo—Italian, white-but-not-white, gone over to the other side—damned, dead.

I didn't die, trying to make a new life for myself out of an old life, trying to be a lover of myself and other women in a place where we were despised. I didn't die, but by spring of the next year, by May, watching the redbud tree drop flowers like blood on the ground, I felt like I had died. I had learned that children were still taken from their mothers in that town, even from someone like me, if by my wildness, by sexual wildness, I placed myself in the wilderness with those feared by white Southern men: if I joined with "every wolf, panther, catamount and bear in the mountains of America, every crocodile in the swamps of Florida, every negro in the South, every devil in Hell."[6] I had learned that I could be either a lesbian or a mother of my children, either in the wilderness or on holy ground, but not both.

I should not have been surprised at the horror of my sophisticated liberal husband; he was also an admirer of the apologists for the Old South, like the poet who named Woman and the Land as the same— beautiful, white, pure: "the Proud Lady, of the heart of fire, / The look of snow...The sons of the fathers shall keep her, worthy of / What these have done in love." But I was no longer pure; I had declined to be kept. I no longer qualified as sacred, eligible for the protection promised by a KKK founder, protection for "the [white] women of the

South, who were the loveliest, most noble and best women in the world. . . ."[7] (I asked my father, in his extreme age, to tell me about his mother, the woman he named me for. He could only say, "She was the best woman in the world.")

Why was I surprised when my husband threatened and did violence, threatened ugly court proceedings, my mother as a character witness for him, restricted my time and presence with the children, took them finally and moved hundreds of miles away? I was no longer "the best of women": what did I expect? But I had expected to have that protected circle marked off for me by the men of my kind as my "home." I had expected to have that place with my children. I expected it as my *right*. I did not understand I had been exchanging the use of my body for that place.

I learned, finally: I stepped outside the circle of protection. I said: My body, my womb, and the children of my womb are not yours to use. And I was judged with finality. Without my climbing the steps to the courtrooms of Cumberland County, I was sentenced. Without facing the judge, since my lawyer feared that "calling the attention of the court" to my lesbian identity would mean that I would never see my children again, I was declared dirty, polluted, unholy. I was not to have a home with my children again. I did not die, but the agony was as bitter as death: we were physically separated; they were seven and six, hundreds of miles away; I had held them before they were born and almost every day of their lives, and now I could not touch them. During this time I discovered that expressions I had thought to be exaggerations were true: if you are helpless with grief, you do, unthinkingly, wring your hands; you can have a need to touch someone that is like hunger, like thirst. The inner surface of my arms, my breasts, the muscles of my stomach, were raw with my need to touch my children.

I could have stolen them and run away to a place where no one knew them, no one knew me, hidden them, and tried to find work under some other name than my own. I could not justify taking them from all their kin, or their father, in this way. Instead, from this marriage I carried away my clothes, my books, some kitchen utensils, two cats. I also carried away the conviction that I had been thrust out into a place of terrible loss by laws laid down by men. In my grief, and in my ignorance of the past of others, I felt that no one had sustained such a loss before. And I did not yet understand that to come to a place of greater liberation, I had to risk old safeties. Instead, I felt that I had no place; that, as I moved through my days, I was falling through space.

I became obsessed with justice: the shell of my privilege was broken, the shell that had given me a shape in the world, held me apart from the world, protected me from the world. I was astonished at the pain. The extent of my surprise revealed to me the degree of my protection.

I became determined to break the powers of the world: they *would* change, the powers that tried to keep me from touching my children because I touched another woman in love. Beyond five or six books on women's liberation, and the process of consciousness-raising, I had few skills and little knowledge of how to act for justice and liberation, and for myself. I had no knowledge of any woman like me who had resisted and attempted to transform our home in preceding generations. I had no knowledge of other instances of struggle, whose example might have strengthened and inspired me in mine.

For instance: I knew nothing of the nearby Lumbee Indians, descendants of the folk who came into first contact with Raleigh's English in the 1500s, who four hundred years later had been part of a three-way segregated school system, white, Black, Indian; who succeeded in the 1950s in breaking up Klan rallies and cross-burnings that had warned them to "keep their place."[8]

Even though I was teaching at an historically Black college, I had no understanding of the long tradition of Black culture and resistance in the town, a tradition which reached back before the Civil War, and which had produced Charles W. Chesnutt, president in the 1870s of the school where I was then teaching, author of novels that described the market house town, political organizing by Blacks, their massacre by whites during the 1898 Wilmington elections, even the story of a white man returning to his hometown who dreamed of, and worked toward, a racially just society.[9]

I knew nothing of the nourishing of Jewish culture in that hostile Bible Belt town, nor of Jewish traditions of resistance. I learned only much later that one of the few townspeople who I knew to be politically progressive, Monroe Evans, was Jewish. His family had immigrated from Lithuania to escape the 1881 May Laws against Jews, the confiscation of property, the limitations on travel and on the right to have homes, the conscription of Jewish children into the czar's army, the violent pogroms. They had struggled to make a place in the town, one of two or three Jewish families, trying to maintain their identity among folk who alternately asked them how big was Noah's ark or called them Christ-killer.[10]

Nor did I know of the huge rallies against the Vietnam War in the 1970s, masses of people around the market house, chanting in the streets, traffic stopped. Nor that Carson McCullers, a woman very like me, living there in the 1930s, had written of the maddening, rigid effects of military life and thinking, and of the resistances of an Army wife.[11]

I knew nothing, then, of the lesbians stationed at Ft. Bragg or Pope AFB, who might spend all day scrubbing out jet fuel tanks, light-headed, isolated inside a metal cavern, and then come out at night to The Other Side to dance with lovers, play pool, no matter that the CID cruised by on Russell Street writing down license plate numbers, no matter the risk of being thrown out of the Armed Services. And later I discovered Bertha Harris' novel of being a lesbian lover, with extravagant stories that might have been told in that bar, being a passing woman in the Wilmington shipyards, being lovers with a movie star who had "hair like gold electricity," hair like my lover's hair, a book that was published the year I moved to the town that outrageous Bertha had long since grown up in and left.[12]

I knew nothing of these or other histories of struggle for equality and justice and one's own identity in the town I was living in. Not a particularly big town, not liberal at all, not famous for anything: an almost-rural eastern North Carolina town, in a region that you, perhaps, are used to thinking of as backward. Yet it was a place with so many resistances, so much creative challenge to the powers of the world: which is true of every county, town, or city in this country, each with its own buried history of struggle, of how people try to maintain their dignity within the restrictions placed around them, and how they struggle to break those restrictions.

But as yet I knew nothing of this. I entered the struggle, adding my bit to it, as if I were the first to struggle, joining with five or six other women like me in the local National Organization for Women (NOW) chapter. For the next few years, I organized educational programs: women working in the home, out of the home, women and health, power, education, the media, the military, women and rape, women in religion, minority women, women and North Carolina law. I worked on self-defense classes for women, on establishing a rape crisis line and a shelter for women who were being beaten, on editing a local newsletter, on producing women's cultural events, on nights and nights of phone calls for the Equal Rights Amendment, on a fight with the local clerk of court to make him admit women's independent name changes, on day care, on Black women's studies courses, and a daily women's news program at the college where I taught. I worked on a county advisory group for women's issues where we struggled with the local Democratic machine to try to get a Black woman appointed as our coordinator, where we pressed for implementation of our recommendations with county money, and were perceived as so radical that the courthouse rumor was that "Lesbians have taken over."

We wanted to change the world; we thought we knew how it needed changing. We knew we were outnumbered: in a town where the Berean Baptist Church owned a fleet of buses and shuttled hundreds of its members to every legislative meeting to oppose the ERA, the handful of us in NOW were the only folks using the words *women's liberation*. We tried everything we could think of to "reach more women."

We were doing "outreach," that disastrous method of organizing; we had gone forward to a new place, women together, and now were throwing back safety lines to other women, to pull them in as if they were drowning, to save them. I understood then how desperately I needed to have a place that was mine with other women, where I felt hopeful, a home to replace the one I had lost. But because of my need, I did not push myself to look at what might separate me from other women. I relied on the hopefulness of all women together; I did not think that perhaps some women would not want to be "saved" by me. What I felt, deep down, was hope that they would join me in *my* place, which would be the way I wanted it. I didn't want to have to *limit* myself.

I didn't understand what a limited, narrow space, and how short-lasting, it would be, if only *my* imagination and knowledge and abilities were to go into the making and extending of it. I didn't understand how much I was still inside the restrictions of my culture in my vision of how the world could be. But I, and the other women I worked with, limited the effectiveness of our struggle for that place by our own racism and anti-Semitism.

With a minimal understanding of history, we knew that, because of civil rights work, Black women in town were probably organized and might be potential allies. So our first community forum had one panel out of six designated with the topic Minority Women, and five of the twenty speakers for the day were Black women. This was in a day's activities which were planned, the speakers chosen, the location selected, and the publicity arranged, by three middle-class white women, me included, who had not *personally* contacted a single Black women's organization, much less considered trying to co-plan or co-sponsor with such a group. We had no notion of the doubts that Black women in that town might have about our endeavor. Neither did we consult our commonsense to discover that "minority women" in Fayetteville included substantial numbers of Thai, Vietnamese, Cambodian, Laotian, Korean, and Japanese women, as well as Lumbee women and Latinas. Attendance at the forum was overwhelmingly white; but we questioned our publicity, instead of our perspective on power.

Similarly, our thinking about allies from the civil rights movement of the sixties did not include the possibility that there might be Jewish women in town who had worked in that struggle, who might be interested in our work. Well-schooled by my past in how Jews (and Communists) were the source of "outsider trouble," the old theory that if Jews are present and visible, they must be in control, I did not turn this teaching around to question if the significant participation of Jews in civil rights work might not have had something to do with their own history of oppression. In fact, I didn't think of Jews as being *in* the town, even though I drove past a large and modern synagogue on Morganton Road every time I went to the grocery store. I did not think of Jews as *living* in the South. Blacks were definitely Southern *and* American even though they'd come from Africa (the continent a blur to me), even though I'd heard men at home mouthing off about "Send them back." But a Black woman had raised me, Black women and men had come in and out of my kinfolks' houses, cooking, cleaning; I knew that they existed. I had no place for Jews in the map of my thoughts, except that they had lived before Christ in an almost-mythical Israel, and afterwards in Germany until they were killed, and that those in this country were foreigners, even if they were here. They were always foreign, their place was always somewhere else.

So I drove past the synagogue, and when we scheduled a discussion on religion, the two women who spoke were a professor of religion and a Methodist minister. No representation was requested from the women of the local Jewish congregation, since *religion* meant denominations of Christianity. We held the session on a Saturday because, after all, Sunday was when folks went to church, or just took it easy. We had no grasp that there might be some Jewish women who would want to come, but not be able since their Sabbath was sundown Friday to sundown Saturday night.

My sense of the history of the town was as distorted as my perspective on its demographics, or its geography, or its theology. When we were organizing a day's program on rape, I was concerned that Black women know and come, so I drove up and down Murchison Road to post flyers, ignoring my uneasiness, the training of years of warnings about which parts of a town were safe for me and which were not. I could have paused to trace that uneasiness to a fear of Black men, but I did not; nor did I wonder about the history of white women in relation to Black men, or white men to Black women, or *then* question what the feelings, not to mention the experience, of Black women in relation to rape might be, compared to mine. I stapled posters to telephone poles; I politely asked permission to place them in the windows of Black-owned businesses, without ever thinking the word *lynching*, or wondering about how sexual violence was used racially by white men to keep Blacks and white women from joining forces.

Nor when we were struggling so hard with ERA ratification, during miserable nights in a doctor's borrowed office, calling strangers' names listed on file cards; during the crisis when one of our key local representatives had a religious renewal and became a born-again Christian just before the vote; during none of the three votes, over six years, did I examine the long complicated relation between the struggle for women's suffrage and Black suffrage through Constitutional amendments. I did not learn that white women's suffrage leaders, including Elizabeth Cady Stanton, had failed to take the long view required of coalition work in their disappointment over the Fifteenth Amendment being passed for male, rather than universal, suffrage. They had refused to make the reciprocal actions that would have pushed for post-Civil War voting rights enforcement for Black men in the South, so necessary for the success of revolutionary Reconstruction governments, and therefore, ultimately, for the establishment of legislatures favorable to Black and white women's suffrage.[13] I did not learn of the deliberate segregationist tactics, used by Susan B. Anthony, of refusing to organize Black women in the South for fear of alienating Southern white women from the suffrage movement.[14] Nor did I speculate over what could have happened had there been more support by Southern white women of voting rights for Blacks in the 1960s: would Black legislators have been elected, more favorable to the ratification of the ERA? I puzzled over why Black women were not more active in the ERA campaign without figuring out how *women's rights* had been a code for *white* women's rights.

When we worked to establish a battered women's shelter, even a temporary place where a woman could come be safe from male violence, I didn't wonder if it would be experienced as a "white woman's home," or if a Thai woman with her own language needs, a Jewish woman with her own food needs, a Black woman with her need to be with another woman of color that night, if any of these women or others might feel so dubious of their safety with *us* that they would choose not to come.

And even as we worked in all these ways to try to change the world, to make it safer (we thought) for all women, I did not reflect on how hesitant I was to mention my lesbian identity except to a trusted few women. I did not feel safe with many of my political co-workers: I had lost my children; I could still lose my job; and I could lose my place in this fragile new space for women I thought we were making. After all, our answer to attacks on the ERA "because it would legalize homosexual marriages" was to say that this just wouldn't happen. *I* didn't answer that there was nothing wrong with lesbians or gay men wanting public recognition of our relationships.

I was, in fact, not seeking liberation as my particular, complex self. I was working desperately to make a new place where I could live safely with other women, while denying publicly a basic part of myself; while not seeing the subtle and overt pressures on other women to also deny their different aspects, in order to exist in the outside world, and in order to come to our place. In newspaper interviews I spoke obliquely of conscious choices, alternatives, possibilities. But I did not yet understand with my heart Lillian Smith's statement that "our right to be different is, in a deep sense, the most precious right we human beings have."[15]

By 1979 I was watching the second wave of the women's movement, which had swept through this Southern town about ten years later than the rest of the country, be increasingly directed into electoral politics and social services, and less and less into grassroots women's work. I knew that I felt painfully isolated as a lesbian, but I did not analyze this in the context of our tiny movement's failure to deal with issues of difference, nor did it occur to me, as Bettina Aptheker has said of women in the first wave of feminism, that ". . . in the context of American politics, the neglect of or acquiescence in racism would inevitably force. . .women into a more and more conservative and politically ineffectual mold."[16]

Instead, I withdrew from our struggling projects. In the evenings I didn't go to meetings but wrote poetry or read, stayed at home; it was so peaceful in my three-room apartment. At night I would burn candles on the mantelpiece, no sounds but the blapping of my typewriter, or maybe the rain on the porch roof outside, fresh smells coming through the screen door. I did not have my children, but I had these rooms, a job, a lover, work I was making. I thought I had the beginnings of a place for myself.

But that year in November my idea of what kind of work it would take to keep my bit of space safe, my very idea of that space, my narrow conception, was shattered. In writing of the change in her own culture-bound perceptions, Joanna Russ speaks of "that soundless blow, which changes forever one's map of the world."[17] For me the blow was literal: the sound was rifle fire. In broad daylight, in Greensboro, North Carolina, about fifty miles from where I lived, Klansmen and Nazis drove into an anti-Klan demonstration, shouting "Nigger! Kike! Commie bastard!" They opened fire, killed five people: four white men, two of them Jews; one Black woman; all of them labor union organizers affiliated with the Communist Workers Party. The next day I saw in the newspaper an interview with Nancy Matthews, wife of one of the Klansmen. She said, "I knew he was a Klan member, but I don't know what he did when he left home. I was suprised and shocked...."[18] But the Klansmen defended their getting out of their cars at the rally, rifles in hand, by saying they saw the car holding some Klanswomen being attacked and were "rushing to their rescue."[19]

And I thought: I identify with the demonstrators; I am on *their* side; I've felt that danger. Yet in what way am I any different from the Klansman's wife? Am I not surprised and shocked that this could happen? Yet it did, and there must be a history behind it. Do I have any notion, *any*, of what white men have been doing outside "home," outside the circle of my limited white experience? I have my theory of how I lost my home because I am a woman, a lesbian, and that I am at risk because of who I am: then how do I explain the killing of Jews, Communists, a Black woman, the killing justified in the name of "protecting white women"?

I set out to find what had been done, what was being done in my name. I took Nancy Matthews' words seriously, and began by asking what had happened outside my home, outside the circle of what I knew of me and my people where I grew up. I asked my mother: she recounted Klan activity in my Alabama home town in the 1920s, marches, crossburnings, a white woman beaten for "immorality," but she didn't know what they did to Blacks. Our family not implicated, but the contrary, she was proud to say: my grandfather the judge stood up to the Klan, political death in that era, by refusing to prosecute Black men who acted in self-defense.

I read Black history: Ida B. Wells' records show that Black men were lynched in my home county, and one in my home town, for allegedly raping white women, in 1893, shortly after my grandfather opened his law practice there.[20] I wondered what he did then: anything? And my grandmother, for whom I was named. What did she do? What did she think? I gathered family letters and documents. They told me explicitly what had never been said by my kin: that on both the maternal and paternal sides of my family, we had owned slaves—twelve to fifteen people, on small "family-sized" farms; that what place and money my family had got by the mid-nineteenth century, we had stolen from the work and lives of others; and that the very ground the crops grew in was stolen. I saw the government form that bountied 160 acres to my great-grandfather Williams for fighting the Seminoles in the Creek Wars, driving them from their homes in South Georgia. Bounty, a bonus for "good work." I read transcripts of legal proceedings from after the Civil War, from testimony about the counties my folks had lived in, and where I had grown up: the voices of Black men and women came to me out of the grave, to tell of homes broken into or burned, beatings, rapes, murders by white men in retaliation for attempts to secure Black suffrage and a redistribution of land, voices telling of the attacks by men determined to keep control in the name of white Christian civilization.

These voices came to me: and I thought of my children and the grief and anger, the shame and failure I felt because I had not been able to fight for them, and have a home for me and them, against the man my husband, and the legal men, and this town, with its market house center where, within some people's memory, families *had* been sold apart from one another. The voices came: and I thought of my small but comfortable apartment, my modestly well-paying job at a Black college, gotten with my segregated-university education, gotten with the confidence and financial help of my family who had held onto a secure place for three and four generations.

During the time that I was first feeling all this information, again I lived in a kind of vertigo, a sensation of my body having no fixed place to be; the earth having opened, I was falling through space. I had had my home and my children taken away from me. I had set out to make a new home with other women, only to find that the very ground I was building on was the grave of people my kin had killed, and that my foundation, my birth culture, was mortared with blood.

Until this time, I had felt my expanding consciousness of oppression as painful but ultimately positive: I was breaking through to an understanding of my life as a woman, as a way to my *own* liberation. The cracking and heaving and buckling in my life was the process of freeing myself. I had felt keenly the pain of being punished for who I was, and had felt passionately the need for justice, for things to be set right. After Greensboro, I groped toward an understanding of injustice done to others, injustice done outside my narrow circle of being, and to folks *not* like me. I began to grasp, through my own experience, something of what that injustice might be like, began to imagine the extent of pain, anger, desire for change.

But I did not feel that my new understanding simply moved me into a place where I joined others to struggle *with* them against common injustices. Because I was implicated in the doing of some of these injustices, myself and my people, I felt in a struggle with myself, *against* myself. This breaking through did not feel like liberation but like destruction.

It felt like the catastrophic ending of a story from my childhood, one of Poe's stories that I read late at night: The walls of a house split, zigzag, along a once barely noticeable crack, and the house of Usher crumbles with "a long tumultuous shouting sound like the voice of a thousand waters." A woman is the reason for the fall of that place of "feudal antiquity"; she is the owner's twin sister who dies and is buried in a chamber deep under the house. The brother, who suffers from a continual and inexplicable terror, "the grim phantasm FEAR," becomes terrified; his friend reads a romance to soothe him, a crude tale of a knight who conquers by slaying a dragon; the sounds in the story, of ripping wood, grating clanging brass, piercing shrieks, begin to be heard in the very room where the two men are seated. In horror the brother reveals that he had buried his sister alive, but he *had dared not speak*; the sounds are "the rending of her coffin and the grating of the iron hinges of her prison. . . ." At that moment, the doors rush open; the lady stands before them, bloody in white robes, and then falls upon her brother in violent death-agonies, bearing him to the ground a corpse, shattering the house over them.

Read by me a hundred years after it was written in the 1840s, a time of intensifying Southern justification of slavery, Poe's description of the dread, nervousness, and fear of the brother, pacing through the house from "whence for many years, he had not ventured forth," could have been a description of my anxiety-ridden father, trapped inside a belief in white supremacy, a need to enforce the purity of (white) women, the fear his world would crumble if anyone, including himself, questioned these taboos out loud.

And the entombment of the lady was my "protection": the physical, spiritual, sexual containment which men of my culture have used to keep "their women" pure, our wombs to be kept sacred ground, not polluted by the dirty sex of another race; our minds, spirits and actions to be Christian, not "common," but gentlewomanly, genteel, gentile; thereby ensuring that children born of us are the sons of their fathers, are "well-born," of "good" blood, skin, family; and that children raised by us will be "well-raised," not veering into wild actions, wayward behavior.

It was this protection that I felt one evening during the height of the civil rights demonstrations in Alabama, as the walls that had contained so many were cracking, when my father called me to his chair in the living room. He showed me a newspaper clipping, from some right-wing paper, about Martin Luther King, Jr., and told me that the article was about how King had sexually abused, used, young Black teenaged girls. I believe he asked me what I thought of this; I can only guess that he wanted me to feel that my danger, my physical, sexual danger, would be the result of the release of others from containment, through the civil rights work of those like Dr. King. I felt frightened and profoundly endangered by King, by my father: I could not answer him. It was the first, the only time, he spoke of sex, in any way, to me.

I had romanticized "protection" in the hot thunderstormy summers of my adolescence as I read Tennyson's poetry, kings and queens, knights and ladies. But protection during the actual Crusades of 1095 to 1270 C.E.* had meant metal chastity belts locked around the genitals of their wives by Christian European knights, who traveled to Jerusalem to free the holy places from "the pollution and filth of the unclean," from the Islamic Persians, who, when Jerusalem was taken in 1099, were beheaded, tortured, burned in flames, while the Jews of the city were herded into a synagogue and burned alive by the Crusaders.[21]

In the United States, the Knights of the Ku Klux Klan have offered such "safety": in 1867 "as an institution of Chivalry" for the purpose of "protecting the homes and women of the South";[22] and in 1923 as "swift avenger of Innocence despoiled" and preservers of the "sanc-

*C.E. or Common Era, is an alternative to A.D., or Anno Domini, "in the year of the Lord."

tity of the home";[23] and in 1964 as working with "sincere Christian devotion" to stop "mongrelization of the white race by Blacks and Jews";[24] and in 1980 as defenders of the family and white civilization who in Klan rituals "advance to the next step of knightly honor," are baptized, and vow that they are white American citizens, not Jews.[25] Within this protection, the role of women, as described by California Klan Corps member Dorraine Metzger, is to have "lots of babies to help the white race along...at least two or three babies because the minorities are just going crazy...babies, babies everywhere."[26] What this "chivalric" behavior has meant, historically, is the systematic rape of Black women;[27] the torture, mutilation, and killing of Black men (over one thousand lynched between 1900 and 1915, many on the pretext of having raped a white woman);[28] the death of Leo Frank, a Jew accused of being the "perverted" murderer of a young white girl, falsely convicted and then lynched by the Knights of Mary Phagan, the beginning of a modern national Klan fifteen million strong at its height in the 1920s.[29] This KKK "knightly honor" has also meant the harassment and attempted intimidation of any of "their women" who rejected the "protection": white women who came South to teach Blacks during Reconstruction,[30] and who asserted their sexual autonomy during the 1920s;[31] white women who spoke out against segregation, racism, anti-Semitism from the 1940s to the 1960s;[32] who asserted economic autonomy by fighting to work in the mines in the 1970s;[33] white women who were openly lesbian at the International Women's Year Conference,[34] and those who are now doing anti-Klan organizing as open lesbians.[35]

It is this threatening "protection" that white Christian men in the U.S. are now offering to white Christian women. In his 1984 State of the Union address President Reagan linked his election to a "crusade for renewal...a spiritual revival" in America, denounced the "tragedy of abortion," stated that "families stand at the center of our society," and announced that this country has "brought peace where there was only bloodshed."[36] All this was in language that paralleled the words of Jerry Falwell's 1984 State of the Union address in which the Moral Majority leader preached a "moral awakening" for the country and condemned the "decadence" of abortion and gay rights.[37] All this in a year when abortion clinics are being bombed by a group called the Army of God;[38] when the Klansmen and Nazis indicted in the Greensboro massacre have been acquitted by an all-white jury because the U.S. Justice Department prosecution allowed them to plead that they were "patriotic citizens just like the Germans," who were also fighting against Communists;[39] when each U.S. citizen under the Reagan budget will pay $555 more to the military and $88 less to poor children and their mothers;[40] when a group of white farm wives visiting Washington, D.C., from the Midwest had U.S. policy in the Caribbean and Central America (including the invasion of Grenada) officially explained to them as a way to prevent "a Brown Horde. . .a massive wave of immigration," if "Communist takeovers" occur in the region.[41]

If I have begun to understand that I am entrapped *as* a woman, not just by the sexual fears of the men of my group, but also by their racial and religious terrors; if I have begun to understand that when they condemn me as a lesbian and a free woman for being "dirty," "unholy," "perverted," "immoral," it is a judgment they have called down on people of color and Jews throughout history, as the men of my culture have shifted their justification for hatred according to their desires of the moment; if I have begun to understand something of the deep connection between my oppression and that of other folks; what is it that keeps me from acting, sometimes even from speaking out? Why do I *dare not speak* against anti-Semitism, against racism? What is it that keeps me from rejecting this "protection" at every level?

The image from my childhood, from Poe's story, returns to me: the woman who escapes with superhuman effort from a coffin whose lid is fastened down by screws, from a vault with iron doors of immense weight. She may free herself, but then she dies violently, carrying home and kin with her, a catastrophe that she seems to cause, though what she is doing is fighting to live. Melodramatic; yet twenty years after I first read the story, when I began to admit to myself how I had been buried by my culture, coffined in heart and body—and how this was connected to my sex, my race, my class, my religion, my "morality"—when I began to push through all this, I felt like my life was cracking around me, that my world was crumbling.

I think this is what happens, to a more or less extreme degree, every time we expand our limited being: it is upheaval, not catastrophe, more like a snake shedding its skin than like death. The old constriction is sloughed off with difficulty, but there is an expansion: not a change in basic shape, but an expansion, some growth, some reward for struggle and curiosity. Yet, if we are women who have gained privilege by our white skin or our Christian culture, but who are trying to free ourselves *as* women in a more complex way, we can experience this change as loss. Because it is: the old lies and ways of living—habitual, familiar, comfortable, fitting us like our skin—*were* ours.

Our fear of the losses can keep us from changing. What is it, exactly, that we are afraid to lose?

As I try to strip away the layers of deceit that I have been taught, it is hard not to be afraid that these are like wrappings of a shroud and that what I will ultimately come to in myself is a disintegrating, rotting nothing: that the values I have at my core, from my culture, will only be those of negativity, exclusion, fear, death. And my feeling is based in the reality that the group identity of my culture has been defined, often, not by positive qualities, but by negative characteristics, by the *absence of: No Dogs, Negroes, Or Jews.* We have gotten our jobs, bought our houses, borne and educated our children by the negatives: no niggers, no kikes, no wops, no dagoes, no spics, no A-rabs, no gooks, no queers.

We have learned this early, and so well. Every spring, almost, when I was in grammar school, our field trip would be an expedition to Moundville State Park, where part of our education was to file into a building erected over a "prehistoric" Indian burial ground; to stand overlooking the excavated clay, dug out so that small canyons ran between each body, bundles of people's bones, separating each from each, as if water had eroded the earth, except it was the hands of a probably white, probably Christian archaelogist from the university, meticulously breaking into the sacred ground. Floodlights exposed people curled or stretched in the final vulnerability of death, while we stood in the safe darkness of the balconies, looking down.

It has taken a long time for me to understand that this place was sacred not because it had been set aside for death, but because it was a place where spiritual and physical life returned to life—bones and bodies as seeds in the fertile darkness of the earth. It took me so long because so much in my culture is based on the principle that we are *not* all connected to each other; that folk who seem different should be excluded, or killed, and their living culture treated as dead objects.

No wonder, then, that if we have been raised up this way, when we begin to struggle with the reality of our anti-Semitism and racism, we may simply want to leave our culture behind, disassociate ourselves from it. In order to feel positively about ourselves, we may end up wanting not to be ourselves, and may start pretending to be someone else. This may happen especially when we start learning about the strong traditions of resistance and affirmation sustained for centuries by the very folks our folks were trying to kill.

Without a knowledge of this struggle for social justice in our own culture, we may end up clothing our naked, negative selves with something from the positive traditions of identity which have helped folks to survive our people. We may justify this "cultural impersonation"[42] by our admiration and our need for heroines, as did one woman at an evening of shared spirituality which I attended: a Euro-American woman, very fair-haired and fair-complexioned, renamed herself in a ritual during which she took three women's names, each from a different tribe of Native American people; she explicitly stated that the names represented powers and gifts she desired—those of healing, leadership, love—qualities she felt she was lacking. We may also justify taking the identity of another as our own by stating a shared victimization, as I have heard from some Christian-raised women when they have mentioned that they have "always felt like a Jew" because of how they experienced exclusion and pain in their lives; sometimes they have then used this feeling to justify a conversion to Judaism, since they are "really Jewish" anyway.

Sometimes the impersonation comes because we are afraid we'll be divided from someone we love if we are ourselves. This can take very subtle forms: as when I wrote a poem for my lover, whom I'd been dealing with about issues of Jewish-gentile differences. Anxious, without admitting it to myself, about the separation that opened at times between us, I blurred our difference in the poem by using images and phrases from Jewish women's spiritual tradition as if they were from *my own*, using them to imply that she and I were in the same affirming tradition.

Sometimes we don't pretend to *be* the other, but we take something made by the other and use it for our own: as I did for years when I listened to African-American church songs, hymns, gospels, and spirituals, the songs of suffering, endurance, and triumph. Always I would cry, baffled as to why I was so moved; I understood myself only after I read a passage in Mary Boykin Chesnut's diary in which she described weeping bitterly at a slave prayer meeting where a Black lay preacher shouted "like a trumpet." She said, "I would very much have liked to shout too."[43] Then I understood that I was using Black people to weep for me, to express *my* sorrow at my responsibility, and that of my people, for their oppression; and I was mourning because I felt they had something I didn't, a closeness, a hope, that I and my folks had lost because we had tried to shut other people out of our hearts and lives.

Finally I understood that I could feel sorrow during their music, and yet not confuse their sorrow with mine, or use their resistance for mine. *I needed to do my own work:* express my sorrow and my responsibility myself, in my own words, by my own actions. I could hear their songs like a trumpet to me—a startling, an awakening, a reminder, a challenge—as were the struggles and resistance of other folk, but not take them as replacement for my own work.

In groups of white women I sometimes hear a statement like this: "We have to work on our own racism; after all, white people are responsible, so we shouldn't expect women of color to help us, or to show us where we are wrong, or tell us what to do." And I believe a similar generalization may sometimes be made about anti-Semitism: "Christian-raised women should take responsibility, and not expect Jewish women to explain our mistakes." I agree with both of these statements, but I think we will act on them only when we know and *feel* them as part of a positive process of recreating ourselves, of making a self that is not the negative, the oppressor.

I believe that we don't want to be like the U.S. government, stealing Native American land for national parks and test-bomb sites; nor like Boy Scouts who group by ancient tribal place names to practice dimly understood dances later performed at shopping malls. If we don't want to perpetuate the Euro-American tradition of theft, of *taking* from others, in large and small ways, I believe we must remember our relation to other women in the context of a national history in which we can tour the U.S. Capitol, with its elaborate murals about freedom and its statues to liberty, but if we ask about the builders, we will *not* be told: "The building was the work of hired-out slaves."[44] We must think about our relation to other women and their work if we can attend a celebration of International Women's Day, and hear accounts of the brave women organizing in New York's garment district, how their work was the foundation for our work, but we are *not* told: "Sixty-five percent of the women in the striking shirtwaist-makers, of the 'Uprising of the 20,000' were Jewish women."[45]

When we begin to understand that we have benefitted, in our privilege, from the lives and work of others, when we begin to understand how false much of our sense of self-importance has been, we do experience a loss: our self-respect. To regain it, we need to find new ways to be in the world, those very actions a way of creating a positive self.

Part of this process, for me, has been to acknowledge to myself that there are things that I *do not know*—an admission hard on my pride, and harder to do than it sounds—and to try to fill up the emptiness of my ignorance about the lives of Jewish women and women of color. It has also been important for me to acknowledge to myself that most of my learning has been based on the work of these women, that I would never have grasped the limits on my understanding and action if I had not read the work of North American Indian women: Leslie Silko, Joy Harjo, the anthology *A Gathering of Spirit,* edited by Beth Brant; the work of Black women: Toni Morrison, Alice Walker, Audre Lorde, *Home Girls: A Black Feminist Anthology,* edited by Barbara Smith; the work of Jewish women: Muriel Rukeyser, Ruth Seid, Anzia Yezierska, the lesbian anthology *Nice Jewish Girls,* edited by Evelyn Torton Beck; and the work of Asian-American women, Latinas, and other women of color in such collections as *The Third Woman,* edited by Dexter Fisher, *Cuentos: Stories by Latinas,* edited by Alma Gomez, Cherríe Moraga and Mariana Romo-Carmona, and *This Bridge Called My Back: Writings by Radical Women of Color,* edited by Gloria Anzaldúa and Cherríe Moraga.[46]

Partly I have regained my self-respect by rejecting false self-importance and by acknowledging the foundation of liberation effort in this country in the work of women, and men, who my folks have tried to hold down. For me this has meant not just reading their poetry, fiction, essays, but learning about the long history of political organizing in the U.S. by men and women trying to break the economic and cultural grip a Euro-American system has on their lives. But my hardest struggle has been to admit and honor their daily, constant work when this means their correction of *my* ignorance, resistance to *my* prejudice. Then I have to struggle to remember that I don't rule the world with my thoughts and actions like some judge in a tilt-back chair; and that by *listening* to criticisms, not talking back but listening, I may learn how I might have been acting or thinking like one of the old powers-that-be.

For me, to be quite exact, honoring this work means saying that I began to reexamine my relation as a white woman to safety, white men, and Black people, after I told as a *joke,* a ludicrous event, the story of the Klan marching in my home town: and a Black woman who was a fellow-teacher said abruptly to me, "Why are you laughing? It isn't funny." So, also, I began to reexamine my relation to the first people who lived in this country because a Shawnee woman, with family origins in the South, criticized my *use* of the Choctaw people's experience as parallel to the experience of the white women of my family: she asked, "Who of your relatives did what to who of mine?" I started to examine my grasp of the complexities of my anti-Semitism when I spoke angrily about the disrespect of Arab male students, from Saudi Arabia and Kuwait, toward me as a female teacher, while *also* saying I resented their loudness, their groupiness, the money that enabled them to take over our financially shaky Black college, while my Black students, men and women, were working night jobs to survive: and a Jewish woman, my lover, who was listening to all this, said quietly, "But your last comments are anti-Arab."

And when a month ago I walked into my corner grocery, D.C. Supermarket, 8th and F Streets, N.E., with a branch of budding forsythia in my hand, and the owners, men and women I had termed vaguely "Oriental," became excited, made me spell *forsythia*, wrote it in Korean characters on a piece of scratch paper so they would remember the name in English; and said it was a flower from *their* country, their country, pronouncing the name in Korean carefully for my untrained ears. Then I had to think again about what I understood was *mine* and what was *somebody else's*. I had to think about what I didn't understand about immigration and capitalism, and how I had taken without thinking, like picking a flower, the work and culture of Asian folk, without even being able to distinguish between the many different peoples.

As I've worked at stripping away layer after layer of my false identity, notions of skin, blood, heart based in racism and anti-Semitism, another way I've tried to regain my self-respect, to keep from feeling completely naked and ashamed of who I am, is to look at what I have carried with me from my culture that could help me in the process. As I have learned about the actual history, and present, of my culture, I didn't stop loving my family or my home, but it was hard to figure out what from there I could be proud and grateful to have, since much of what I *had* learned had been based on false pride. Yet buried under the layers, I discovered some strengths:

I found a sense of connection to history, people, and place, through my family's rootedness in the South; and a comparative and skeptical way of thinking, from my Presbyterian variety of Protestantism, which emphasized doubt and analysis. I saw that I had been using these skills all along as I tried to figure out my personal responsibility in a racist and anti-Semitic culture.

I found that my mother had given me hope, through the constancy of her regard for her mother and sisters and women friends, and through her stubbornness in the undertaking and completing of work. I found that my father had given me his manners, the "Pratts' beautiful manners," which could demonstrate respectfulness to others, if I paid attention; and he had given me the memory of his sorrow and pain, disclosing to me his heart that still felt wrongs. Somehow, my heart had learned that from his.

In my looking I also discovered a tradition of white Christian-raised women in the South, who had worked actively for social justice since at least 1849, the year a white woman in Bucktown, Maryland, hid Harriet Tubman during her escape from slavery, in her house on the Underground Railroad.[47] From the 1840s to the 1860s, Sarah and Angelina Grimké of South Carolina, living in the North, had organized both for the abolition of slavery and for women's rights, linking the two struggles. Angelina had written:

> True, we have not felt the slaveholder's lash; true, we have not had our hands manacled, but our hearts have been crushed.... I want to be identified with the negro; until he gets his rights, we shall never have ours.[48]

In 1836 in her *Appeal to the Christian Women of the Southern States*, she said:

> I know you do not make the laws, but... if you really suppose you can do nothing to overthrow slavery, you are greatly mistaken.... 1st. You can read on this subject. 2d. You can pray over this subject. 3d. You can speak on this subject. 4th. You can act on this subject....[49]

When copies of the *Appeal* reached Charleston, the sisters' home town, the papers were publicly burned, like other abolitionist literature, by the postmaster; and the police notified the Grimkés' mother that they would prevent Angelina from ever entering the city again. In a letter to her family to explain her and her sister's writings, Angelina said:

> It cost us more agony of soul to write these testimonies than any thing we ever did.... We wrote them to show the awful havock which arbitrary power makes in human hearts and to incite a holy indignation against an institution which degrades the oppressor as well as the oppressed.[50]

From the 1920s to the 1940s, Jessie Daniel Ames of Texas led an antilynching campaign, gathering women like herself into the Association of Southern Women for the Prevention of Lynching. Begun several decades after Ida B. Wells first organized, as a Black woman, against lynching, the ASWPL included, by the early 1940s, over 109 women's organizations, auxiliaries of major Protestant denominations, and national and regional federations of Jewish women, with a total membership of over four million. The women used a variety of methods to stop the violence done by the white men who were of their kin or their social group, including: investigative reporting for the collection and publication of facts about lynching locally; attempts to change white-run newspaper reporting of lynchings toward a less sensational and inflammatory treatment; signature campaigns to get written pledges from white sheriffs and other law enforcement officers to prevent lynchings; publication in their communities of the names of white "peace officers" who gave up prisoners to lynch mobs; mobilization of local peer pressure in the white community and face-to-face or over-the-phone confrontations with white men by the women; and direct intervention by the women to persuade a mob to stop its violence, including one ASWPL woman in Alabama who stopped the lynching of a Black man accused of raping her seven-year-old daughter.[51] The Association repudiated the "myth of mob chivalry"; its statement of purpose said that ". . .the claim of the lynchers [is] that they were acting solely in the defense of womanhood. . .we dare not longer permit this claim to pass unchallenged nor allow those bent upon personal revenge and savagery to commit acts of violence and lawlessness in the name of women."[52]

Lillian Smith of Georgia, who traced her political roots to the ASWPL, was an eloquent novelist, essayist, and speaker against the force of segregation from the 1940s to the 1960s. She edited, with Paula Snelling, the magazine *South Today,* and ran a summer camp for girls where she raised social issues like racism and nuclear war by having her campers create dramatic enactments of the struggle between justice and injustice as they saw it in their daily lives. She is the woman who wrote in "Putting Away Childish Things":

> *Men who kill, riot, use foul words in the name of race will kill, riot, use foul words in the name of anything that safely provides outlet for their hate and frustrations. . . . They are the "bad" people. And we? We are the people who dream the good dreams and let the "bad" people turn them into nightmares. . . . We need ourselves to become human. . . . When we reserve this humanity of ours, this precious quality of love, of tenderness, of imaginative identifi-*

> *cation, for people only of our skin color (or our family, our class), we have split our lives. . . .*[53]

In the 1940s Nelle Morton of Tennessee was also actively organizing interracial college chapters of the Fellowship of Southern Churchmen in the South, specifically to protest anti-Semitic and Klan activity, as well as starting Southern interracial summer camps for Black, white, Arab, and Asian students.[54] During the same time, Anne Braden from Alabama was moving from being a reporter on the 1945 trial of Willie McGee, a Black man accused of rape, into a lifetime of activist work. She is the woman who has said:

> *I believe that no white woman reared in the South—or perhaps anywhere in this racist country—can find freedom as a woman until she deals in her own consciousness with the question of race. We grow up little girls—absorbing a hundred stereotypes about ourselves and our role in life, our secondary position, our destiny to be a helpmate to a man or men. But we also grow up white—absorbing the stereotypes of race, the picture of ourselves as somehow privileged because of the color of our skin. The two mythologies become intertwined, and there is no way to free ourselves from one without dealing with the other.*[55]

And in the late 1950s and early 1960s many young Southern women came out of their church experience to work in the civil rights movement, and later in the women's liberation movement: Sandra "Casey" Cason and Dorothy Dawson from Texas, Sue Thrasher and Cathy Cade from Tennessee.[56] In my looking I found these women who had come before me, whose presence proved to me that change is possible, and whose lives urged me toward action.

I have learned that as the process of shaping a negative self identity is long, so the process of change is long, and since the unjust world is duplicated again every day, in large and small, so I must try to recreate, every day, a new self striving for a new just world. What do we *do* to create this new self? Lillian Smith said: Do *something* to overcome our "basic ambivalence of feelings," by which we move through our way of life "like some half-dead thing, doing as little harm (and as little good) as possible, playing around the edges of great life issues."[57]

There *are* lists of "Things To Do"—Smith published one herself in 1943.[58] We can learn something from such a list, but most of it is common sense: we already know that work against anti-Semitism and racism can range from stopping offensive jokes, to letters to the editor, to educational workshops, to changing the law, to writing poetry, to demonstrations in the street, to a restructuring of the economy. But because knowing what to do in a situation that you suspect may be racist or anti-Semitic involves judgment, and ethics, and feelings in the heart of a new kind than we were raised with, we will only be able to act effectively if we gather up, not just information, but the threads of life that connect us to others.

Even though we may have begun to feel the pull of the ties that connect us to women different from ourselves, we may not have the confidence to follow that connection toward a new world. For, as Bernice Johnson Reagon says: "We aren't from our base acculturated to be women people, capable of crossing our first people boundaries— Black, White, Indian. . . ."[59] When we discover truths about our home culture, we may fear we are losing our self: our self-respect, our self-importance. But when we begin to act on our new knowledge, when we begin to cross our "first people boundaries," and ally ourselves publicly with "the others," then we may fear that we will lose the people who are our family, our kin, be rejected by "our own kind."

If we come from backgrounds where anti-Semitism and racism were overt and acceptable, then our deep fear may be that action against these hatreds will be, as Lillian Smith says, "a betrayal of childhood love for our parents—for most of us have never learned to separate this love from the 'right' and the 'wrong' which our parents taught us."[60] If we betray them, then they will repudiate us. But even if we are from liberal backgrounds, I believe we know, also on a deep level, that we can go "too far."

If we ally ourselves with the "other" group, in a direct, personal, or public way, even if it is an issue of justice, and if this threatens our folks' self-interest, or definition of self, then there is the risk of our being "thrown out" by them. It is a real fear. We know the stories: the white Southern woman whose family rejected her when she began civil rights work; the woman whose mother didn't speak to her for seven years after she married a Black man; the woman whose parents disowned her after she became a lesbian and wouldn't see her for twenty years.

This is a fear that can cause us to be hesitant in making fundamental changes or taking drastic actions that differ from how we were raised. We don't want to lose the love of the first people who knew us; we don't want to be standing outside the circle of home, with no-where to go.

Sometimes it is possible to make a fundamental change and still reenter the familiar circle: when this happens it can seem like the future, not the present, like a new world happening. I have been there for a day, in that place, as a grown woman with my mother when she welcomed me at home with the woman who, as a lesbian, as a Jew, as my lover, I feared she might treat as an enemy. But she made a place for us, fed us in the kitchen, family not company, noon dinner. As she cooked butterbeans, she told us stories: how she'd talked to the tortoise she'd found while weeding in the daylilies. "I spoke to him. I said, 'Mr. Tortoise, now where are you going to?' but he still didn't answer me." We talked of none of our differences that day.

But when we act on our beliefs close to home, there is also the possibility of upheaval in that familiar place. Then we may again dread destruction: as when I told my mother, last August, that I had gone on the March on Washington for Jobs, Peace, and Freedom, the twentieth anniversary of the march led by Dr. King. I hadn't gone to Selma in the sixties, thirty miles from my home: where white police drove marchers who were heading toward Montgomery back up the bridge arched like a hill, high over the cold water of the Alabama River, drove them like cattle back into town. I had not marched in Selma, so I made a beginning at the anniversary march.

Walking as a lesbian, with a group of Third World and white lesbians, with the thousands, with the half-million people streaming slowly between the monumental government buildings, past the hot marble walls, I affirmed to myself that I finally was grasping the interconnectedness of me and "the others."

My act seemed more symbolic than challenging; nevertheless, what I had done quite safely in Washington was wrong to my mother: "Some day you will understand that what you all are doing is wrong." From her conversation, and later letters, I learned that the "you" doing wrong included not just the marchers, mostly African Americans, but also myself, Joan, lesbians, feminists, and Jews who named themselves Zionists because, according to my father, such Jews were "trying to control the world." She loved me and felt much pain, and shame: I was going the wrong way. I had walked away, and seemed to have turned my back on home.

The profound differences in our beliefs opened like a chasm between us, and I couldn't help but fear a separation more sharp than the old love between us was strong. (And yes, Mama, even here I risk it again, in this writing, which I have hesitated over so long, out of that fear: I say I do love you, and I am compelled *by my own life* to strive for a different place than the one we have lived in.)

I believe that as we begin to act, to try to do something about anti-Semitism or racism, it is not just kin we fear losing, but friends who are our family now. If we define ourselves as feminist, we may have worked hard to gather together women friends who will be a replacement for our blood-kin, from whom we are separated by the disruptive economics of our culture. Over the last ten years we have been building a women's community: festivals, yearly conferences, political organizations, land groups, businesses, magazines, newspapers. But if we are from families and a culture that enforced, either overtly or subtly, separation by skin and blood, I believe we need to look seriously at what limitations we have placed in this new world on who we feel close to, who we feel comfortable with, who we feel "safe" with. We can ask ourselves what we are doing *actively* to make our lives and work different from that of women who say they joined the Klan because it gives them a family closeness, a "white family," like "sisters," Klanswomen who support the Equal Rights Amendment, and express sympathy with the women's movement that has helped them gain confidence to work outside the home, start their own businesses, be more independent.[61]

I believe we can question what pressures we may put on women in our communities to be *like* us, to assimilate to our culture, be like our family, so we can feel comfortable, "at home." In what ways do we press women to talk like us, think like us, fight like us: the Arab woman who is told by Anglo friends that she fights "too angrily," the Black woman who is thought to be "too loud" by white women at a party. How does what we do differ from the obliteration practiced by the rest of the dominant culture?

When women differ from us by ethnicity, by "blood," but are white-skinned, how much does our desire for them to be like us have to do with our thinking racially in either-or categories—either you are white, or you are not—and how much does that have to do with our desire to ignore the history of rape by white men, the forced assimilation caused by rape? How much does avoiding the complexities of women's existences have to do with our not wanting to ask: Who, actually, is *in* our family? What are the possible connections by blood? And what have been the intimate daily connections, like mine to the Black woman who raised me, that we have been taught not to honor with the responsibility of family?

When we begin to ask ourselves in what ways we have re-created in our new world, our women's world, a replica of our segregated culture-bound homes, then we also raise other questions: What will happen if we challenge the racism or anti-Semitism here? Will this mean destruction of our work?

We hear the objections made by women like ourselves, in many different kinds of women's gatherings, when issues of diversity have been raised: from academic feminists at the 1981 National Women's Studies Conference who feared a "loss of unity. . .a disintegration," because the focus for all workshops was "Women Respond to Racism"; from women activists at an organizing conference who asked why we had to talk about homophobia and racism, couldn't we "just be women together"; from lesbians at a cultural conference who didn't want "divisive issues" raised during one of the few times they had "to be together as lesbians"; from women who felt that bringing up anti-Semitism was just adding another troublesome item on a list of political correctness.

We hear these objections, and we know how much they echo our own. We ask: What if I say I need this to change? Will I be the next one unwelcome here? Then comes the fear of nowhere to go: no old home with family; no new one with women like ourselves; and no place with folks who have been systematically excluded by ours. And with our fear comes the question: Can I maintain my principles against my need for the love and presence of others like me? It is lonely to be separated from others because of injustice, but it is also lonely to break with our own in opposition to that injustice.

But the fear of loss of community because issues of diversity are raised is like the fear of loss of self when we discover the connections between racism and anti-Semitism and our life as women: if we can go to the other side of this fear, we can see where there are also gains. Every time we speak or act we will likely find out more about how we need to go on changing, and meet other women who also want their lives to be the creation of a more just, more loving world.

Every year for the past five years I have gone South to a lesbian writers' conference, driving between red clay banks, past walls of kudzu. It is a small gathering, maybe sixty to eighty women, sometimes two or three Black women, a few Jewish women, the rest of us white, Christian-raised, of different classes. Every year we struggle over the same ground: over when, and how, and even whether, issues of racism and anti-Semitism and other matters of difference will be faced in that brief, four-day community—which *is*, objectors point out, about *writing;* which *is*, those of us on the other side say, about *life*. I have learned from the going back and back to the same place, and to the same people often, since many of us return every year, what a struggle it is to change my habits of a lifetime, and the beliefs of centuries we all inherited. I have learned from trying to explain *exactly* how issues which seem to be about "other" people are connected to my life as a lesbian. I get tired of trying to do this, and I get scared doing this, but every year it is a place also of great hope for me because of what I learn there.

I learned to think more clearly about the context of "safe" women's space, when I researched the land where our gathering was located to make specific the connection between our women's world and the surrounding countryside. When I discovered it was land taken from the Creeks by the State of Georgia with the collusion of a man who was also a slave trader, and that it had been, in the 1960s, a regional Klan organizing site, I could comment that as lesbians we shared these enemies, men who even today wished us dead because of who we were. What I also learned was that these facts alone merely discouraged and depressed women who were already struggling with daily small-town repression as women and as lesbians, and that I needed to figure out positive reasons for our dealing with racial and cultural difference.

From this conference, I learned how *structural* racism and anti-Semitism are, not just in male-dominated national government, but in a women's organization when it is started by a nondiverse group. If the diversity is not in the planning sessions, a shift later, in how and what decisions are made, is exceedingly difficult. I learned that this didn't stop us from struggling with the issues of difference anyway. I learned that there are ways of creating songs, rituals, stories, poems, not to escape, but to carry us forward with some hope in the struggle, so that we do not become suicidal with self-criticism.

I learned something of how the process of criticism has been shaped, for women like me, by Christianity. When I objected, strongly, to a woman's writing which I felt to be racist, another woman told me later that she didn't listen to my explanation, because I had reminded her of her self-righteous grandmother, who used to be sweet to her in private, and then, when they got to church, would expose all her sins publicly before the congregation.

I learned from this that I had to be more clear about why *I* was personally hurt by something that was anti-Semitic or racist, so that I wasn't criticizing another woman like me in a way that seemed to be I'm-good-and-you're-bad. In this particular case, I realized that my fumbling comments had been that the writer's description of a Black woman (from a historical novel) was stereotypical, based on "jungle animal" metaphors: I had criticized the *words* as racist. But my actual distress came because the Black woman was graphically portrayed in the act of being an erotic slave to a white woman; I realized that the reading of the passage out loud had intrigued me, sexually, and that then I had felt angry and ashamed because I was being drawn into, and was participating in, the degradation of a Black woman. And though I didn't understand this at all at the moment, I was able to figure it out in the process of trying to explain my objection to other women, who were upset that I had voiced my criticism.

From this experience and others, I also learned that unless a method or a time for criticism is structured into a gathering, I am on my own responsibility to comment on something I feel is insulting. When and how to do so is usually confusing, and I've learned that speaking-up is often seen as inappropriate or disruptive or threatening to the unity of the group, even when I have felt that the insulting comment or act is what has really been disruptive. And I have learned that folks may criticize the style, timing, and appropriateness of a challenge to racism or anti-Semitism to avoid examining the questionable act or comment.

When I passively witness the repetition of the old ways of doing things, and do nothing, I feel my rigid circle close around me, tightening, painful: I feel myself closing into a narrow world, away from the friendships and the creative possibilities of a place where diverse women live. In my inertia and ignorance, I do not always speak or act. When I do, there is fear, but also the exhilaration of going forward toward that place.

If we push our work against racism and anti-Semitism beyond our "home," beyond our women's groups, what fears make us hesitate to act, what gains come from acting? Last fall I went home to speak publicly, outside my women's community, about my struggles to free myself as a woman, as a lesbian, and about the connection of this to my struggle to reject what I had been taught as a white person and as a Christian. As I prepared for the trip, I began to have nightmares; and what I feared was this:

On the night before my birthday, I slept and thought I heard someone walking through my apartment. I wanted it to be my lover, but it was my father, walking unsteadily, old, carrying something heavy, a box, a heavy box, which he put down by my desk. He came through the darkness, smoking a cigarette, glints of red sparks, and sat down on my bed, wanting to rest: he was so tired. I flung my hands out angrily, told him to go, back to my mother; but crying, because my heart ached: he was my father and so tired. He left, and when I looked, the floor was a field of sandy dirt, with a diagonal track dragged through it, and rows of tiny green seed just sprouting.

The box was still there, with what I feared: my responsibility for what the men of my culture have done, in my name, my responsibility to try to change what my father had done, without even knowing what his secrets were. I was angry. Why should I be left with this? I didn't want it; I'd done my best for years to reject it; I wanted no part of what was in it—the benefits of my privilege, the restrictions, the injustice, the pain, the broken urgings of the heart, the unknown horrors.

And yet it is mine: I am my father's daughter in the present, living in a world he and my folks helped to create. A month after I dreamed this, he died. I honor the grief of his life by striving to change much of what he believed in; and my own grief by acknowledging that I saw him caught in the grip of racial, sexual, cultural fears that I am still trying to understand in myself.

The second fear came in a dream on the same night: I was in a car parked near a barn in the country, at night, at home, near a field that could have been the green seeds grown to corn. A young white man drove his tractor past me, then walked toward me; he could have been any of the boys I went to high school with. He had a shotgun in his hands and he *looked* at me: he knew *who I* was, not just by my family, but as the kind of person I was, and he knew I was no longer on his side. He aimed the gun and fired; I felt a hot shock in my head: death.

It was the first time I'd had this dream, but other women dealing with similar issues in their lives have since told me of having such nightmares. It is, in its most extreme form, the fear that can make us hesitate to act: the fear that if we challenge the men of our culture, if we break with them by saying publicly, *Do not do your violent work in our names,* then we will be punished.

But this is a dream of their inventing, where all the power lies in *their* hands. It is a dream based in their fear, and if we let ourselves be ruled by that fear, we are acquiescing in the lies taught us about who we are as women: the lies that say we are isolated, helpless, can not work with other women to widen the place of change.

Instead of this nightmare, I prefer to think of this possibility: In the early 1960s, as men in White Citizen Councils in the South planned severe economic reprisals against political Blacks, they counted on "their women" to agree to fire the Black maids and cooks working for their families. What if all the white women had refused? Had understood their place at the edge between the force of containment and the power of liberation? And had chosen to stand with the other women?

Instead, I prefer to remember that when I went South last fall I *was* with such women who were making that choice: A gathering of workers from battered women's shelters, the Southern Coalition Against Domestic Violence, met to work intensely at finding the connections between racial and cultural hatreds and woman-hating, as part of their work of making shelters into places where women could be safe from male violence, and also safe in their own complex identities.

We are offered some false gains to keep us from making the choice to stand with women different from ourselves. One is a material security equal to the men of our culture, if we side with *them* as we move outside the home, into the larger world. To draw us toward them, we are offered, not the nightmare image of the slaughtered woman, but images like the one that, as a girl, I saw flashed on the screen in a darkened theatre: a beautiful young white woman is weeping because her past affluence is gone, her plantations and her slaves; her family is without food, the garden trampled. But she digs her hands into the red clay and vows: "I'm never going to be hungry again. No, nor any of my folks. If I have to steal or kill—as God is my witness, I'm never going to be hungry again." She goes on to become financially secure, using white men for protection when necessary, using everyone she can during the social revolution of Emancipation and Reconstruction.

When I was a child, Scarlett O'Hara was a heroine as a woman within the myth of my land; today she is to me a person ready to take what is offered to her as a woman who is white, a lady of the culture, with no caring about where the land came from and who has worked it, willing to leave all others behind except her immediate family, in order to seize a narrow place of safety that she foolishly thinks is secure: the place of equality with white men.

That this is foolish security is evidenced by the number of women in poverty in this country, white women as well as women of color, a number increasing every year.[62] Anne Braden points out that historically the struggle for economic and social justice for the most disadvantaged group, which in the U.S. are African Americans once held in slavery, has substantially benefitted all other folk who were not in control of land and money; she likens this to a shift in the foundation stone of a house that causes all else to move.[63]

Today the economic foundation of this country is resting on the backs of women of color here and in Third World countries: they are harvesting the eggplants and lettuce for Safeway, they are typing secretarial work sent by New York firms to the West Indies by satellite.[64] The real gain in our material security as white women would come most surely if we did not limit our economic struggle to salaries of equal or comparable worth to white men in the U.S., but if we expanded this struggle to a restructuring of this country's economy so that we do not live off the lives and work of Third World women.

A second false gain that we, if we are privileged women, are being offered now is more "protection": this time not just in our "sacred homes," but protection of us living in the U.S. from the "powers of evil" in the rest of the world. The foreign policy of the Republican administration is being influenced by evangelical Christian beliefs that hold the U.S. has a divine calling to "protect the free world" from godless, "perverted" Communism, and from "domination" by any world leaders whose religion is not within a narrow "Judeo-Christian" tradition.[65] This apocalyptic thinking interprets all world events as enacting Biblical prophecies, especially those in Ezekiel, Daniel, and Revelations, which predict, evangelicals think, a struggle between the "forces of good and evil," culminating in the battle of Armageddon in Israel.

Christian evangelical theology believes that the forces of "good" *will* win such a battle in order to bring the second coming of Christ, the destruction of the present world, and the creation of a new heaven and earth.[66] Thus, theology-shaped U.S. foreign policy has supported Israel, but *not* because of the recognition that Jews who have been expelled from or killed in other countries for thousands of years need a place to be, as Jews. Instead, President Reagan has said, as have Christian evangelicals, that Israel is important to the U.S. as the only "base for democracy" in the Middle East, as a place that the Christian forces of good can *use* in their battle with the "evil empire."[67]

In fact, in evangelical theology, the establishment of the state of Israel, the growth of an "Arab-Moslem confederacy," the rise of "red"

Russia and China, are seen as important only as preparation for the second coming of Christ; the Christian messiah will come again only when Arabs and Jews in the Middle East "fight a battle into which all the world's nations will be drawn"—Armageddon.[68] All non-Christians will suffer horribly in these "end-days," which are described as specifically a time of "purification" for Jews. *Christian* believers will escape this holocaust, which some of them think might be a "limited" nuclear war, because they will be caught up into heaven in "the Rapture," and return to earth only after Christ's coming has prevented the destruction of the planet. Such Christian believers, in their Arab-hating and their Jew-hating (disguised as Jew-loving, the right-wing Friends of Israel) have no motivation to work for peace in the Middle East, no interest in mutual recognition and respect between Arab countries and Israel, no interest in the needs of *both* Palestinians and Israelis for safe homelands. Reagan has said, to Jerry Falwell, that he believes "We're heading very fast for Armageddon."[69]

The U.S. economy is being mobilized to enact a Christian morality play, with U.S. soldiers, or forces in the pay of the U.S., acting as an Army of God, fighting "anti-Communist" interventions throughout the world, in the Caribbean and in Central America, as well as in the Middle East. In the statements of the men running this country, I hear echoes of the condemnation, by my folks, of the civil rights movement of Black people; impoverished Third World people fighting for economic and political freedom are condemned as "Communists" and "Godless." Under these comments are the old racist beliefs: that people of color are "uncivilized," "immoral," "dirty," "naturally evil," "need to be controlled." Meanwhile, Third World countries, like Nicaragua, that need to use limited resources for literacy and health campaigns, for building a self-sufficient economy, instead must spend enormous sums of money for arms to defend against a U.S. that is reenacting the Crusades, trying to "save" the Western hemisphere.

And the people at home supposedly protected by these actions are suffering also. To fund the military build-up, cuts have been made in health programs, educational programs, job training programs, with disproportionately severe effects on all women and children, and on people of color, while about ninety-five hundred jobs for all women are lost for every one billion dollars shifted from civilian to military spending; and 63 percent of the current U.S. budget goes to pay for preparation for war and for the debt of past wars.[70] The Children's Defense Fund has said, "One third of President Reagan's proposed military increase could lift every single American child out of poverty."[71]

Again, it seems that if we are women who want a place for ourselves and for other women, and our children, in a just, peaceful, free world, we need to be saying: *Not in my name.*

From where I live I can walk down Maryland Avenue to the Capitol; it's just a few blocks. Nowadays the oak trees are blooming and there is a green pool of fallen pollen under each tree. There are concrete barricades all around the Capitol building now; around the White House, too. After we invaded Grenada last fall, October of 1983, the barricades went up; they are suppposed to prevent "terrorist attacks." Sometimes, when I'm down near the White House, I veer around the barricades and stand at the fence, just to speak to the President through the railings, toward wherever he is behind the guards and the ground-to-air missiles buried in the lawn: to tell him I think he should be ashamed of himself.

From the White House, along the Mall, up to the Capitol, all the buildings are on a monumental scale, but the Capitol dome could be the courthouse in my home town, just larger and better lit at night: the same men running things. It is hard not to feel discouraged, hard to hold on to the power of change. Nevertheless, as I walk around my neighborhood, I hang on to these bits of possibility:

I got hopeful, after the invasion of Grenada and the bombing of U.S. Marines who were occupying Lebanon, when I talked to my oldest son on the phone; he asked me, urgently, what I thought of these events. He said that he, himself, was "ashamed" of the United States, that we were "acting like a bully"; he dreaded war, his generation being called up to fight. We ended up talking about the draft, about the possibilities of resistance.

Going down to the Air & Space Museum, at the Mall, to leaflet against U.S. invasions in Central America with my small action group, gave me hope, and that we are planning a gay and lesbian protest of the North Carolina Klan/Nazi acquittals, down in front of the Justice Department. And I get hope from being in a consciousness-raising group of white women, Christian-raised and Jewish, who meet to try to grasp the impact of racism on our lives, in this town that is now our home town, and within the communities of women we belong to. We try to help each other think of ways to change, actions to take.

And I get hopeful when I think that with this kind of work there is the possibility of friendship, and love, between me and the many other women from whom I have been separated by my culture, and by my own beliefs and actions, for so long. For years, I have had a recurring dream: Sleeping, I dream I am reconciled to a woman from whom I have been parted—my mother, the Black woman who raised me, my first woman lover, a Jewish woman friend. In the dream we embrace, with the sweetness that can come when all is made right. I catch a glimpse of this possibility in my dream. It appears in waking life with my friends sometimes, with my lover: Not an easy reconciliation, but one that may come when I continue the struggle with myself and the world I was born into.

Notes

I thank Joan E. Biren for her insightful comments and careful editing without which I could not have developed this essay from its original sketchy form. Elly Bulkin's persistence and vision ensured completion of the book she co-edited with Barbara Smith and me, *Yours in Struggle: Three Feminist Perspectives on Anti-Semitism and Racism* (New York: Long Haul Press, 1984; reissued by Firebrand Books in 1988).

1. Barbara Deming, *We Are All Part of One Another,* ed. Jane Meyerding (Philadelphia: New Society Publishers, 1984), p. 326. Other works by Barbara Deming that have helped me include *Prison Notes* (New York: Grossman, 1966); *Revolution and Equilibrium* (New York: Grossman, 1971); *We Cannot Live Without Our Lives* (New York: Grossman/Viking, 1974); and *Remembering Who We Are* (Pagoda Publications, 1981). *Prison Notes* was reissued as *Prisons That Could Not Hold* with an additional essay, and photographs by Joan E. Biren, on Deming's civil disobedience in connection with the Seneca Women's Peace Encampment (San Francisco: Spinsters Ink, 1985).

2. Deming, "Confronting One's Own Oppression," in *We Are All Part of One Another,* p. 237.

3. Published since 1969, except for a one-year lapse, this newsletter went through many transformations and became *Feminary* magazine, a lesbian-feminist magazine "for the South." It was edited by a Durham, North Carolina, collective of women, which, in its last year there, included Cris South, Eleanor Holland, Helen Langa, Raymina Y. Mays, Minnie Bruce Pratt, Mab Segrest, and Aida Wakil. In 1984 it was transferred to a collective of women in San Francisco; the last issue of *Feminary* was published in the summer of 1985.

4. Sara Evans, "Southern White Women in a Southern Black Movement,"

in *Personal Politics: The Roots of Women's Liberation in the Civil Rights Move- ment and the New Left* (New York: Vintage, 1979), pp. 23–59.

5. Patsy Sims, *The Klan* (New York: Stein and Day, 1978), pp. 108–109.

6. Susan Laurence Davis, *Authentic History of the Ku Klux Klan, 1865–1877* (New York: S.L. Davis, 1924), p. 121.

7. Mrs. S.E.F. (Laura Martin) Rose, *The Ku Klux Klan or Invisible Empire* (n.p.: 1913), p. 22.

8. John Stewart, *KKK Menace: The Cross Against People* (Durham, North Caro- lina: John Stewart, 1980), p. 30.

9. Works by Charles Waddell Chesnutt include *The House Behind the Cedars* (1900), set in Fayetteville, North Carolina; *The Marrow of Tradition* (1901), set in Wilmington, North Carolina; and *The Colonel's Dream* (1905).

10. Eli Evans, *The Provincials: A Personal History of Jews in the South* (New York: Atheneum, 1980), pp. 73, 79–84.

11. Carson McCullers published *Reflections in a Golden Eye* in 1941.

12. Bertha Harris' *Lover* was published in 1976 (Plainfield, Vermont: Daugh- ters, Inc.). More information and creative discussion of Southern lesbian writers can be found in Mab Segrest's articles, "Southern Women Writ- ing: Toward a Literature of Wholeness," in *Feminary,* vol. 10, no. 1 (1979); and "Lines I Dare Write: Lesbian Writing in the South," in *Southern Ex- posure,* vol. 9, no. 2 (1981), both collected in Segrest's *My Mama's Dead Squirrel: Lesbian Essays on Southern Culture* (Ithaca, New York: Firebrand Books, 1985).

13. Bettina Aptheker, "Abolitionism, Woman's Rights, and the Battle Over the Fifteenth Amendment," in *Woman's Legacy: Essays on Race, Sex, and Class in American History* (Amherst: University of Massachusetts Press, 1982), p. 32.

14. Ida B. Wells-Barnett, *Crusade for Justice,* ed. Alfreda M. Duster (Chicago: University of Chicago Press, 1970), p. 230.

15. Lillian Smith, *The Winner Names the Age,* ed. Michelle Cliff (New York: W.W. Norton, 1978), p. 154.

16. Aptheker, p. 50.

17. Joanna Russ, *How to Suppress Women's Writing* (Austin: University of Texas Press, 1983), p. 137.

18. "Death Suspects 16 to 60," *Fayetteville (N.C.) Observer,* November 6, 1979, p. A1.

19. "Klan/Nazi Defendants Claim Self-Defense," *(Durham) North Carolina An- vil,* October 31, 1980, p. 10.

20. Ida B. Wells-Barnett, *On Lynchings: A Red Record* (New York: Arno Press, 1969 reprint).

21. Will Durant, *The Age of Faith: A History of Medieval Civilization* (New York: Simon and Schuster, 1950), pp. 591–593.

22. Rose, p. 1.

23. *Papers Read at the Meeting of Grand Dragons, Knights of the Ku Klux Klan* (Asheville, North Carolina: July, 1923), p. 136.

24. Sims, p. 243.

25. Jerry Thompson, "My Life with the Klan," special report from *The (Nashville) Tennessean*, December 11, 1980, pp. 1, 14.

26. "The 'New' Klan: White Racism in the 1980s," special report from *The Tennessean* (n.d.), p. 31.

27. Gerda Lerner, "The Rape of Black Women as a Weapon of Terror," in *Black Women in White America* (New York: Vintage, 1972), pp. 173–193.

28. *The Chronological History of the Negro in America*, comp. Peter M. and Mort N. Bergman (New York: New American Library, 1969), p. 376.

29. Leonard Dinnerstein, *The Leo Frank Case* (New York: Columbia University Press, 1968), pp. 19, 51, 71, 119, 132, 150.

30. *Testimony Taken By the Joint Select Committee to Inquire Into the Conditions of Affairs in the Late Insurrectionary States* (Washington, D.C., 1872), vols. 8–10.

31. Henry P. Fry, *The Modern Ku Klux Klan* (Boston: Small and Maynard, 1922), pp. 189, 191.

32. Anthony P. Dunbar, *Against the Grain: Southern Radicals and Prophets, 1929–1959* (Charlottesville: University Press of Virginia, 1981), pp. 230, 241.

33. Letter from Mary Weidler, American Civil Liberties Union of Alabama, Birmingham, September 26, 1979.

34. "Klan at IWY," *Do It Now: Newspaper of the National Organization for Women*, September/October 1977, p. 5.

35. Conversation about National Anti-Klan Network organizing in North Carolina with Eleanor Holland, Washington, D.C., April 30, 1984.

36. "U.S. 'Is Too Great for Small Dreams,' " *Washington Post*, January 26, 1984, pp. A16–17.

37. Letter from the Moral Majority, Inc., February 9, 1984.

38. "More Abortion Clinics Firebombed," *off our backs*, May 1984, p. 3.

39. "Green Light to Get Reds," *The Guardian*, April 25, 1984, p. 18.

40. "Less for Kids," *off our backs*, April 1984, p. 6.

41. "Chief Sees Migration, Not Mining, as Public Worry," *New York Times*, April 16, 1984, p. A7.

42. Cynthia Ozick, "Cultural Impersonation," in *Art and Ardor: Essays* (New York: Knopf, 1983).

43. Mary Boykin Chesnut, *A Diary from Dixie* (Boston: Houghton Mifflin, 1949), pp. 148–149.

44. Constance McLaughlin Green, *The Secret City: A History of Race Relations in the Nation's Capital* (Princeton, New Jersey: Princeton University Press, 1967), p. 15.

45. Charlotte Baum, Paula Hyman, and Sonya Michel, *The Jewish Woman in America* (New York: New American Library, 1975), pp. 140–141.

46. *This Bridge Called My Back* has an extensive bibliography of writing by and about women of color; it is now reprinted and available from Kitchen Table: Women of Color Press, P.O. Box 908, Latham, New York 12110. *Cuentos* and *Home Girls* are also published by and available from Kitchen Table Press. *A Gathering of Spirit*, originally published as a special issue of *Sinister Wisdom* magazine, is now reprinted by Firebrand Books, 141 The Commons, Ithaca, New York 14850. *Third Woman* was published in 1980 by Houghton Mifflin. *Nice Jewish Girls* was reprinted by Beacon Press in 1989. The most recent comprehensive anthology of writings by women of color is *Making Face, Making Soul: Haciendo Caras*, ed. Gloria Anzaldúa, published by Aunt Lute Foundation, P.O. Box 410687, San Francisco, California 94141 in 1990. Specific books by the authors I named which have helped me are: Leslie Marmon Silko's novel, *Ceremony* (New York: New American Library, 1977); Joy Harjo's poems, *She Had Some Horses* (New York: Thunder's Mouth Press, 1983); Toni Morrison's *The Bluest Eye* (New York: Holt Rinehart, 1970) and *Song of Solomon* (New York: Knopf, 1977); Alice Walker's novel, *The Third Life of Grange Copeland* (New York: Harcourt Brace Jovanovich, 1970), stories, *You Can't Keep a Good Woman Down* (New York: Harcourt Brace Jovanovich, 1982), and essays, *In Search of Our Mothers' Gardens* (New York: Harcourt Brace Jovanovich, 1984); Audre Lorde's essays, *Sister Outsider* (Trumansburg, New York: Crossing Press, 1984); Muriel Rukeyser's poems in a collected edition by McGraw-Hill in 1982; *Wasteland*, a novel by Ruth Seid [Jo Sinclair] (New York: Harper, 1946); Anzia Yezierska's autobiography, *Red Ribbon on a White Horse* (New York: Persea, 1950).

47. Aptheker, p. 35.

48. Gerda Lerner, *The Grimké Sisters from South Carolina* (New York: Schocken, 1971), p. 353.

49. Lerner, p. 139.

50. Lerner, p. 267.

51. Jacquelyn Dowd Hall, *Revolt Against Chivalry: Jessie Daniel Ames and the Women's Campaign Against Lynching* (New York: Columbia University Press, 1979), pp. 175, 223–253.

52. Jessie Daniel Ames, *The Changing Character of Lynching, 1931-1941* (Atlanta, Georgia: Commission on Interracial Cooperation, 1941), p. 64.

53. Lillian Smith, in *From the Mountain: Selections from. . . South Today,* ed. Helen White and Redding S. Suggs, Jr. (Memphis, Tennessee: Memphis State University Press, 1972), pp. 131, 136–137.

54. Dunbar, p. 230.

55. Anne Braden, *Free Thomas Wanley: A Letter to White Southern Women* (Louisville, Kentucky: Southern Conference Educational Fund, 1972).

56. Evans, pp. 33–36.

57. Smith, "Addressed to Intelligent White Southerners," in *From the Mountain,* pp. 116–117.

58. Smith, pp. 116–131.

59. Bernice Johnson Reagon, "Coalition Politics: Turning the Century," in *Home Girls,* p. 361.

60. Smith, "Putting Away Childish Things," in *From the Mountain,* p. 135.

61. Bonnie Wolf, unpublished paper, Cambridge, Massachusetts, 1981, p. 17. For other discussions about femaleness and white Christian culture, from the point of view of white women, see: Maureen Brady, "An Exploration of Class and Race Dynamics in the Writing of *Folly,*" in *13th Moon,* vol. 17, no. 1–2, pp. 145–151; Pamela Culbreth, "A Personal Reading of *This Bridge Called My Back,*" in *Sinister Wisdom 21* (Fall 1982), pp. 15–28; Andrea Dworkin, *Right-Wing Women* (New York: Perigee, 1983); Nadine Gordimer, "Living in the Interregnum," *New York Review of Books,* January 20, 1983, pp. 21–29; Marilyn Frye, "On Being White: Toward a Feminist Understanding of Race and Race Supremacy," in *The Politics of Reality: Essays in Feminist Theory* (Trumansburg, New York: Crossing Press, 1983); Adrienne Rich, "Disloyal to Civilization: Feminism, Racism, Gynephobia," in *On Lies, Secrets, and Silence* (New York: W.W. Norton, 1979), pp. 275–310; Lillian Smith, *Killers of the Dream* (New York: Anchor, 1963).

62. "The International Feminization of Poverty," *off our backs,* August/ September 1983, p. 5.

63. Anne Braden, "Lessons from a History of Struggle," *Southern Exposure,* vol. 8, no. 2, p. 61.

64. "International Feminization," p. 5.

65. Robert Zwier, *Born Again Politics: The New Christian Right in America* (Downers Grove, Illinois: InterVarsity Press, 1982), pp. 42, 45.

66. Hal Lindsey, *The 1980's: Countdown to Armageddon* (New York: Bantam, 1981), pp. 9–16.

67. "Does Reagan Expect A Nuclear Apocalypse?" *Washington Post,* April 8, 1984, p. C4.

68. Lindsey, p. 53.

69. "Does Reagan Expect...?", p. C4.

70. "Your Income Tax at Work," *The Washington Peace Center Newsletter,* March 1984, pp. 1, 5. In this article, figures are from *The Budget of the U.S. Government-FY 1985;* percentages were computed *after* amounts for Social Security were removed.

71. "Less for Kids," p. 6.

"I Plead Guilty to Being a Lesbian"

All weekend the grey rain has come down, the first fall rain in the city, melancholy, isolating, shutting us behind a cold curtain, inside apartment buildings and narrow rowhouses. This is the weekend when night becomes longer than day; by early evening the daylight is gone, rain muffles the noise from the street, outer realities vanish. I'm left alone in my three rooms, in silence in-

This essay about the lesbian and gay mass civil disobedience of October 13, 1987, was written with the help of narratives from other members of the LIPS affinity group: "We believe in getting the word out."

terrupted by a few small sounds: the ping of the elevator, a thump on the wall from Sharon's two-year-old next door, the rattle of my typewriter.

All weekend I've been trying to write about what happened a year ago, to write as a way of marking the anniversary and the significance of events almost the opposite of what I am feeling now. A year ago reality was briefly, hugely, communal. In days of brilliant sunshine or bright greyness, hundreds of thousands of men and women like me gathered in D.C. for the biggest-ever civil rights march, to demand gay and lesbian rights. The March itself was a conglomeration of the contradictions of our community, from the dancing man costumed as a purple-and-green velvet pansy to the three-piece-suited young Republican; from the women snare-drumming behind a phalanx of U.S. flags to the women in rainbow colors with clanging bells and hand drums, who looked as if they could have just arrived from a women's peace encampment.

The March was evidence of how we've worked for the last twenty years to live our lives out in the open, to have our love not be hidden as a secret, or punished as a sin and crime. We saw ourselves in the proliferation of organizations and groups from a geography as wide as the States, as the world. We saw the art of our flamboyant costumes, the monumental pieced-together quilt for those dead of AIDS; we heard our defiant, mocking, mournful chants and songs; we gathered the papers scattered through the crowd that announced concerts, workshops, lobby sessions with members of Congress, the giant wedding of queers, the town meeting on sex and politics, the benefit dances to raise money for political causes. The March was the evidence given by half a million lesbians and gay men that none of us had to be isolated or alone.[1]

When I was out walking on Maryland Avenue the Saturday before the March with my friend Jo Angela, butch to my femme, we met a young Black man who might have been a neighbor passing by, who could have passed for heterosexual, except he smiled at us and said, "Going to the Wedding this afternoon?" And when my lover Joan and I were on our way to Sherill's for breakfast, we were greeted by an older white man walking his poodle who also smiled and said, "Welcome to D.C., ladies." To which we replied, "But we live here. We *live* here!"

Except this was a place I had never lived in before, a place where my walking out with another woman brought smiles and approval from strangers on the street. It was a place of joy where I had never lived, and where, despite that weekend, I still do not live: men routinely taunt women with the catcall *dyke* on the street corner on Saturday nights; I am a potential felon for any loving acts I commit in my own home in the District of Columbia, where sodomy, my "unnatural" love, is still a crime.

Despite my insistence on being myself as a lesbian to my family, to my students, in my writing, and on the streets with my lover, I had not realized, until the weekend of the March, how constantly I had guarded against a destroying look, a hateful sneer. I had been cut off from the joy of being recognized as who I am and welcomed, not in spite of, but *because* of this. In the past, a friendly knowing look in some dangerous public space had been a solitary, fugitive exchange between other women and my lover and me: a glance like a secret code. But that weekend these glances were no longer hidden; they were given like blessings on every street corner. I had known the raw oppression of being a lesbian and, because of my sexual self, of being declared unfit as the mother of my children. And I had felt the danger of the names thrown at me on the street corner. But until that weekend, I did not understand the tense inner barrier that had guarded me for years from how I might be recognized as a dyke out in the world; the barrier that kept one aspect of my self always apart, expecting hate, not joy.

On the Tuesday after the March, I walked over to the Supreme Court building with my friend Elly: only eight blocks to walk, right in the neighborhood, but crossing over to some new place in myself, a little after seven o'clock on a lush golden morning, in the promise of slanting sunlight and in the clamorous cries and shouts of thousands of people gathering there. We were on our way to meet our affinity group beside a fountain with bronze naked women at the Library of Congress, on our way to being part of a public protest against those who hated us, those who had made the laws that made us criminals.

The Supreme Court was chosen for the protest by March organizers because of the 1986 *Bowers v. Hardwick* decision in which a majority of the Justices had rejected an appeal by Michael Hardwick for Constitutional protection of his right to privacy in his own home for his intimate sexual relationships. An Atlanta policeman, harassing Hardwick for being gay, went to his house, was admitted by a roommate, went into Hardwick's bedroom, walked in on Michael and another man making love, and arrested them for violating the Georgia sodomy statute.

(When I heard of that arrest, I imagined looking up from the passion of lovemaking with Joan, naked, sweaty, hot, dreamy with sex, to see a tall, tall white man standing over us in trooper grey and a wide-brimmed hat, or would it be a blue uniform, gleaming with metal? I remembered when our friend Barbara told us about her recurrent nightmares of being caught in bed with her woman lover, searchlights hunting them, blazing on them, caught, naked, criminals.)

In June 1986, Justice White, writing for the majority, reminded the country that sodomy was a criminal offense at common law when the Bill of Rights was written; said that love between people of the same sex violated the Judeo-Christian tradition of America. And said that for Hardwick "to claim that a right to engage in such conduct... is 'implicit in the concept of ordered liberty' is, at best, facetious." White compared Hardwick's lovemaking to "possession in the home of drugs, firearms, or stolen goods"; and compared this act of consensual adult sex to "adultery, incest, and other sexual crimes." In the end he declared:

> Even if the conduct at issue here is not a fundamental right, respondent asserts that there must be a rational basis for the law and that there is none in this case other than the presumed belief of a majority of the electorate in Georgia that homosexual sodomy is immoral and unacceptable. This is said to be an inadequate rationale to support the law. The law, however, is constantly based on notions of morality, and if all laws representing essentially moral choices are to be invalidated under the Due Process Clause, the courts will be very busy indeed. Even respondent makes no such claim, but insists that majority sentiments about the morality of homosexuality should be declared inadequate. We do not agree, and are unpersuaded that the sodomy laws of some 25 States should be invalidated on this basis.[2]

Clear enough from the highest court in the land: They are the majority and they rule. They can treat us as they please, no reasons needed. They are good, we are bad, and to say that we, as a minority, expect our right to privacy to be protected is "facetious"—laughable. They condemn as immoral our love that extends far beyond a specific sexual act, a love as necessary to our living as breath. They attempt to condemn us to different kinds of death.

They do not acknowledge: The gay man thrown off a bridge, drowning because of who he loved. The lesbian raped and murdered when she walked out of a gay bar late at night. Those of us forbidden the children of our bodies; kicked out of our parents' house, or out of the college dorm, or out of our apartments; fired from a job. Those of us denied medical treatment; spat at or threatened or beaten in the street; locked up as mentally ill, castrated, or half-electrocuted by shock treatments.[3]

In our defense, Justice Blackmun commented that not so long ago the religious tradition of the majority was used to make interracial marriages illegal. He wrote, "A State can no more punish private behavior because of religious intolerance than it can punish such behavior because of racial animus." He emphasized that ". . .the right of an individual to conduct intimate relationships in his or her own home seems to me to be the heart of the Constitution's protection of privacy."

But his opinion disclosed no understanding that our lives as lesbians and gay men are more than one kind of sex act performed behind a closed door; no statement that our kind of loving, made public, could be a liberating possibility for others. Justice Blackmun didn't mention that the majority might have some lesson to learn about themselves if they could bear to look at the joy of me and Joan, walking down the street after dinner, Saturday night, holding hands; if they could bear to consider why our sexual pleasure has been condemned by them as sexual crime.

The group of women I was walking toward through the golden morning light had begun several years earlier as a collective anarchy of five-to-ten dykes, calling ourselves LIPS. Not an acronym for anything, Eleanor said: "It's just like Coke; LIPS stands for itself and that's it." But, of course, the double meaning of *labia* was always there, underneath, slightly lurid, lascivious. After the 1986 Hardwick decision came down, we talked about having a kiss-in at the Court, inside the courtroom. We imagined making out on cue in the hushed judicial silence. Could we get arrested just for French-kissing, as lesbians, in public?

We had been doing political work together since 1983 when we began meeting because of the U.S. invasion of Grenada. We had demonstrated against the Klan, against Attorney General Meese's Pornography Commission report, against the Rehnquist appointment to the

Supreme Court. We'd done voter registration, graffiti spray-painting, and street theatre. We'd been arrested and done support work at South Africa anti-apartheid and Central America anti-intervention rallies. We'd written and handed out leaflets about citizen rights if the FBI came calling, and leaflets about the connection between sexual pleasure and the right to abortion. We'd made songsheets for marches and stickers for park benches: *Open Your Eyes To Reagan's Lies*. In our statements and press conferences we were always clear that we were lesbians and that our analysis was from a lesbian perspective. Everything was signed: *LIPS: We believe in getting the word out*.

But we'd never done a public action that was just for us. For us as lesbians.

So after the decision came down, we fantasized about a kiss-in at the Supreme Court. We had no particular discussion of nonviolent philosophy or civil disobedience. We did not consciously try to search out the point of pressure, the essence of action, that could free us as lesbians. We didn't talk about how Black folks in Selma had crossed a police line made of string, guarded by brutal force, a crossing made not for symbolic reasons but to get into the courthouse to register to vote. We didn't discuss how in India, despite violent beatings by the British soldiers, Gandhi had led people in walking down to the sea, again and again, for a salt that was not metaphor but necessary for life.

But we knew that a kiss between us was as necessary to our lives as salt or bread. Without talking strategy or philosophy, we chose that illegal gesture: a public display of our affection for each other as lesbians, made in the highest court in the land, that would defy the official judgment that our lives were forbidden and criminal.

We didn't discuss, even among ourselves, what it had cost us in the past to make loving gestures, declarations of ourselves, in public; how seldom we had risked touch, how sometimes we had, and had suffered. We didn't say to ourselves that our lives as lesbians and gay people had been one long act of civil disobedience, because we had continued to find and love each other, no matter what the law said. We simply sat in chaotic meetings at Betsy's or Jennie's or Urvashi's house and fantasized about kissing in the Supreme Court chamber.

But in the end, summer and fall of 1986, we didn't feel ready for an action at the Court with our handful of people. Even though the folks in our group had grown bolder and bolder as "out" lesbians over the years, there were still women who worried that someone from work would see them at a demonstration on TV and make trouble. A few of the lawyers in LIPS began to speculate on how a conviction for contempt in the Supreme Court could affect their careers: was disbarment possible? And I began to imagine, with a shiver, what it would be like to be one of four or six women kissing in that vast chilly chamber.

We weren't ready to go on our own then, but, by the time of the 1987 March, we were ready for the plans for mass civil disobedience. When Michelle Crone, national coordinator for civil disobedience (CD), came to visit, Joan and I drove her one moonlit night to the Court, reconnoitering its possibilities as a location for massive protest. We pulled up to the front sidewalk to look for traces of a LIPS graffiti—*In Search of Reagan's Brain* (thanks to Doonesbury)—spray-painted there, at the White House, the Heritage Foundation, and elsewhere on the eve of the second inauguration. We told Michelle of our fantasies of an erotic political action, and we circled the building to look for entrances, for large public spaces where people could sit down, lie down, and embrace each other.

I can't remember if, in the dim light, I could see the words *Equal Justice Under Law* carved above the columned entrance, over the heavy bronze doors, above the wide stone plaza. Not until much later, perhaps after the civil disobedience was over, did I realize how literally I was protesting the injustice that had been done to me in my life as a lesbian: The legal pressures brought to bear on me by husband, lawyer, court. The attempts to make me think of myself as an unfit mother. The sordid interview in the courthouse when I had to swear I was signing the divorce agreement "under no duress," when there had been verbal and physical threats that I give way or never see the children again. The legal attempts to break my spirit: How helpless I had felt as the idea of justice became a mockery to me, and the legal system but another way to punish and restrain me. How I'd felt for months and years a huge rage, and the pressure of doors shut on me, against me, separating me from myself. How I had imagined breaking that barrier with my hands, with bare fury.

We sat uneasily in Betsy's living room, a group of twenty lesbians talking hardly at all to each other the day after we'd marched with more lesbians and gay men than we'd ever seen before. We were waiting for the meeting to start when we would decide what to do the next day during the civil disobedience at the Court. LIPS had been at a standstill by the time of the March, but I had wanted us to do one more action, to be the core of an affinity group for the CD, so I had coordinated this meeting. Now we sat, awkward, virtually a new group, with many out-of-towners. Most of us knew only two or three other lesbians there, who, in turn, knew a few of the others present. We were a chain, flexible and durable, of lovers, ex-lovers, friends.

From New York City came Jill Harris and Lauren Young, a lawyer and a typesetter, and ex-lovers; as well as Amber Hollibaugh, an AIDS educator and video artist who had been active in writing and speaking about sexual pleasure. Elly Bulkin was also down from New York City, where her political work had ranged from the lesbian literary magazine *Conditions* to antiracist coalition work to New Jewish Agenda. Jennie McKnight had traveled from Boston, having just moved there from D.C. to work as an editor for *Gay Community News*. Jenifer Firestone, also from Boston, performed with the Ten Percent Revue, a cabaret act with lesbian and gay themes.

We had Tacie Dejanikus, a local March coordinator for D.C., who'd worked for years on the radical feminist newspaper *off our backs (oob)*. Tacie brought with her a friend, Beck Young, who had done antiapartheid organizing in college. Others from D.C. were Lauren Taylor and Wendy Melechen who had done organizing on many Jewish, lesbian, and feminist issues. DeDe de Percin, who had been involved with the Seneca Women's Peace Encampment, was there; she knew Lauren Taylor from karate class. Sue Lorentz, who said she was inspired by the nonviolent activism of Barbara Deming, had done civil disobedience and peace work since the anti-Vietnam War movement.

During the meeting these were the women who decided to be arrested, as I did. Other women there, all in-towners, decided to do support work. They included Priscilla Hayner, another karate friend of Lauren Taylor's; Angela Marney, Tacie's lover, who also worked on *oob*; Betsy Cohn, who was head of a Nicaragua information service; Bonnie J. Berger, Beck's lover, a staff member at a national women's organization; Laura Flegel, a government lawyer; and Terry McGovern, Laura's lover, who until recently had practiced poverty law in New York City.

LAURA: *Over the weekend it came home to me, through the vision of what life might be like without it, that lesbian and gay oppression really does distort my life and impair every human relationship in a way that is absolutely intolerable. And so unnecessary. I found that I couldn't not participate in this history that was happening on my own behalf in my own city.*

TERRY: *During my first year at Georgetown Law School, a D.C. trial court*

*declared the University's policy of discrimination against gays permissible as
an expression of religious belief. At that point in my life, I realized that justice
and fairness were not concepts that applied if you were gay.*

*I wanted to participate in the Supreme Court action because, among other
things, I am a lawyer. I understand that all rights are contingent upon inclusion and protection by the Constitution, and I understand that the Hardwick
decision wrote lesbians and gays out of the Constitution. Moreover, I have
learned watching my gay friends die of AIDS that we may as well live kick-
ing and screaming for our rights, and validate our own pain. AIDS and the
Hardwick decision have taught me that no other cause or political movement
is worth my life's fervor if it cannot recognize and respect my choice to live
as a lesbian.*

In the newly created affinity group, only four were from our original LIPS group: Betsy, Jennie, Terry, and I. Other LIPSters were working at large in the Supreme Court action: Urvashi Vaid and Sue Hyde,
Jenifer's lover, both of whom were on the staff of the National Gay and
Lesbian Task Force (NGLTF); Ruth Eisenberg, also a government lawyer; and Joan E. Biren (JEB), my lover, who had been photographing
the gay and lesbian movement for sixteen years. But of those lesbians
in Betsy's living room that afternoon, most of us were strangers to one
another.

And there were many issues, undiscussed, that lay between us.
Doing civil disobedience was an economic hardship for some of us,
who'd had to raise bail money from friends, and others simply couldn't
afford to take the time off from work. Some who were still not out at
work risked losing their jobs by such a public lesbian action. There
were no women of color in the CD group, and, once again, we had
to question, as white women, how racism worked in our personal
lives, in our political and friendship connections. Some of us had bitterly and publicly disagreed over political issues in the lesbian community, including the sexual pleasure/pornography debate. The one
woman who was mother of a small child carried a different weight
from the others in trying to guess the risk she undertook.

All of these conflicts, and more, lay unspoken between us when
we met for the first time that Monday. We had only an hour to come
to some kind of agreement before we had to move on to the gathering of the affinity groups at All Souls Church. As I facilitated, we
agreed on a lot of issues rather quickly. Most women felt that they had
a forty-eight-hour limit on the time they could stay in jail before paying a fine to be released; most wanted to forfeit out on bond as soon

as they could; many wanted to cooperate fully, although a few decided to go limp and noncooperate on arrest.

But our serious debate began with the question of which "wave" to join, which group of people to walk forward with in an attempt to approach the doors of the Court, in our effort to go in and be *heard.* The three choices for waves which had been set up by the CD organizers were "national lesbian and gay rights groups," "people with AIDS and their supporters," and a "women's wave." At first we had decided without discussion to go in the all-women's group. But several women challenged that decision because the wave was not being called *lesbian,* even though most, if not all, of the women's wave affinity groups were probably lesbian. Elly said, "I've gone to a lot of trouble to *be* a dyke, and I want to be arrested *as* one." We had a spirited, somewhat anxious, discussion until we all agreed that we would try to get the organizers to designate a wave as *lesbian* and we would go forward in that group.

We were a gathering of women who knew, but did not know, each other. We sat and talked together with the power of our shared lives as lesbians in this country and in the shadow of bitter conflicts between us. Power shimmered in each of us and in the group, while beside each of us stretched a shadow, the memory of having been the isolated one, outlawed, excluded, alone. And yet we sat trying to make some way to walk together, as lesbians, for at least a few minutes the next morning.

In the late afternoon, in the long slant of sun and shadow, we straggled from Betsy's house through the streets of Mt. Pleasant, toward the gathering at All Souls of participants in the next day's civil disobedience. As we walked in clumps of two or three with the women we knew best, we met and passed people coming home from work, mostly Latinos, some of the refugees and immigrants from Central America who lived in the neighborhood, men and women swinging wearily down off the bus. For them, for most of the others on the street, the evening we walked toward was nothing more than the end of a long day's work. I felt slightly dizzy, standing on the traffic island between inexorable, anonymous streams of cars, waiting to cross over to prepare for an action that I hoped would somehow change everyone's daily life, by making more of a place for lesbian and gay lives. Standing on the street, I found it hard to imagine how.

But when we entered the church, we saw more than eight hundred people in the sanctuary, filled with an exhilarating spirit. A camera person from Channel 7 came in to pan the crowd for the evening news, thinking, perhaps, that we would just sit and look like a big committee meeting. When he turned on his lights, everyone jumped up, shouting "WE WANT JUSTICE" with fists in the air. We didn't stop until the lights went off, and we knew that the only picture he had was our outcry: "JUSTICE."

During the evening, we sent representatives from our affinity group to various information meetings: medical, cooperation/noncooperation, media, legal, support, spokespersons. But our main work was a long process of trying to reach consensus over our group identity. Our representatives, Tacie and Elly, managed to get the organizers to agree to rename the women's wave *lesbian/feminist*. They returned to us elated, thinking they had solved our problem. However, Amber, and to some degree, Jill and Lauren Young, said they could not participate under that name. Amber said she had suffered too much as a lesbian from the actions of feminists during the sex debates of previous years to feel right about identifying with that group. We didn't talk at all at the time about why any one of us felt that she couldn't go out under *lesbian*, or *lesbian/feminist*, or *gay*. We seemed simply to agree to respect each other's serious feelings. Tacie, and others, then said they they could not go in the mixed gay men and lesbian first wave. I thought at this point that we would split up as a group.

Yet I thought we were all being amazingly calm with each other and that perhaps if we split up, we might do so with no harsh feelings. Later I wondered if we did so well because there had already been many divisions and heartaches in our different lesbian communities; perhaps we had no illusions about community. I also wondered if our perseverance came in part because many of us had been doing coalition work, and we had learned something about the differences among us.

Finally, during this discussion about group identity, someone, Wendy I think, elaborated by Elly, suggested that we demand that the first group to cross over to the Court be lesbian, though as part of the gay/lesbian wave; and that there would be alternating all-lesbian and mixed groups within that wave. With me still facilitating, we all agreed to this in the name of lesbian visibility. We sent Amber and Tacie together to the spokespersons' meeting, the meeting of representatives from all affinity groups. I thought that if the two of them, who had often held opposing positions in political matters, could get a plan through that they both agreed on, we could all agree to it.

The spokespersons' meeting was run by a woman who buried our concern until the last five minutes, then let two people speak against us (one woman and one man); both condemned our plan as separatist.

JENIFER: *The significance to me of us being the ones to raise the issue of lesbian visibility is that a tremendous amount of heavy-duty consciousness-raising needs to be done among our gay brothers. They do not yet recognize the way sexism operates, and they aren't hip to the fact that they must share and give up some of their undeserved but matter-of-course power as (usually) white men. I can't tolerate being treated by my gay brothers in the same fucked-up ways that straight men have always done, ignoring our lesbian experience, expertise, and hard work. I do not think of this as separatism.*

BECK: *One of the comments made in our group about the objections set off bells for me. Someone said, "Those people thought it was about lesbian separatism, but that's not it—our plan didn't have anything to do with that." But if any of the group felt that her actions were dictated to some extent by lesbian separatism, then they were.*

The splits that have been forced upon us by political coalitions in the past came screaming through that night: Am I more a woman, or am I more a lesbian? Am I queer, or feminist? Am I motivated by good sex or politics? Part of my motivation for demanding a lesbian wave was my outrage at being forced to split myself (again), to segment my identity.

Another clue to the real issues behind our articulations is to remember our reaction—unified reaction—to the protestations against a lesbian wave by a man during the final general discussion. When he said, "Why are you being divisive now? We're all in the same boat," the immediate response of "No, we are not!" was, I believe, thoroughly shared within the group.

Though I must qualify this by admitting that my own definition of lesbian separatism is unorthodox, the demand for a distinct lesbian wave was in part, for me, a separatist demand. We all responded that night to an outrageous comment in the full knowledge that we, as lesbians, are in a separate boat from gay men. By ignoring that, by pretending that our lives, needs, and motivations are the same—as the entire March/CD weekend had pretended—any possible feminist agenda was buried. We are separate, and until we take control of those distinctions and make the inequities and simple differences visible on our own terms, our work and our energies will be naively spent on an imaginary "common agenda" that in reality keeps us invisible.

The one person the chairwoman let speak *for* our proposal was a man, a Radical Faerie, who understood exactly why the first wave needed to be identifiably lesbian in an action that would be reported as exclusively about gay men unless we were more conscious and aggressive at advancing lesbian visibility. He said he didn't want to open the *New York Times* and see lesbians tacked on in a paragraph at the end—again. After he talked, the spokespeople agreed to a compromise, also proposed by a man, that the first group up the steps of the Supreme Court be all-lesbian, but they would not accept the proposal of alternating groups of lesbians with gay men and women. Back in our affinity groups, we all agreed (though some reluctantly) to this plan.

When the meeting as a whole reconvened, Amber went to the microphone and announced our plan, which had already been presented to the individual groups by their "spokes"; she got rousingly cheered when she said the first affinity group to be arrested would be lesbian. Then some people started booing and yelling that consensus had been abandoned. The chair of this meeting, who was also a woman—most of the significant CD people were lesbians, including head of medical, head of legal, publicity spokeswoman, and overall coordinator—put her foot down. She said that we had had consensus in the spokespersons' meeting, and that was that. Some complaining continued, but finally one of the two men who spoke from the podium asked for an acknowledgment of women's leadership in the action: he said that everyone had worked together, but that lesbians had provided key experience and guidance. At this point everyone cheered satisfactorily. (But, thinking back, I can't remember if he actually said *lesbian*. Perhaps he only said *women*. Did he say the L word?)

At the close of the meeting we waited by the front door for other lesbian groups to meet us, as we had asked, so we could plan the first wave. But no one else came. We left thinking that we would have to go forward the next day first and alone, just the thirteen of us. This was not what any of us had planned to do; we thought we'd be hidden away in a mass of people, not walking out front.

On Tuesday morning, as we crossed the East Lawn of the Capitol, facing the Court, we were still trying to figure out what we were going to do as civil disobedience. We had used all our energy and time in an effort to stay together as lesbians. We had made no plans about what our action would be.

We crouched in the green dewy grass, in the beautiful light, in the ecstatic energy of four thousand people. Intense joy condensed around us as we gathered there, a nimbus of light.

As we made our plans, Betsy kept an eye on Mary Lee, who was in charge of starting the action, to make sure that we *would* go first, after all our trouble. Amber looked for other dyke groups to join us. Suddenly, the Sojourners affinity group appeared—women from Ohio, New York, and Virginia; the nine of them wanted to go with us.

Together, we decided we would walk across the street in a line, holding hands, singing, *When the dykes go marching in* to the tune of "The Saints Go Marching In." And we'd sing, *I've been cheated / been mistreated / when will I be loved,* my suggestion, my memory from being for the first time a lesbian in public with other lesbians, sitting in an auditorium with hundreds of women singing this song, waiting for the Red Dyke Theatre to begin, Atlanta, 1976, the Great Southeast Lesbian Conference.

And this day, marching across, we'd sing, *My body's nobody's body but mine / You run your own body / Let me run mine,* written with infinite raunchy stanzas, but we knew only the chorus. After singing, we would stop on the steps, kiss each other at length, then go forward and speak individually to the police in front of us, explaining why we were there. Finally we would try to cross the barricades. We ended our planning by practicing our songs with great enthusiasm, off-key and loud.

Everything went according to our plan at first. What we were not prepared for was the immense energy—physical, spiritual, political—coming from everyone else. When we started moving across the street, and we were the first to go, the voices of people rolled over us like a huge wave, a cry of love and hope, a sound that usually only the lover hears from the beloved, shut away in some private room, but on that day, enormously loud, heard by us all, meant for us all. As if that energy, anger, love, determination were going through my body, through all of us, as if my molecules were being altered in some permanent way. I was profoundly happy, as happy as I've ever been in my life. It was very sexual, like going through to some deliciously sweet place, but also tumultuous and noisy.

We had to push through our folks, and through the media, which was the other part we weren't ready for. Some male reporter at my elbow was speaking into a microphone, describing us as if he were reporting on a prizefight, blow by blow. The video cameras seemed to be focusing on our teeth, they were so close. Yet it was as if these observers were in one place, and we were in a place entirely different. When we finally got up to the police, singing all the while, though barely able to hear ourselves, we stopped and kissed.

JENIFER: *Going across to the courthouse was terrifying. I was afraid of the cops. I was afraid there would be a riot and they would beat the shit out of us. It was thrilling to hear and see those huge throngs of people and media people. I felt protected by all of that. I felt like I didn't really know what to do when we got up there. I couldn't talk to the cops. It was hard for me to keep breathing and singing. I was proud to be there and felt like it was the right thing to do. But once we were up there I just wanted them to get it over with and arrest me. I was glad I didn't cooperate so they had to drag me. I think I was the first one not to walk and I knew seeing me would make it easier for others to do the same. I remembered the other times I got dragged away doing CD and I thought of the great CD role models I had. I tried to keep in mind how they would act.*

DEDE: *I was trying to remember what I knew about power and control. To do CD, for me, requires that I struggle to be very centered on what power is, where it comes from in me, how not to give it away—all very important when I give up my freedom and get arrested.*

After we kissed, we stepped forward to the police line, where I started talking pleasantly to the officer in front of me, who was a trifle wall-eyed with terror. My best manners, you may be sure: "How are you today? A bit wild, isn't it? We're here nonviolently and we don't want anyone to get hurt." But I had not collected myself enough to speak about why I was there as a lesbian, when suddenly the police removed the yellow barricades and let us walk through to the plaza, a wide, flat space between the lower steps of the Supreme Court and the upper steps leading to the big bronze doors. In court, later, we were charged with entering unlawfully, but of course we did not: the police let us in.

Later, after we had been arrested, we learned that the police were regulating the pace of the demonstrations and of the arrests by controlling the flow of groups onto the plaza, partly by when they opened a barricade, partly by pushing and sometimes clubbing protestors, who maintained nonviolent discipline, though they could have moved to physically overwhelm the police they outnumbered. Because we were the first group, we did not have to face the question of how to respond to this "cooperative" control by authorities. Some weeks after this action we met to look at video clips and photographs, and we asked: What would we have done if we had faced this control, later in the day? What would our goal have been then? Would we have sat and waited to be let in by the police at their convenience, waited in line to be arrested? Would we have attempted to get into the building by some other entrance, the back door if necessary, as one affinity group tried to do, galloping around the building, clad in matching yellow plastic gloves and hats, mocking the police who raced in a panic behind, some wearing plastic gloves in their irrational fear of AIDS contamination? Would we have tried to convince other groups to abandon the sit-in, and attempted to surround the building, to close the Court, which continued its business through the day?

But at that moment, we simply pushed on through the crowd and police toward the open space. I passed Joan, jammed in the middle of the pandemonium. She was photographing without pause, while a policeman was shouting at her, "You have to move back." She was talking to him, saying, "There's nowhere to move back *to*," without taking her eye from her camera as the policeman pushed at her. I said, "Joan, be calm," to which she replied, "I *am* being calm." The policeman continued to shout.

In the open, police ranged behind us and in front of us, but we were free to move. We hadn't anticipated these moments when we were free to do whatever we wanted, and hesitated, then circled and sang, briefly, *We are a gay and lesbian people / We are singing, singing for our lives,* which I felt was a song of last resort since it is so slow-tempoed, like a hymn at a Wednesday night prayer service. But then we broke out into *I've been cheated* and began to dance around, as everyone cheered wildly. A bit more time and we might have jitterbugged, but meanwhile an officer was reading the statute about how we couldn't assemble and demonstrate on the plaza, and gave us the standard warning that unless we moved, we would be—The police began to arrest us. Our having a good time was too much for them.

We were whisked away quickly. Some of us tried to stay for those who went limp, but couldn't delay. I got flustered and forgot to wait. My officer was a member of the Supreme Court force; there were only seventy of them, joined by much larger numbers of the D.C. Metropolitan Police and the Capitol Police. This policeman was young, white, and terrified. His hands shook so hard he could just manage to write my name on the arrest form. However, once I started talking to him, he calmed down. In his terror, he had jerked the plastic cuffs painfully tight on my wrists; after we began talking, he loosened the cuffs by pulling my wool jacket sleeves from underneath. He talked politely as we waited for the Polaroid snapshot of me as a criminal to materialize. Just before I was put on the bus bound for the jail, he said, "I can't say anything to you all; I come here every year and demonstrate with the right-to-life movement."

Others in our group had a different experience. Some who went limp were rolled onto their stomachs and dragged or jerked around. Jill, a tough-looking lesbian, recognizably a butch, got a policeman who insisted that she get on her knees to him.

JILL: *I was standing up and felt a hand on the back of my neck, gripping the collar of my jacket. A male voice said, "You're under arrest." Even though I expected to be arrested, it took me by surprise; I guess I thought I would see it coming. Then the voice said, "I want you on your knees." Oh, shit! I looked over my shoulder at the officer—he wasn't much taller or bigger than I am— and then around at the others who were starting to be arrested. No one was on her knees. I said to him, "I don't think that's necessary." He gave my neck a little shake and said, more firmly, "I want you on your knees." I definitely had not expected this, and my mind began to race: should I go limp, should I fall to the ground, should I just stand there, should I try to talk him out of it? Kneeling was not an option. I said, "Look, I can't do that. I won't resist, I'll let you put the cuffs on, I'll walk, but I can't do that." We had a little stand-off for a few seconds, and I guess he decided it wasn't worth insisting. He put the cuffs on me, and we walked to the buses. I asked around afterward. No one else I spoke to was told to kneel.*

BONNIE: *After the women had been taken off of the Supreme Court plaza and were being led to the bus, we stood and watched them being booked from behind yet another police barrier. There were two women police officers just smiling and having a great time. I asked them why they weren't on this side of the barrier. Almost in unison they replied, "We couldn't get the day off."*

As we were hustled off the plaza, we could still see our support folks, who had pushed up against the barricades, waving our banner and singing. We'd joked about how the banner was generic, designed by former LIPS members Eleanor Holland and Helen Langa with many different demonstrations in mind. That day it was perfect: huge red lips speaking giant words, *LESBIANS PROTESTING INJUSTICE.* Concerned marchers had often explained to us that LIPS was not the acronym for our slogan, that we'd gotten it backwards, to which we always replied that our banner was as perverse as we were.

The lips smiled enigmatically on, matching the bright red lipstick lips Lauren Taylor had kissed on our cheeks early that morning, matching my silly red plastic lips earrings. Marcia called from Tuscaloosa the next day to say she and Rose had seen me and my earrings, and the group, lead the way on CNN. Another friend called from San Diego because she'd seen us on the "MacNeil/Lehrer Report." An acquaintance in Michigan said she was listening to National Public Radio and heard us singing *When the dykes go marching in;* she had burst into tears, she was so happy. Though many newspapers, both mainstream and movement, described those being arrested mostly as gay men with AIDS, the *Washington Post* said, "The first wave of demonstrators, about two dozen women, carried a large banner decorated with a pair of bright pink lips and the words 'Lesbians protesting injustice.' " We felt we had been seen.

Later I regretted that we had not turned toward the Court, marched up the steps past the police, and tried to enter through the metal doors. Why didn't we? Our original image of the action had been to take ourselves into the very place, before the very people who denied our human love, and speak to them. But giddy with the brief freedom allowed us after the barricades, we paused to dance; and that was all the time we were allowed. We had not expected as much movement as we got after crossing the forbidden line. We had expected and had prepared for restraint, not freedom; and we weren't ready to seize every possibility when freedom came, even the bit of freedom that we gained for those few minutes on the plaza.

We were arrested sometime after 9:30 A.M. By ten o'clock we watched northeast Washington rush by through the rusted mesh of the police bus windows. I jounced on a hard plastic seat and guessed at where we were being taken. I tried to keep my balance with my hands cuffed behind my back. I considered how to explain to my students what I was doing in jail that afternoon instead of in our class on feminist theory. Many had expressed fear and distrust of radical actions: why couldn't we work through the legislatures, the court systems? How would I make real to them, these young mostly heterosexual women who felt protected by our legal system and our government, what it meant to me to be made a criminal, to be placed outside the system by the ultimate law of the land? How to show them the narrowing distance between lesbians punished for our sexual behavior and heterosexual women denied abortions, denied access to birth control, by men intent on controlling the sexual lives of women? I thought how strange it would be to stand in front of them as their teacher, after a day or more in jail.

We were bused to Building B, part of the judiciary complex in the northwest part of the city, where we were offered a chance to forfeit out: $100 collateral and no record at all. In keeping with their original decisions, Elly, Lauren Taylor, Tacie, and Wendy left at that point. The rest of us managed to stay together as a group through most of the day, which was miraculous, since the police later began to deliberately break up affinity groups, having figured out that this lessened resistance.

Although in the earlier meetings we had said we probably would try to get out as soon as we could, somehow for those of us left it was too galling just to hand our money over. So we were searched, fingerprinted, photographed, and put in a holding cell crammed with squeaky bunk beds, where we sat eating trail mix that hadn't gotten confiscated. I didn't mind the fingerprinting; I'd had that done before when I was arrested at the Valentine's Day action at the South African Embassy. What scared me the most was having the grim-faced police photographer take my picture, so severe and hateful a contrast to seeing Joan's face in serious concentration behind the camera.

We watched other demonstrators brought in, many who noncooperated, including one man who stayed limp while the police tried to get his fingerprints, so that they had to hoist his body completely up into the air to get his hands in place. We heard later that some lesbians arrested in the women's wave were strip-searched—their vaginas forcibly searched by rubber-gloved police matrons. We wondered if the police, in a homophobic panic after dealing with the wave of people with AIDS, had decided to take out their fears on the women.

We each were interviewed separately in a small, dark cubicle by a policeman who wanted name, birthplace, social security number, mother's maiden name; mine also made jokes about asking me out for a date after I was released. I laughed nervously; I wondered if he would track me down later, like the Georgia policeman who harassed Michael Hardwick about a traffic citation and later showed up at his home to arrest him for sodomy. Some of us gave names not our own or refused to name our mothers.

Then we were bused to D.C. Superior Court, with a bunch of gay men from Los Angeles who sang, *Homo, homo, it's off to jail we go.* Though we marched into the holding area jauntily, singing *Ain't no court supreme enough / to keep me from my dream* led by Jenifer, the court jail was a high-tech spooky place, cold iron and blank-faced guards staring at banks of black-and-white TV monitors. We were searched again, shoes and jackets off, everything out of our pockets on the floor: quartz crystals, love notes, dimes and quarters, vitamins. Some things were confiscated, but the only thing taken away from me was my ballpoint pen, part of a set Joan gave me when I finished my last book; it was imprinted with the message, *We Say We Love Each Other / My Honey Babe, and We Do, We Do / Oh How We Do / Always Remember.* It was removed from my little pile on the cement floor by the woman who also patted us down amid great excitement, a handsome African-American woman, very butch. She talked at length to Jennie, who perhaps said she was a journalist, because I heard the woman offer to take her through the jail on a pass sometime. She seemed baffled by us but, in the end, sympathetic.

Not one of us women in the first wave was a woman of color. All of the women we saw working in the court jail were Black. And the walls of our cell were scrawled with the names of scores of women who'd been held there, probably prostitutes, many undoubtedly African-American, arrested for working, not for demonstrating, but arrested as sexual criminals as surely as we were, arrested because the State was regulating their bodies also.

But we didn't see any of these women; we were kept entirely segregated from the other prisoners.

We were kept in holding cells in the court jail from noon until about 6:00 P.M. For a couple of hours no one came in, not other demonstrators and not our lawyers. I kept remembering the clang of the cell doors behind me. This was when I got scared and began contemplating the possibility of sixty days in jail, the maximum sentence for what we'd done. I thought I might manage it, if I just could have a pencil and paper.

They had put us in three cells: a large one with most of the group, who also had the most difficult decisions to make because many of them had fouled-up paperwork; a small cell with Jenifer, Linda from Ohio, and me; and a cell next to us with Jill and others. Finally two more dykes were brought in, Maria from D.C. and another dyke who was a PWA. Then Nancy Polikoff, who was head of the legal team, came in with love notes and information, and we all began to cheer up.

NANCY: *I was the last person to leave the site of the action, as I wanted to make sure the arrests were really all over before I joined the other lawyers*

and the support people at the courthouse. I went back to the lock-up area be-
hind one of the courtrooms, and there were my friends, and my lover. Behind
bars. They knew their choices—forfeit $100 and leave with no criminal rec-
ord, plead guilty to one misdemeanor, or plead not guilty. No one knew then
what the sentence would be if they pled guilty. The first person to make that
choice would find out. Some of them desperately wanted my advice. I adhered
with difficulty, and with strong resistance from some, to the cardinal princi-
ple of client-centered counseling: it was their decision; I would discuss
consequences—advantages and disadvantages—and I would help assess risk.
But I would not answer the question some asked: what would I do if I were
they?

While we waited, we had conversations about lots of different
things: how Jill felt, as a lawyer, at the possibility of having a criminal
record; how Linda hoped her goats were being cared for properly;
where we had first heard of the planned CD—through gay political
organizations, through the women's music festivals. During the afternoon there were times when it seemed some of us might be released,
but not others whose paperwork had been lost or mislaid. When this
happened we would try to reach a decision, talking through the bars
and across the corridor, on how to stay together.

After many threats to the guards that we would noncooperate if
our group wasn't kept together, we were all walked to a third set of
holding cells directly behind a courtroom. Here we were given another
chance to forfeit collateral by paying the $100, and at this point Lau-
ren Young, Sue, Jill, and Amber went out: Lauren because she had
to get back to work; Sue because of her health; Jill so she would not
have a misdemeanor on her record; Amber because she'd given her
name as Michael Hardwick and her paperwork was a mess.

Amber was actually the very first arrest of the action, so Hardwick's name was the first given to the police, but they couldn't deal
with a report that said *Michael Hardwick—female*, so they had taken her
photo off the form and attached the picture of a man who was arrested, presumably someone who had given a woman's name. Later
Joan suggested that a foolproof plan for bamboozling the court system during civil disobedience would be for everyone to give cross-
gender names.

As we were trying to decide whether to forfeit out, Jenifer introduced a new suggestion: that we demand community service instead of a fine. She argued strongly against paying our money into the
judicial system we were protesting. We started fussing with each other

over what to do. In the cells with us by then was Kathy from Boston, who had been one of the Capitol rotunda defendants in a Central America anti-intervention action. She said, "This is always when everyone starts quarreling." The temptation of wanting to leave the others, to get *out*. The difficulty of understanding, as the first people arrested, what impact our decisions would have on all who followed.

We finally agreed that the five who remained—Beck, DeDe, Jennie, Jenifer, and I—would plead guilty, but Jenifer would ask for community service. By this time we were in the holding cell area with a lot of other people, mostly gay men; when our folks forfeited out, so did all of them but one man. So we were to be the first people to actually plead guilty and be sentenced. To what, we had no idea.

I was tired and wanted to go home; I'd pushed far beyond where I had thought I could go; I couldn't imagine standing in front of the judge and demanding community service instead of a fine, and being ready to go to jail if I didn't get that. Yet, by then I also felt that if I pled guilty and made a statement about myself and my children, and about how that loss was related to my being a lesbian and this demonstration, and if then the judge could still give me sixty days, I would go, furiously.

Our lawyers were a white man, and a white woman who was distracted but supportive. The man was awful, roaring and pompous, a contrast to the sweet and self-deprecating gay men we'd been locked up with. I ended up shouting at him to lower his voice: me behind bars yelling at my lawyer on the other side. The court marshals, who led us into court, were older Black men, very encouraging, saying, "Good luck." Our commissioner was a middle-aged Black man who listened carefully.

Then we pled guilty, reading these statements out loud before Commissioner Byrd, and our friends and lovers, in D.C. Superior Court:

MINNIE BRUCE PRATT: *Twelve years ago I lost custody of my two small children who I loved (and do love now) very much, because I chose to live as a lesbian. The Supreme Court's decision last year in* Hardwick vs. Bowers *established as the opinion of the highest law in the country that I, and other lesbians like me, do not have the right to be the mothers of our own children. I feel this is an outrage to both my human love and to my citizenship in this country under the Constitution. I did protest this today at the Supreme Court, and I do so plead—guilty, voluntarily.*

JENNIE McKNIGHT: *I plead guilty to the charges, but I want to say that my actions today at the Supreme Court were about who I am as a lesbian. They were an appeal for justice for lesbians and gay men. I protested because I don't believe that any institution or any person has the right to tell me who I can love.*

DEDE DE PERCIN: *I am here today because I do not recognize the authority of any court or any person to tell me who I can choose to love. I believe that there is a higher moral imperative based on the rights of all people, all women, all lesbians, that requires me to take action when these rights are violated or jeopardized.*

I plead guilty to being a lesbian, and to demonstrating as such at the Supreme Court today.

Beck spoke of Sharon Kowalski, severely injured in a car accident, confined to a nursing home by homophobic parents who would not let her lover Karen Thompson see or communicate with her; Beck said she had demonstrated so nothing could keep us from each other again. Paul from New York, the only one of the gay men with us who did not forfeit out, spoke of working with homeless people and seeing them die in the streets because of AIDS. Jenifer pled guilty and asked for community service.

After a short recess, the judge returned and sentenced us: $50 or three days in jail, and six months unsupervised probation, no community service possible. I handed my lover Joan the money, which I'd hidden in my sneakers. We were returned briefly to the holding cells while the support people paid our fines, and released around 9:00 P.M. After all that fierce working together, we wandered aimlessly into the lobby of the courthouse. A few brief kisses, then we drifted out the doors into the night.

I paid the fine, but wished later I had done the days, since the folks who pled guilty and did not pay were released at 12:01 A.M. Thursday morning, a little over a day later. Of course, I felt like this after I had eaten, showered, slept, and been free twenty-four hours.

Seventeen busloads of people waited behind us after we were released. The courts closed at 2:00 A.M., and about 130 people had to spend the night, including some on AZT who didn't have their medication. The official press release from the Supreme Court reported 572 arrests; sources inside the police department placed the number closer to 800. In either case, it was the largest mass arrest in Washington since the anti-Vietnam War demonstration in 1971, and the largest ever at the U.S. Supreme Court.

When she was arrested, DeDe was wearing a jeans jacket with a pink triangle on the back and the words, *Nonviolent resistance is the only reality.* At the CD rally, Pat Norman had said, "Civil disobedience is not new to gays and lesbians. Each and every day we commit the act of civil disobedience by loving each other." Eric Rofes, at the Town Meeting on Sex and Politics, had said, "No matter what, we find a way to be who we are." I have remembered those words for a year as "No matter what, we find each other."

The reality of our being together is hard to remember on a day like today, when I struggle to write about that weekend, distracted by worry. About money, how I'll make enough to pay my rent and my medical insurance this month. About the ninety-two-year-old neighbor who I found on the floor of her room in her own shit and urine earlier in the week, and had gotten to the hospital, an ambulance ride spent thinking about her penurious, isolated life.

Today I haven't seen any of my neighbors on the fifth floor. Not Sharon next door, nor Rod, my white gay male neighbor who works as a secretary. He's usually cheerful, except at Christian holidays like Easter and Christmas, when he sometimes lights candles and sticks them, waxy burning lumps, out in the hall in front of his door. When he becomes suicidal during the holidays, he puts himself into a psychiatric institute for a "rest." I haven't seen him, or the new neighbors, two dykes, Latinas, stylish dressers, friendly. Today I have felt only an intense isolation, the absence of even the frailest ties of community, and my life tightening and closing around me.

During the day I saw no one but Miss Elsie on the first floor. I went down to keep her company because the doctor was coming to see to her feet, and she didn't want to be alone with a strange man. I sat in her efficiency apartment, where she lived for nine years with her mother, and for thirty years alone, and listened to her talk as the doctor trimmed her bone-thick toenails and smoothed her grainy, rough, old feet. In her shadowy room I sat and thought about the glowing reality of the days a year ago, and the chasm between that and the reality weighing heavy on me today.

DEDE: *Someone said to me, ''Remember this in the middle of winter when it feels like you can't do anything.'' I was absolutely flabbergasted at the reactions of my close friends. They showed more excitement, love, concern, and support for me than I ever expected. I knew doing CD was a big decision for* *me and a major event in my life—but I really didn't understand beforehand the effect it would have on my friends. They were so proud of me! Support even came from the least expected places—the red-neck Republican at work who gave $10 to my bail money fund. I've used the strength I got from the CD to take more risks and be more open about who I am as a lesbian, and that is empowering—it's a circular energy.*

In my feminist theory class this week, I assigned a set of readings, oral herstories by a poor white Appalachian woman, a poor Southern Black woman, a Latina who did migrant farm work, a Jewish woman who was a peace activist, and a Native American lesbian mother. The class, which included all these ethnic groups, wanted to talk about only one issue: should lesbian mothers be *allowed* visitation rights to see their children? The question rested on the assumption that we should not be allowed *custody* of our children. I choked on my old familiar rage as the discussion shifted from point to miserable, predictable point. Until Laura, mother of four and a lesbian, told of raising her children and her constant fear of losing them. Until Diane, my teaching assistant, spoke of being a lesbian and of the son she had raised with another woman, a child who was now a man beginning college just as she finished her degree. Then Laura's partner, Linda, talked more about their life with their children, of the love they shared as a family. And I spoke of my sons and my struggle to be their mother, even when told, by a world that shared my students' assumptions, that I, as a lesbian, was not fit to be a mother. The class ended; the students quietly left. I stood in the empty room and realized I'd never been in a place, out in the world, where that many lesbians who were mothers had spoken spontaneously, passionately, openly, of our lives.

BECK: *I love the idea of social disobedience (SD) direct actions. I think these are perhaps more important than CD actions for the gay rights movement, because the strongest laws we must oppose are social, ''moral,'' and religious rather than penal.*

When I last talked to Elly, I told her that LIPS was over with. We had ended as a group, though without any group decision; we'd simply stopped meeting. She said, very regretfully, "What a pity." That's what I felt until I realized that the group had ended because we had *expanded:* Jennie had moved to work full-time on *Gay Community News*. Bonnie had become a leader of Lesbian and Gay Democrats in Montgomery County. Urvashi had left her job as a lawyer with the ACLU Rights Project and, instead of her volunteer work doing leaflets and publicity for tiny LIPS actions, was in charge of the 1987 March and CD publicity, and then on to full-time work as public relations director for the National Lesbian and Gay Task Force. Ruth had quit her government job to do full-time legal work for the Whitman-Walker Clinic, a gay and lesbian health clinic. Tacie was working on a national campaign to Free Sharon Kowalski.

And others had gone on to increased activism:

JILL: *After the CD I was looking for a place to do political work, and I wanted it to be as a lawyer. I joined ACT UP New York and in October 1988 was the co-coordinator of the legal team for the ACT NOW Food and Drug Administration (FDA) action. It was great, one year later, to be in the middle of another group of angry and courageous demonstrators. Currently I'm planning a pro se teach-in for ACT UP, where people can learn to represent themselves in court; I see my work for the group as helping people feel empowered in relation to the criminal justice system so they don't have to look to lawyers to do things that they can do for themselves.*

SUE: *I have spent the last ten years working as an electrician and electrical inspector. I am certainly proud of my success in this field, but during those long hours spent in jail, I realized how stifling it was for my creativity and my activism. I resolved to somehow find a more holistic way to support myself. I am now taking care of plants and doing small arrangements in a flower shop owned by a gay man. During the planning in the weeks before the action, I realized I needed to change my activist work as well. With much sadness I said good-bye to my nonviolence committee at the Washington Peace Center. I am now a coordinator for my North Arlington neighborhood lesbian group.*

BECK: *I'm not sure I've ever experienced an event that was measurably transformative before. In one day I made the sort of "leap of consciousness" that generally evolves over a long time. I think it has made me more composed in the face of hostility and more able to be scared and do something anyway. I also think the CD was the final push I needed to quit my job with a national organization in order to begin work with direct service—coordinating an AIDS outreach program for IV drug users.*

LAURA: *At the time of the CD, I worked with the Department of Labor where, for the first time in my life, I wasn't out as a lesbian on the job. I worked in a small agency for a man who was quite openly antigay (among other things) and who I think would not have hesitated to find a way to fire me if I'd been out. I went home the night of the CD, coming down from the euphoria and into my exhaustion and my fears about my job, to a message from my friend Hillel on my phone machine. He said, "I was happy to see your smiling face under the LIPS banner on the national news tonight." So I had taken the step for myself, toward dismantling that huge block of fear at being visible as a lesbian at my work.*

Since the CD I've made my workplace safer for other lesbians and gay men. I coordinated the formation of a policy for employees with AIDS, and found it remarkably easy to get the administrators to agree to a really sound, humane policy. I've used that as an opportunity to talk with many people at work, with whom I might never have talked, about issues of lesbian and gay liberation, and I'm out to more and more people here.

On that blazingly sunny day a year ago, I saw us find each other in a new reality, one that had never existed before. Afterwards I wrote to Elizabeth, my friend of eighteen years, the first lesbian I ever knew *was* a lesbian: "I don't know what it means, not at all. Except that I do feel changed in my body." And I wrote in my journal:

> *What does it mean? That we've been working on this for a long time, and that's partly why we can be here together? Joan says there's less anger toward each other, more appreciation. Why? More self-love? We're sober, more of us; less ignorant of our different cultures; more proud of our own lives; more evolved spiritually; less isolated because we have built a movement; more drawn together because of the mortal threat of AIDS and its use by those who hate us; more conscious of the need to be beyond, yet with, ourselves. What does it mean? That in the middle of death, and hate, and meanness, we are healing ourselves? That we are asking for health and happiness? That we finally believe we deserve to be loved?*

All weekend the grey rain has come down, and, with darkness, night has become longer than day. Yet in the end, the recollected words of the women are louder than the sound of the rain, and affirm the reality that we have lived beyond despair, that we danced on a fragile island of hope one morning, beneath the brilliantly blue sky, beneath the promise of justice.

Notes

Thanks to all the LIPsters who wrote CD accounts and agreed to have them included here. A longer version of this essay, with additional narratives by members of the LIPS affinity group, is on file at the Lesbian Herstory Archives (LHA), P.O. Box 1258, New York, New York 10116, (212) 874-7232. Lauren Taylor and Elly Bulkin did heroic work in compiling and editing the narratives and getting them into the computer. Many thanks also to Priscilla Hayner for her computer work; and to Joan E. Biren (JEB), Judith Arcana, Elly Bulkin, and Elizabeth Knowlton for editorial comments.

1. *For Love and For Life: The 1987 March on Washington for Lesbian and Gay Rights,* a video by Joan E. Biren (JEB), vividly documents all these events during the six days of the March, as well as the civil disobedience action. In addition, the video shows the importance of the March within the historical context of other U.S. liberation and protest movements. To obtain the video, contact Joan E. Biren (JEB), Moonforce Media, P.O. Box 2934, Washington, D.C. 20013.

2. The Justices' opinions, here and later, are from the Supreme Court decision, no. 85–140 (June 30, 1986), *Michael J. Bowers, Attorney General of Georgia, v. Michael Hardwick, and John and Mary Doe.*

3. Those who, after reading "I Plead Guilty to Being a Lesbian," still wonder why we chose to commit civil disobedience, might read the accounts of physical and emotional abuse of lesbians and gay men recorded in *Gay American History* by Jonathan Katz (New York: Avon, 1976). The National Gay and Lesbian Task Force documents contemporary U.S. persecution in *Anti-Gay/Lesbian Violence, Victimization and Defamation in 1990,* available from the NGLTF Policy Institute, 1734 14th Street N.W., Washington, D.C. 20009, (202) 332-6483. Information about the persecution of lesbians and gay men internationally is available from the Information Secretariat of the International Lesbian and Gay Association, c/o Antenne Rose, 81 rue Marché-au-Charbon, 1000 Brussels, Belgium, (32-2) 502-2471.

My Mother's Question

I first started to understand about work in my early teens when my mother began to take me with her as she drove out in the county on her job, in the summers, early 1960s in Alabama, about thirty miles north of Selma, when no one much outside of Alabama had heard of Selma yet. We drove on dirt roads, red as blood, choked with dust or slippery in the afternoon thunderstorms, to see her clients, people getting public assistance from the Department of Pensions and Security, known as Welfare now. Now my mother would be called a social worker; then it was said more clearly: she worked for the State.

I saw only the outside of the lives of the folks she visited, for she didn't let me go with her into their homes. I saw searing poverty, nevertheless, and something of the attempt to survive it, in the crumbling houses, the struggling patches of okra and tomatoes,

This is an expanded version of a speech given at the "Afro-American and White-American Women: Culture, Community, and Organizing" Conference, Ithaca, New York, February 20, 1988.

the children in tatters of clothes. I saw what now the media would present as "images of a starving Third World," except that then it was reality in this country, and is still: a poverty that was and is mostly women and children, Black women and children, or Latinas, Native American women, and their children, women of color and their children. As a white child in the South I had lived, and sometimes even played, in the middle of this poverty. But in those summers I finally understood that this was the place I would grow up into, and have to find work in, as a white woman like my mother.

My mother hardly talked about her work. She sometimes said, "If people were only given a chance," and once, grimly, "How will anything ever change?" when a woman with several young children had a failure in her birth control and was pregnant, again. I absorbed my mother's despair. During visits I sat in the car, waiting for her and reading the Bible, the book of Revelations: how there would be "a new heaven and a new earth" because this reality would pass away, and then "God shall wipe all tears from our eyes, and there shall be no more death, neither sorrow, nor crying, neither shall there be any more pain." I sat reading this promise that all would be different some day, after we had died, thinking about how I had to escape before that day.

So the first oppression I understood was not abstract words— *racism, class inequities, sexism.* What I saw with my own eyes were people, mostly Black women and children, caught in crushing poverty; what I understood was that any work open to a white middle-class woman in my hometown meant facing this poverty and taking some kind of responsibility for it; and what I knew was that I could not stand the despair and pain of this. I hardened my heart; I resolved that, instead, I would *get out.*

What would I have had to know not to have felt this despair, not to have chosen the escape available to me because of the scrapings of privilege? I would have had to understand, then, things whose lack still keeps us from acting now. I needed to know how to stay yet not repeat my mother's life, to stay and try for some kind of fundamental change.

I would have had to understand my mother's seeming acquiescence to "the state welfare system," her despair that the *women* had failed, and her lack of analysis of how the state was attempting to control women, specifically women of color, through birth control, sterilization policies, through money policies. I would have had to under-

stand that she had no analysis available to her, was unable to offer herself or me any except Christian stoicism, our kind of Christianity that
reinforced racism and class structures: *There will always be someone on
the bottom. The poor you will always have with you.*

I needed an economic history of my region, my country, that
would have disclosed the irony and injustice of a state government dol-
ing out, through my mother, pitifully inadequate sums of money to
women, and men, and their children, the sale of whose *selves* and
whose slave labor, prison labor, hired-out convict labor, unpaid and
underpaid domestic work, factory work, all kinds of work, had erected
the white state, universities, houses, hospitals, factories, office buildings, fortunes. I would have had to understand that I had no knowledge of this economic analysis because there had been systematic and
often violent state suppression of information and organizing about
class issues, from the beginning of the country until the most recent
example—at that time the McCarthy purges.

I would have had to see that the red-baiting and Communist-
hunting of McCarthy was based not on patriotism or love of democratic freedom, but on the assumption that capitalism *is* freedom. That
there was a terrible fear of any questions about whether the U.S. economic, and therefore political, system was really fair and democratic.
That this fear, which McCarthyism tapped into, was a constant but unacknowledged fear, then and now, on the part of anyone in this country who has accumulated a scrap of anything—money, property,
privilege—those of us who are not "the bottom" but know we will not
be "the top" either, never direct the economic affairs of the country,
or even the company we work for. That this is the fear of most of us
in the U.S. A fear constant for me in my family precariously situated
on the edge of the lower-middle class, holding on mostly because of
professional or clerical jobs reserved for white people who could be
put in charge of those below us in the economic structure.

To have stayed home and worked for a fundamental change in
that economy, I would have had to understand how white skin was,
and is, as good as money in this country. That one reason for the insistence of white Southern men on sexual purity in white women was
so skin privilege could be passed down to their sons, and daughters,
just like land. That my white skin was what was going to help me escape, while my femaleness bound me to those in poverty. So that I
pushed away my femaleness, thought of myself as body-less, as someone who was *mind.* I would have had to understand that I resolved
to get out, escape, leave the despair behind, simply because I *could:*

I had the resources, the privilege, to make the attempt. To have acted differently, I needed some vision beyond this illusory individualism, some vision of how to meet with others and fight together with them for change. I needed some glimpse of a future beyond the end of the book of Revelations.

I got that vision, eventually, from the women's liberation movement, the lesbian and gay movement, the civil rights movement. Except these words are abstractions, and the movements came to me through living people. But what I learned about work and class came not from these movements, or the people active in them, but from my life, from the fact that I came out as a lesbian and began to understand the abstract word *privilege.*

As soon as I wanted to live as a woman independent of my particular white man, and men in general, I became a threat; my existence called into question the ways in which we as women are bribed and coerced into staying in our place, into hanging on to the little bit of security we think we have. I understood what heterosexual status was only when I had lost it *and* custody of my children; the first privilege that my husband and the state tried to take from me was that of being a mother, and then I understood I had been a mother only by their permission. In order to leave my husband I had to have a job, had to be able to support myself as a woman alone, and yet could not be open about my life, the essence of my joy, my sexuality, in an ordinary, everyday way; I thought if I were openly lesbian in my conservative town I would never get hired as a teacher. And then I understood, bitterly, that I might choose freedom, to live as myself, and lose the means to live at all. And all of this I grasped only half-consciously. To have acknowledged what loss of privilege meant, I would have had to face the enormity I was living everyday; and face the question, *How will anything ever change?* A question I could answer only by living out the answer.[1]

The job I finally got, the only one I was offered, was teaching at a historically Black college in the North Carolina town where I was living. Which returned me to face what I had tried so hard to leave: The brilliant female colleague who had been a child in a house like those of my childhood, who raised her brothers because her mother was dead early from breast cancer, because there was no health care available for a poor Black woman. And my students: The young mothers on welfare, including one woman, left by her abusive boyfriend, who wrote eloquently about hours of travel on public transportation to public clinics, talking all the while to her baby, saying how *they* would stay together, *they* would love each other. The smart young mannerly men, the one struggling to find a job who signed up for the military because that would be steady work, and I do not know if he ended up sent to Grenada. The young dyke student who tutored teenage girls in the impoverished neighborhood on the edge of campus, trying to give them skills to get themselves out, out from under.

How do we get us all out together? The question my students put to me, silently, year in and year out, when I came back ready to learn something from them. I started teaching at historically Black colleges, first Fayetteville State and then Shaw, in the mid-seventies, after the historically white North Carolina universities had at last begun to admit Black undergraduates. Since many middle-class Black students who had formerly attended Black schools were able to go to these universities, and did, most of my students were poor and working-class. These students set their lives against my memory of the poor ragtag children in dirt yards, a memory that carried the ideas *aimless, doomed, pitiful* into the present for me.

The students set themselves against these ideas, against my assumption that poverty was connected to laziness, and that laziness was Black. The woman student just older than me, raising three children, working one full-time job nursing, one half-time job cleaning, going to school full-time also, sleeping two or three hours at night: this student put herself against my idea of laziness and my assumption about how much work was necessary for a person to get an education, to get a decent standard of living, to get ahead.

The students set themselves against my assumption that a poor or working-class person was not as smart or as intelligent as a middle-class or "educated" person. The woman student who revealed that she had handed in a paper weeks late because of the painfulness of the topic, racist violence; who wrote of the loss of her family's farm to the Klan, the death of her father, the rape of her mother: in her strong words, with her clear understanding of power and history and poverty and race, this student placed herself against my assumptions about intelligence.

By their lives and by their words, these students said that they did not exist merely as images of pain from my past, nor as accusations of my guilt, nor as exposers of my ignorance. They were not my assumptions. They were fighting and struggling to get somewhere that was not the past. They were themselves, and I faced them every day in a classroom that, finally, I could not call *my* classroom. I began to see much of what I had considered intelligence was simply what I had learned about what white men knew. I began to realize I knew little of my life as a woman, or of the culture and history of women of any background, while my students knew their own history as a people and were proud of their struggle—a history I was profoundly ignorant of, although it was a history linked to mine and to my people. I began to think about how little work I had done to acquire my education: the summers I spent reading during high school, doing little else, while a Black woman took care of my mother's house; my years in school on scholarships; my ability to continue in my studies when my children were born because I hired Black women and working-class white women to do daycare at wages so low that even then I must have been ashamed, because I can't remember now what I paid them.

As I did my teaching, I thought of all these things, half-consciously at first. Pondering my work with ideas, with books, I remembered how my family always said, affectionately, that I was just like my aunt Betty Pratt, a great talker who loved books. Most of her life she was a widow, and spent long stretches of time in bed, reading, while Ross (I never knew if this was her last or first name), the Black woman of her household, waited on her, cooked, cleaned, did all the dirty work.

How to keep from repeating this pattern? The question my students put to me, with their lives, their work, their feelings, their thinking. How do we all get out together? The question I am still asking.

I finally got to *see* my mother work one summer when I was home and she took me with her to visit Beulah Jennings, a former client who sometimes called her in emergencies; over ninety years old, she was confined to a wheelchair, one leg amputated because of misdiagnosed diabetes. Mama was emphatic about how she admired Beulah's fight to get back to her own apartment after the surgery, how impressed she was with the skill with which Beulah took care of herself, cooking meals, getting in and out of bed. But I was a little uneasy when Mama said how she had to be careful not to do much for Beulah, who needed to "do for herself." I thought I heard an echo of comments made by people who had no idea how hard it was to help yourself up from the bottom of this country.

But in Beulah's apartment in Brent Gardens, the tiny public housing project, my mother sat down solidly on a padded trunk, knees spread, and Beulah rolled her chair up between them, and a quietness settled on the room. They gave each other a long familiar look and began, with no hurry, each with absolute patience, to go to work on solving the problem at hand. Beulah was paying a woman $100 a month for day help, but the Meals-on-Wheels lady thought Beulah's day help might also be getting paid for this work by the State. To get confirmation and save Beulah paying the extra money, my mother needed the name of the Meals-on-Wheels lady, but Beulah couldn't remember: "Is it so-and-so?" "No, no, why can't I call her *name?*" "As soon as I go, you'll remember." A slow nod, then, "It's Emma Green's mother-in-law!" Mama laughed. "That doesn't do me any good. I don't know who her mother-in-law *is.*"

They went on slowly, the Black woman facing the white woman, trying to piece together the solution, asking each other questions, puzzling over the women in town who might be the possible answer. They sat there like opposites, yet so similar in style, pace, method. Beulah said, "I pray to God at night." Mama said, "Yes, that's all we've got." I was shaken by the regard of my mother, her intense concentration on what was being said by this Black woman old enough to be her mother, as if her words were the only words being uttered in the universe at the moment. And I was shaken by knowing the inherent inequality of their relation, that my mother was the one with the power to "help," and always had been. Beulah echoed this ambivalence by calling Mama *Miz Pratt* and *ma'am* half the time, and the rest of the time calling her *child.*

Beulah wanted us to do some errands before we went, a money order for her rent, some juice from the Dixie Super-Saver. Mama carefully and meticulously ascertained Beulah's wishes about each item: "The cranberry juice has only 10 percent juice, is that what you want? I'll get it for you if you want it, I just want you to *know.*" She made no assumptions about these small daily desires. Beulah waved us off when we left, sitting in her doorway, having managed by her tenacity and ingenuity, and the cooperation of my mother, to get her problem solved. As we said good-bye, she said of my mother, "She won't miss the Kingdom."

But when I said to Mama that I could see she must have helped many people in all the years of her work, that she must be proud of what she'd done, she lamented that she had helped only two or three ever. She said she got "too involved" and had to struggle to "stay back." She said that what *really* helped women in the town was the garment factory (where both white and Black women were employed): they were so grateful for a chance to work and make some money.

That afternoon I saw how much she had given me, her sorrow

and despair, the care of her attention, and her hidden passion. By her life she challenged me to work with more than words and theory, to learn from her strengths and her mistakes. She showed me the stubbornness with which she faced the daily needs of poor women in our county; despite isolation and inadequate information, she went on trying to figure how things could change, if only in some small way.

Last semester, at the historically white state school where I sometimes teach part-time, I put the students in my feminist theory class, all women, in a circle and asked them a question.[2] They were mostly white women (gentile and Jewish), some African-American, one Chinese-American. Many were middle-class, and many others on the edge but planning to become solidly middle-class. Intending to be the managers, the lawyers, the professional women, the women with others under them, women who would not think of themselves as workers or as owners, but as independent women, in control of their lives. New women.

I asked them: How might it be possible to end the cycle of female impoverishment, the growing poverty of women and their children in this country, and in the world?

I proposed an experiment: Imagine that we are creating a new economic work system in this room, in miniature, like a business. But we have only ourselves; all work has to be done by ourselves alone. No one else can come in the room. How can we create a system that will end poverty, provide everyone a say-so about the system, and give everyone the work that she wants? Someone proposed that men be brought in to do the dirty work, and I had to repeat again that all work has to be done by us in the room. The women looked at each other, face to face. Left only with each other, each admitted that since she did not want to get stuck with work she didn't like, at wages that weren't fair, she couldn't do that to other women in the room. So a new system had to be devised. Someone said, "It looks like capitalism is the first thing to go."

They had put aside, momentarily, the differences by skin color, by class background, by body size, by lesbian and heterosexual, differences that become advantages or disadvantages in a system based on privilege, differences that usually become divisions that split our circle. But I, of course, had made the rules, an artificial situation where they were inescapably face to face with each other, with no escape, and no way to avoid the dirty work, no upward mobility possible to tempt them. No way out.

So then I asked a second question: If you brought money and skills into the system, and disagreement about your common goals began, what would you do? And of course someone said that if she couldn't convince the others to agree with *her*, she would take her money out and leave. Because, she said, "My money is mine." So I told her, and the others, how I felt about the idea *my money*. And this is what I said:

Mostly I earn my living now through part-time teaching and poetry readings and guest lectures. I don't make a lot of money; actually in Washington, D.C., I'm classified as one of the "almost poor," living on the margin above the official poverty line, but below the middle-income bracket. Nevertheless, I have a nice car; my mother gave it to me. I have a Ph.D. and work that I love; I could take higher-paying jobs which are available to me. I could choose to live on different economic terms.

Instead I live on the margin, in an attempt to define my own work, as a visible lesbian who writes and teaches from a feminist and political standpoint. My position means many bosses would not hire me for many jobs; yet there are academic jobs open to me through women's studies. Because of my class background, despite my lesbian identity and politics, because there has been a women's liberation movement and a gay/lesbian movement, I could earn more and have a bit of job security within the university. But, I fear, only at the cost of increased pressure to pass, to hide myself, to become indebted to the academy.

So what I think about my money is very complicated. Where does my attractiveness to women's studies come from, at least in part? Why do they hire me and pay me? Because I have a Ph.D. and a way with words? A skill with language, derived from those long summers of reading, from my family's expectations about books and knowledge, slight in my small, anti-intellectual Southern hometown, but present. Because with this skill I write poetry? A form which in the women's movement has been heard, often, as the voice of the movement, and has been seen as an elite form, a prestige form. Because I have written some feminist theory, because I'm a good teacher? Both skills based in a significant way on what I learned from my students at historically Black schools.

I'm a good teacher, a skillful writer. Seen from another angle I am an extremely low-paid instructor, with the same or better qualifications as higher-paid full-time faculty, in a university where class-action suits against gender discrimination have been filed by the tenure-track female professors. I give poetry readings and talks for audiences who think of culture and work as separate realities, who think poetry, in particular, is a luxury; not something that could be both my dream and my livelihood.[3] And the Ph.D. that, in part, got me my skill with words, that enables me to take the teaching, that keeps me financially afloat, what am I to make of that? A university graduate degree that I got with a scholarship awarded to me because there was a shortage of white men, because they were off being killed in Vietnam, a scholarship that I should have been able to get anyway as a woman, but probably wouldn't have. But in my grad school class there were no Black women or men; they weren't getting any of those excess scholarships.

How am I supposed to feel about the money I earn with this degree? How do I think about what to do with this money? And what about my undergraduate degree? Obtained from a segregated university, an education that I grew up expecting to get because most of my family was college-educated, including the women: my aunts and my mother had all worked hard and put themselves through school. An education I also was expected to get because of a family class position built on land taken from the Creek Indians, given to a great-grandfather who fought against them, and farmed with slave labor. A middle-class status hung onto through a grandmother teaching in segregated white schools, getting paid, I'm sure, more than Black teachers were at that time. Hung onto through a grandfather who worked as the coal company's deputy sheriff, security guard, working for the owners in order to get his family through the Depression. And was the company using convict labor then? And were those the years when Bull Connor, before he became sheriff of segregationist Birmingham, worked as head of security for the same coal company?

What do I feel, what do I do about "my money" obtained through this grimly held class position?

And, yes, my mother worked hard, so hard all her life, and taught me to work hard, to be a working woman. But I remember that she worked for the State, and meanwhile I was being raised by a Black woman being paid, I know, not enough. How do I figure the cost of her life, of Laura Cates' life, into the idea my money? How do I question what is mine? How do I responsibly return what privilege has bought me? How do I do this beyond an individual effort? How do we all?

And I said to the women:

We each decide these questions from where we are now, from our position wedged in this country's class structure. Only we can know our own history that got us to that place. If we are middle-class, it is easy to make excuses for ourselves and our family; to say we are the exceptions, or the victims, somehow, in this grinding system. But we are fooling ourselves if we admit no responsibility. If our family is now middle-class, it often isn't easy to find out our economic history; in family stories a veneer of respectability gets brushed over how people earned their living, how they survived. I've had to reconstruct what I know of my history from bits of conversations, library research, essays on class theory; and against my own reluctance to understand how the money that I earn now is suffused with the pain and blood of people in the past and in the present. I have had to struggle to see how I am implicated, in the present, in the acquisition of this money, blood money. It is so much easier just to deposit my paycheck and let the banks launder it clean.

Then Megan asked, "Does that mean that we can't make money at all, we can't take jobs that pay well?" And I said, "No, I'm just asking that you question yourself about your money, your privilege. How do we take whatever has given us power in the world, money power, decision-making power, power with words, any power that is ours, and return that, or pass that on, to others in a way that will break out of the closed cycle of power?"

This is what I asked them, and you, and myself.

I made another attempt to answer this question with a different, smaller group of white women, Jewish and gentile, with whom I met recently. Several women in the group were managerial staff in national women's organizations that had announced some commitment to being nonracist. The organizations had proposed changes that these women were to implement, but our careful scrutiny revealed that all of the proposed changes were cosmetic plans to make women of color more visible in the group so as to imply that the organizations were doing something about racism, without, in fact, altering in any way the allocation of decision-making or money toward the needs of women of color. In the weekly meetings of our group, we went over budgets, departmental structures, policy statements; we strategized about how the white women from their positions of power could implement *structural* changes in their organizations as a way of beginning to redistribute some of *their money,* of beginning to rethink the idea that what we make or acquire is exclusively ours to control, to rethink the idea of *mine.*

When I consider what to do about changing the idea of what is mine, so we can all get out together, I think mostly of small steps; it's easy for me to despair of fundamental change (an echo of my mother's despair). I know bigger strategies are being talked about, are under way: demilitarization of the budget proposed by the peace and justice movement, new organizing in women's jobs by the labor movement, economic innovations in comparable worth by the women's movement. But, in my daily life, I am still wrestling with the specific actions I can take.

I struggle to make ethical decisions about money and power in whatever ways I can. When I go, for instance, to the supermarket, the drugstore, a department store, and there is the lavish array of material goods, and there is my impulse to buy, buy something with my bit of extra money, I examine my desire to acquire security through things, rather than through the process of remaking the world or the creative impulse of my writing.

I try to assess my idea of what I *need*, to question my idea of *comfort*. I attempt to keep my standard of living down, buy my clothes mostly at Value Village, because I distrust my ability to resist my learned middle-class habits of need and comfort. If I made much more money, would I be able to hold out against spending it on books, presents for my children, things for the house, and instead rechannel it to others, return what privilege brings me? Now, if I get a windfall, I have trained myself to let go of at least part of it, in contributions to movement organizations. I try to make some kind of monthly allocation of money and time to political work; we called that tithing in the church, but my proportion is quite small now. Yet I am working on disciplining myself in relation to money, so that if I do earn more, I will have to be thoughtful about what I do with it.

I attempt to keep my income low for another reason: to resist paying any, or to pay hardly any, federal taxes; to resist feeding my money into a system that supports militaristic capitalism rather than the old women who live on social security and very little food in my apartment building. I do some organizing in my building, have worked with other tenants to prevent rent increases, have assisted the older women in applying for exemptions from rent pressures—all partial, erratic efforts. When I face the women I see my own old age, living not merely on the margin, but sunk, going under, my old age unless I grab at security, make more money, contribute constantly to a retirement fund. I struggle to resist this fear, the fear of losing my little bit of security unless I pour my work *into* the system.

Instead I try to push myself to overturn these fears, to stress the need for change in the structure of privilege in this country. At the university, I organize faculty/staff discussions on issues of power and difference in our work and teaching. In designing my classes I shift white women out of the center, so that my students learn about social change, the women's movement, and feminism through an inclusive range of artists, writers, and theorists of different ethnicities and class backgrounds. I always have us study work by lesbians, and I always discuss my life as a lesbian, in class, with my students. Some of them murmur, "All we study about are lesbians, Blacks, and Jews." The more polite ask why we aren't reading Katherine Anne Porter instead of a novel about an impoverished Chinese-American immigrant, writing that isn't as "artful." In the discussion that follows, I have a chance to pass on, by speaking about my own life, what I have learned about power, privilege, and how we can make change, and why we can want to make change. In teaching predominantly middle-class students, usually white students, usually white women, who in some ways remind me of myself twenty-five years ago, I have a chance to encourage them to learn and act in a way that my teachers never challenged me to do, in a way that I learned from my students at Fayetteville State and Shaw.

And in the work that is my poetry, and my writing, I am beginning to understand that I can effect material change. A woman writes to me that she has read over and over something I have written, to keep herself from going crazy, from killing herself, to help herself go on with a new way of living. When this happens, I know that I can speak and write in ways that can make something possible that has not existed before. My words are not deeds, but they can lead me toward another reality.

So I push myself to say out loud what I'm not supposed to talk about: lesbian sex, or the racism of my family, or my own fears and failings about money. I find myself repeating, in a way that seems strange and obsessed even to me at times, things we are supposed to hide. This embarrasses people: I'm being too personal, I'm telling secrets. But I remember how my entire childhood was lived inside secrets, and how the keeping of these secrets *in* prevented the beginning of change *out* in the material world. So I write, I speak; it is a way of living my mother's question, making with words a space inside which I can consider change, and out of which I can step to make something happen.

Toward a way that will change the fact that I went into my corner grocery in the fall, and a young Black woman was wandering around, waving a lamp: "Anybody want this lamp for a dollar?" Her children, three of them, were standing outside, each lugging a huge paper sack. She said her boyfriend had thrown them out; she had no money and nowhere to go, that's why she needed to sell the lamp. Someone must have told her about the House of Ruth two blocks away, because they started across the bare dirt playground in that direction, a straggling line of mother and children, looking like refugees on the evening news, looking like a woman and her children walking toward another life, out of her past, out of my past.

Notes

I thank Elly Bulkin for her helpful comments on early drafts of this essay.

1. I have written about this at greater length in my essay, "Identity: Skin Blood   Heart," in *Yours in Struggle: Three Feminist Perspectives on Anti-Semitism and Racism,* coauthored with Elly Bulkin and Barbara Smith (Ithaca, New York: Firebrand Books, 1988; reprinted from the original 1984 Long Haul Press edition).

2. I heard this question and experiment proposed first in a guest lecture by the poet Irena Klepfisz, in an introductory women's studies class on women, art, and culture at the University of Maryland-College Park.

3. I rely in this on Audre Lorde's "Poetry Is Not a Luxury," from her *Sister Outsider* (Trumansburg, New York: Crossing Press, 1984).

When the Words Open

Last Friday I cleaned out Miss Brown's apartment, full of old newspapers, roaches, leaking canned goods, empty tubes of zinc oxide for bedsores, greeting cards from the women she'd once clerked with at Lansburg's. I saved some of the cards, her brush and comb, underwear, a few dresses; she can't keep much in a two-foot-wide closet in the nursing home. I found letters that she'd written last spring when she'd been so worried about money: the same sentence, written over and over, instructions to Social Security on how to send her money to her home address, not to the bank, she was ninety-two, couldn't go out anymore, couldn't get her money unless they sent it to her

This essay first appeared, in a different form, in *InVersions: Writing by Dykes, Queers, and Lesbians*, edited by Betsy Warland (Vancouver, Canada: Press Gang Publishers, 1991).

home address, 518 Ninth Street, #203, she was ninety-two, not strong enough to to go out, wouldn't be able to get her money unless they sent it to her at home, not the bank, not strong enough to go out, she was ninety-two. . . . Pages and pages of the same letter, stuck in old phone books, in a dictionary, in her kitchen cabinet in piles of folded wax paper, between paper plates with quarters and pennies in case of an emergency. Pages of pleading messages, never mailed, but written over and over, a prayer, a magic incantation, the words willing that some action be taken, that help appear: the words calling up action.

Back in town that spring, after a long absence, I had heard from the janitor that Miss Brown was distraught. I went to her, and together we figured out how she could get her money. The written word had not brought me; but she had fixed her need inexorably in her fading mind by writing over and over, by repeating to herself and then to others what was necessary, until something was done.

Now her piles of old newspapers, clippings of celebrities and atrocities, remind me of my own boxes of yellowed papers, cut from the newspaper of any town where I've lived, and saved as notes for some future poem or essay. I finger her desperate letters to the authorities and think of the book of poems that I've just finished, the poems where I tell over and over the story of my life, my love for another woman, the loss of my two boys to their father: anger, injustice, grief, almost unendurable pain, isolation, joy, reconciliation, defiant laughter, poem after poem. But was my writing the same as hers? A shout to someone to do something. A reminder to myself of what I needed to remember, words to center me in a hostile and chaotic universe. A prayer, a justification of need. A repetition to keep my sanity, a stubborn clinging to what I needed in order to go on with my life on the edge, on the margin of power. I shudder with recognition at the repeated phrases, at her grip on the centrality of her need.

After a poetry reading in the winter, at a small new women's bookstore, a woman approached me and said, "I feel that if I said what you just said, lightning would strike me." I had just read some poems that were explicitly sexual and lesbian; I'd talked about my children, my lover, my mother; I'd said the word *lesbian* several times. Her reaction to this wasn't uncommon. Sometimes after I read my work, people are silent, or shrink back from me as if there is some scorched smoking circle of dirt around me, as if I'd been struck, for my sin, with lightning by God. Or as if I might be struck down, for my rebellion, by some unseen power.

During this reading, I had had a flash, a jump of my heart, that I was saying the word *lesbian* too many times. After all, it was a new bookstore; perhaps this first reading would give it a reputation as "too lesbian" and women would be afraid to come. And the program for which I was in town as a resident writer was a community program; maybe it would damage them somehow that I and my poems were being so unmistakably clear. A flash of doubt, though I didn't change anything I was saying or reading, a flashback on other moments when I opened my mouth and *lesbian* came out in one form or another, and I feared a blow in return. The power of my own word turned against me.

After the reading, I talked to another woman who came up to thank me. I spoke of my fear of saying too much, of being "too lesbian." She was surprised that I still worried about this, surprised that I would hesitate. She thought of me as "brave," as "strong," as beyond that fear. I don't think of myself as brave or strong. The only way to understand that I exist from one day to the next, one year to the next, is to write down my life, and in the end, send the words out to others. The poems sent or read aloud, as if by someone writing an obscure sacred document. Is this power? It does not feel like power, but necessity.

Yet there are moments when the words open into some not yet open space. Then I feel I am stepping into power. And perhaps it is then, hearing those words, that others think, "This is the moment she will be struck down."

Walking down the hall, with its institutionally green walls, its smell of stale food, I pass every day the dark varnished doors of my neighbors, each life closed and hidden, like an unread book, like an unwritten story. Miss Brown says to me, "I pray to God; He will take care of me; I've been a good girl." I have long since lost faith in the kind of prayer that appeals to a god who rewards or punishes. Yet I write poetry, and the first poetry I knew was the voice of God saying to a poet-prophet: "Whom shall I send, and who will go for us?" as the poet's lips were touched with a live coal, and given the power of words. I would read these lines from Isaiah and yearn for that mysterious fire on my mouth. And for the freedom given when God said to John: "Write the things which thou hast seen. I have set before thee an open door, and no man can shut it."

But in my small Southern town the poetry of my religion was shut up in narrow, literalist interpretations. What was written in the book of God was the truth, and there was only one way to see it—the way we, the people of my church, lived it. There was no room for a leap of faith through metaphor, for the uncertain truth of poetry, for the inexplicable connection between poet and listening stranger. I lived in that town as I was taught, a good girl, the fire of my own words, and my life, closed up and sealed away from me.

When I was thirteen I began keeping a journal in spiral-bound flimsy notebooks. I never promised myself that I would be a writer. Instead I summarized the hodgepodge of books I read, and wrote: *I'll learn to fly a plane, I'll travel around the world.* Escape, escape. I quit writing in my journals when I left home for college, though, groping for myself, I wrote a few poems during my first two years at the university.

Of these poems, I entered two in a contest sponsored by the campus literary magazine. In one, a piece of lyric desolation in traditional meter, I compared an abandoned house to a beached seashell; I wrote it as an exercise, an abstract idea of despair. That poem won first prize and some money. In the second poem I described another house, that of my grandmother, great-aunt, female cousins; I wrote in a sprawling branching form, the house given life and eyes, some hidden power reclaimed. This poem was declared by the contest judge to be "not a poem."

I was allowed to sit in on a class in poetry writing. I don't remember that there was another woman in the room. The professor criticized me for writing so little; he said that I wanted to be a poet without writing. One of the men smiled and, to console me, said, "Beauty is its own excuse for being."

Finally, I married the man who was the editor of the campus literary magazine, a poet. At a party not long after we married, in a smoldering cloud of cigarette smoke and a fog of alcohol, our philosophy professor pointed at me and declared, "You'll go to grad school; you can have an academic career." Laying his hand on my husband's arm, he said, "You will be the poet."

I stopped writing poetry after I married at twenty, had a child at twenty-two, and another child eighteen months later. For a long time after I married and bore my two sons, I heard nothing inside me, nothing at all, as if a door had closed on some inner voice, a heavy wooden door, thick, impenetrable.

Ten years later, I began a new poem, one about my husband trying to kill me in various ways—with a homemade bomb, by handing me over to men who shot me, by turning me over to the police. A poem about my running away from him with the children, across the

South on a Greyhound bus, in strangers' cars.[1] A poem in which I left out the reason I feared him: I had fallen in love with another woman, was mad for her, mad about her, and he knew. I drank power from her body and mine, sexual power that opened and unfolded into another future, an ecstatic vista, unseen, unknown, taken on faith. I was afraid he would pursue me down that mysterious way, coming after the power that had become mine: my sex, my secret, my words, my need, my key to the door that opened before me.

At my typewriter, with a splitting headache, in the summer's vile, smoggy heat, I try to believe that I am not crazy to write poem after poem about being a lesbian and a mother and a lover and a poet, as I sit naked in my white enamel kitchen chair, sweat sticking me to the paint.

When I first began to write again, all I could hear was the voices of women screaming. They seemed to be voices torn by pain, fury, grief; but they could also have been cries of orgasmic pleasure, joy, ecstasy. Were they the trapped voices of the damned? Were they the chanting voices of the released? My mouth touched the body of my lover, live coal, fiery spirit burning through my numbness, but all I could hear was the voices of women screaming. Which was my voice? How was I to follow one tongue of flame in many?

Now I follow the voice inside me as if I hold a cleft divining rod that bends, not toward the water, but toward some fiery source. Haltingly I write myself through to a place where I simply live every day, not in a heaven of self-justifying righteousness, not in the hell others have condemned me to.

In my teens I read poets who were fascinated with hell, or with the moment just before someone entered hell because *he* had attempted to seize spiritual or political power, or *she* had sought sexual power. There was Dante who put people in smoky or stony circles, in tortured punishment for all the varieties of sin, with Satan at the icy center. Tennyson allowed the Lady of Shallot one step forward toward the window before he destroyed her art because she had looked at the forbidden sensual world. I read Poe, and Rossetti also, for their poems of women dead, rotting, but still powerful, opening the tomb or the earth to come back to claim the living. The poets expressing the fears rampant in a culture of masters, owners, and spiritual overseers who were nervous and obsessed, as usual, with the possibility of rebellion among those below. The poems hiding my own desire to break free.

But when I was punished as one of those rebels, when, with forbidden sexual power, my belief in my own words came back to me, nothing—not loss of my children, not estrangement from my family—could convince me that I was speaking from hell, that mine was the voice of one who was damned. I knew my power came not from God's curse or blessing, but from the god of myself, yet to be known.

A few weeks after the beginning of my first love affair with a woman, I attended with her a conference where one night's "entertainment" was a poetry reading. First Robin Morgan read: I admired her work as ambitious; I envied her rolling lines, her weightiness. Yet now I can't remember a single line she spoke. But I have carried with me ever since the words of that night's other poet, Audre Lorde.

She was the first writer and the first poet I heard speak publicly as a lesbian. That evening she began with the revelatory words of her love poem to another woman: "Speak earth and bless me with what is richest." Words praising her life, my life, spoken out loud before thousands of other women. She was a guide through the compelling uneasy landscape that had opened before me with the words, *I am a lesbian.*

I was blessed that I could turn to Lorde's writings for hope; and to Judy Grahn's poems for an answer to those who would condemn lesbians to bitter suffering and death. I was blessed that I began my life as a writer when women who loved other women were creating a world of politics and culture from their lives. I was able to live as a lesbian and work as a poet only because other lesbians asserted that there *was* an *us.* Slowly, I began to think of myself, not yet as a poet, but, in Grahn's words, as "a woman who believes her own word." These two women, close to me in age, but seemingly separated from me, one by class, one by race, gave me the clearest answers to the question, "What would happen if one woman told the truth about her life? / The world would split open."[2]

When I turned for guidance to the woman who had asked this question in her poetry, a woman of my mother's generation, Muriel Rukeyser, I learned that she also was a lover of women, and I looked in her work for this love. But in the few possible poems the pronoun was *you;* there was no *she.* I thought her most explicitly lesbian poem was "The Conjugation of the Paramecium," a description of nonprocreative sex, the slow "inexplicable" exchange of "some bits of nucleus" between two of these simple one-celled animals. She did assign "renewal / strength   another joy" to this process, but hardly the grandeur that she gave to the life of Käthe Kollwitz, wife, mother, artist, who was the inspiration for her lines on truth.[3] I could find in Rukeyser's poetry no similar nakedness of truth about a lesbian life. I felt a huge condemning anger, the anger of betrayal: why had she not told her *own* life clearly?

I felt the same anger when I turned to Lillian Smith, who was, like me, white and Southern-born, also of the generation before me, whose work I had leaned on, who knew how each person had within her "a poet and a demagogue," one creating, the other attempting to destroy. But I learned that Smith had loved Paula Snelling for forty years, and had lived with her, and was her lover for at least some of this time, yet she could not bear the word *lesbian,* and with despisal had denied her own name.

Smith spoke of "the beats and the smokers of pot and the kids in high school who are now drug addicts and the young homosexuals flaunting their deviations and the young heterosexuals flaunting theirs. So few thinking in terms of the *quality* of relationships. . . ."[4] But what of the quality of her relationship with Paula, distorted by denial for all those years?

Smith said: "It is the omissions, *the absence of context,* that so dangerously distorts things." Did she think she would be struck down, blown up, if she spoke of her love for another woman? Did she think she would lose everything she loved, beyond what she lost by speaking out against segregation in the South? I have spoken angrily to myself and to her, dead now twenty years: *What about the omission of "the deep truths" of your life with Paula? What about* this *distortion?* Angrily, because I needed her life as a way of understanding how to live my own.

Yet I know I am angry because I have to do now, as a lesbian, the work she did not do: the splitting open of the self over and over, the telling of the story, the risk of condemnation, the risk of loss. I know that Lillian, and Muriel, did not have an *us,* and that I can write of my lesbian life only because we have created a circle of women to speak within.

As I work at my desk, under my window, two stories down, the next-door church is having Sunday morning service, and the day vibrates with gospel song, hand claps, the beat of drum and tambourine crying out to God. When I was little, at home on Sunday mornings, I could hear our church bell clanging through the silence—flat, brassy, calling us to come hear the voice of God in his Word. Three times a week I sat and listened to those beautiful and terrifying words, spoken by men who firmly believed in leading me to their way.

I had no place to go, three times a week, to hear a lesbian voice. How have we ever found each other? For a long time we sought each other only through a wordless look: searching for the other woman who was also looking, *really looking at you*, and seeing you, the woman who was the other lesbian. For a long time there were no public respectable words for us, no definition for *lesbian* in the dictionary that described our life, no books in the library that named us except as "sick," "unnatural," "kin to thieves, murderers, and liars," and even those books usually kept behind locked doors where perverted books belonged.

How did we find each other? We made a political movement and a culture; we taught ourselves to speak, to write, to sing; we heard each other and we found each other. For instance: Traveling south one winter after I had left my husband, I went to a house the Atlanta Lesbian Feminist Alliance had opened. At a solstice ritual there I met Mab, a lesbian, a writer, also heading home to Alabama. I gave her a ride, and a friendship began that led to a decision: we couldn't wait for the world to name us writers, we must create ourselves. Mab asked me to work on the editorial collective of *Feminary,* a literary journal for lesbians in the South, based in North Carolina, a publication rooted in a local women's liberation newsletter. Later we both self-published our first chapbooks of poetry. With other lesbians, we went on to organize a yearly writing conference for lesbians in the South, WomanWrites, also collectively run, with the firm rule that no "stars" would be paid and brought in to teach us how to write; we would teach each other.[5]

And that is how I learned to be a lesbian poet: other lesbians taught me. I learned by driving through the South in my VW bug to do poetry readings that lesbians organized at a conference against domestic violence in Little Rock; at a women's health club in Fayetteville, Arkansas; at an abortion clinic in New Orleans; at a gay Metropolitan Community Church in Jackson, Mississippi; at someone's home in Gainesville, Florida; at a women's salon in a Quaker meeting house in St. Petersburg; at a women's bookstore in Birmingham; at a women's studies program in Tuscaloosa. I learned in writing groups with other lesbians; I learned from the comments and encouragement of lesbian editors and publishers.

They gave me the hope to keep on writing, the faith that there is another energy, another being, alert, looking for me, looking back at me. The faith that the words will find someone, not as a prayer to a god, but as the vibration of a sound that evokes sound in another.

Not long ago in a shabby alternative radio station, I waited to be interviewed. A young woman, splicing tape, recognized me, said rather harshly, "So how does it feel to be a star?" I answered, uneasily, "I don't think of myself as a star." She clearly didn't believe me. She had *recognized* me. Because I had written some poems, some essays, and these had been published, I had power, and sat far from her in the distance, a coldly burning light. It meant nothing that I thought no one would remember my name in a hundred years, that I had no idea how I'd pay my rent or health insurance after September, that some few thousands, not millions, of people had ever read my words. But she knew: I had power.

Mab has said, "I have to find a way to be Somebody that does not make other people into Nobody."[6] To be a writer, a poet, is to be somebody in the lesbian community. Outside, to be publicly a lesbian is to risk many things, including being assaulted on the street. Inside, among us, to speak and write openly as a lesbian is to be someone who gains power from saying she is a lesbian; is to be someone who is admired, and envied perhaps, when we cannot say who we are because of dangers, shame, self-doubt. To be a lesbian writer is to be somebody who connects us, who calls up another reality where we do not have to be split with grief. And, therefore, perhaps, we think we are nobody, and the poet/writer is somebody, is the only voice answering the question, *And who will go for us?*

But my answer is, *We will all go, and as ourselves, every woman the poet of her own life.* Yet there are other questions: Who can afford to go *as* a lesbian, saying this out loud? What does it cost to live the life of a lesbian writer? I have been able to write as a lesbian partly because of the economic foundation given to me by my middle-class education; I got trained in the skill of words in those years of study, a skill I used eventually to write about my lesbian life. But I have also been able to write because I was driven to the edge of madness by my losses and punishment as a lesbian. I wrote because I could not *afford* to acquiesce in that reality; I had to use words to prove to myself, if to no one else, that I was someone.

Still, the one who speaks has power. Rukeyser wrote of poetry as the exchange of energy between the poet and the listener/witness.[7] But I do not always know whether I am using my power to reach toward another, or whether I am just using words like money, to gain admittance to a separate reality, mine alone. I have called a poem "the truth," I have called a poem "a gift" for someone I loved, and I have had others name the same poem lies and torments. My first lover, when I gave her a poem that I had written in love and anguish about women friends who had been raped, including her own rape, cried out and said, "You have stolen my life."

When are my words an opening of myself to a new place? When are they the appropriation of another's life? For me to speak of another lesbian may be to reveal her secrets; yet when another woman's life crosses mine, she is part of my life. I have struggled over how to use words to search out a connection between me and others, the way lightning from the ground meets lightning in the air, a fiery spirit that calls but does not command another.

Years ago, in the warm steam of us cooking supper together, I sat talking to the other women gathered by Susan and Betty from across the South: lesbians, poets, all talking at once. I said loudly that I had vowed always to put something in my writing so people would *know* I was a lesbian. At the corner of the table, one of us leaned forward to speak out of the bitter experience of years: "No matter what you say, they'll always deny it."

Years later, my lover Joan and I, holding hands, were catcalled and harassed by a bunch of young white men, the usual ridicule and shouts and the car speeding by. From a friend, some weeks after, I heard that a print artist was looking for poems inspired by specific locations in D.C. I wrote a poem about that night, as if to a passerby, "To Be Posted on 21st Street Between Eye and Pennsylvania"; I wrote about being a lesbian, about being hated because of how I love, about trying to open my life into places not yet open to me.[8] The man rejected my poem because it was "too long for the printing format," and also, he said, "Is it *really* a poem? It's so *direct*."

Unless I write explicitly of how I am a lesbian, I will be denied my identity, my reality. When I do write explicitly, I am denied art.

I could choose an aesthetic of indirection, like a flash of lightning, white, on blank white paper, a subtle illumination of nothing that can be named. Instead I keep trying to write poems that hold, in some way, the idea of *lesbian*.

Yet again, in a recent literature seminar, a student asked, "Why do you *need* to describe yourself as a *lesbian poet* on the back cover of your book?" Sometimes I feel like I'm writing a letter, the page covered with scrawled words like a prayer, the same letter over and over, without knowing who will read or understand it.

But I have been answered. Sometimes the listener raises her hand to still my words because they clash with her life. Sometimes her hand and her voice send her own words back to me:

> In the very beginning, Donna and Lucy in our living room, making me recite poems out loud to them, over and over, shaping my meaning, tone, phrasing, so I could go to my first public reading as a lesbian: "So you won't disgrace us."

> The woman who wrote from prison to say: "I have sincerely enjoyed your poems. In your writings, you have expressed so many of the walled-up feelings that women have had in their hearts, and many of your poems brought tears to my eyes. You said so many things that we carry locked up inside from generation to generation passed on from mother to daughter, from a grandmother! Sisterly, I remain, Helene."

> At a conference on battered women, the lesbian who walked out while I was reading, who later told me she couldn't bear the splitting images of violence which offered her no relief from her work every day.

> The woman who wrote to say that as a lesbian she'd been unable to look at her past, the forced sex with men which she had always named "not-rape," until reading some of my poems she began to remember, and remember.

> The young sorority women, reminding me of myself twenty years before, who chatted loudly as I read of the rape of a woman lover; who were silenced by the cold fury of my look; who walked out in the middle of the next poem when I spoke, with a sacred meaning, the word *cunt*.

> The women friends who told me they kept my poems by their bed and made love after reading them; the dyke who said she read the love poems in her bathtub; the university colleague, a lesbian,

who said, uneasily, that she felt like a voyeur listening to me read erotic poems.

The woman who came up after a reading and said, "I don't usually like poetry; it seems too distant, nothing to do with me; but I like your poetry."

The woman reviewer who, after finding me lacking in comparison to Milton, said my work wasn't poetry: I should simply stop writing.

The friend, a writer and a lesbian, who heard me read some of the poems about my children; who gave me nothing afterwards but a hug and a burning look; who told me later she went home and started a new short story; who said, "I kept thinking of all the *work* in them."

My mother, sitting at the kitchen table, who said of my work: "I can't be proud of you; I want to be, but I can't." My acceptance of that statement, as both rejection and love, in my reply: "I know, but I'm proud of what I do." Admitting this moment as a flash of truth between us, painful, intense, my mother's honesty traveling with me into my work.

The first time I read my poetry publicly and as a lesbian, the woman who said to me, "Write more. I want to know what happens next."

The letter from Helene is tacked to the white plaster wall near my typewriter, close to the open window. The letter trembles in the hot summer air, the fading words call out to me, a shout: *Go on. Go on.*

Notes

I thank Betsy Warland for her suggestions about how to edit early drafts of this essay; Mab Segrest, Cris South, and the women I worked with on the *Feminary* collective for my education as a lesbian poet; and the lesbians who have organized and attended WomanWrites over the last fifteen years. I especially thank Joan E. Biren (JEB) for all she has taught me about being a lesbian artist, and for her years of work in creating lesbian culture.

1. The nightmare poem was "But Cato Said: Attach No Importance to Dreams," in my chapbook, *The Sound of One Fork* (Durham, North Carolina: Night Heron Press, 1981).

2. "Speak earth. . . ." is from "Love Poem" in Audre Lorde's *The New York Head Shop and Museum* (Detroit: Broadside Press, 1974). Her other books of poetry include *From a Land Where Other People Live* (Detroit: Broadside Press, 1973), *Coal* (New York: W.W. Norton, 1976), *The Black Unicorn* (New York: W.W. Norton, 1978), *Our Dead Behind Us* (New York: W.W. Norton, 1986). Some of her essays and speeches are collected in *Sister Outsider* (Trumansburg, New York: Crossing Press, 1984). Judy Grahn's classic poem of lesbian defiance of our punishments is "A Woman Is Talking to Death," included in *The Work of a Common Woman: The Collected Poetry of Judy Grahn, 1964–1977* (New York: St. Martin's Press, 1978; reissued by Crossing Press, 1983). "The woman who believes her own word" appears in the "She Who" series in the same collection.

3. "The Conjugation of the Paramecium" and "Käthe Kollwitz" appear in Muriel Rukeyser's *Collected Poems* (New York: McGraw-Hill Book Company, 1978).

4. Lillian Smith's essay, "The Role of the Poet in a World of Demagogues," is included in a collection of her prose edited by Michelle Cliff, *The Winner Names the Age* (New York: W.W. Norton, 1978).

5. Information about WomanWrites, held yearly for Southern lesbian writers, can be obtained from the Atlanta Lesbian Feminist Alliance (ALFA), P.O. Box 5502, Atlanta, Georgia 30307.

6. See Mab Segrest's essay, "Mama, Granny, Carrie, Bell: Race and Class, A Personal Accounting," in *My Mama's Dead Squirrel: Lesbian Essays on Southern Culture* (Ithaca, New York: Firebrand Books, 1985).

7. Muriel Rukeyser, *The Life of Poetry* (New York: Current Books, 1949).

8. "To Be Posted. . ." appeared in *Sinister Wisdom 35* (Summer/Fall 1988). The address for *Sinister Wisdom: A Journal for the Lesbian Imagination in the Arts and Politics* is P.O. Box 3252, Berkeley, California 94703.

The Friends of My Secret Self

When I began living as a lesbian, and began to wonder why I had not known this about myself before, I also began to wonder about the girlfriends I had grown up with. I would sometimes look through my senior high school yearbook with its fake leather gold cover, look at the faces of a small rural Southern town of the mid-sixties, white boys with slicked-back hair in overalls, white girls with teased hair in dowdy plaid dresses, and speculate on who might be gay *now*, who might be a *lesbian*. For I needed to know I wasn't an aberration, someone who had strayed off from the rest of humanity, from those I had been raised with. I needed to know I wasn't the only one, not now, but

This essay was first presented, in a different form, on May 29, 1988, at the Southern Women's Music and Comedy Festival, in Cleveland, Georgia.

139

then, at the beginning.

I have a memory for one of the smiling faces, bold-eyed, short-haired Cathy, with her scrawled "Love ya," one of my earliest memories: she and I are wading barefoot, after a thunderstorm, in warm, clear water rushing through a grassy ditch in front of our houses. We are four years old, perhaps, and with us is a neighbor boy a year older, Randy; we three are sliding and splashing together as the sun shifts from behind storm clouds. I remember looking down to see my feet, surprisingly strong, like strange animals in the transparent water. I remember standing there, being perfectly happy, some energy running through me and my friends, holding us in the clean-washed late afternoon.

When I moved to the other side of town the next year, Cathy came to visit for a while, until the day we had a terrible fight. Grubbing around in the garage, we discovered an old wooden gavel, belonging (I think) to my grandfather, the judge, who, though recently dead, still was alive to me in his authority. Sitting on the dirt floor, Cathy and I began to play with, and then quarrel over, this object of unmistakable power, arguing passionately, with no pretense at being nice girls. We were willful, well-matched in our belief in our *selves*, yet friends, well-known to each other since before we could even walk. But finally, to my astonishment, Cathy raised her fist, with gavel, and hit me, then announced she was leaving, was walking home (a mile or more for a five-year-old and beyond belief to me). She set out, a small determined girl, disappearing down the long slope of the hard red-clay road. And that was the end of our friendship for a long time, this quarrel in which we did not know how to negotiate power when it broke into the love between us.

As for Randy, the only memory I have of him after our afternoon wading in the water is this: I was walking home from school with him and Em Hornsby some years later. I was eleven, and in Miss Lucille Splawn's fifth-grade class we had been studying geology and weather, the earth, winter, water turned to ice, and how, in New England fields, frost enters deep into the ground to heave up granite stones that the farmers have to gather in the spring before they plow. I was explaining this to Randy, excited by a new idea. I said to him, "Today we learned how stones *grow* in the fields in the North in winter." I was making a metaphor, perhaps my first consciously created line of poetry. He rejected the statement as an impossibility; I tried to explain the connections between my metaphor and "facts"; I asserted that stones *did* grow. He became angrier and angrier that I was insisting on something that could not *literally* be true. Finally, he hit me in the face, then ran off as blood began to gush from my nose. I touched my face, and my hands were covered with blood. Em, concerned, baffled, and ever socially prepared, had no kleenex, but handed me a pair of white cotton dress gloves to mop up the red, red blood.

I don't remember Randy being able to look me in the eye after this, in his shame at having committed that action most revealing of a loss of male power, hitting a girl. As for me, I learned, for the first but not the last time, something of the violence that lay all around me, in my town, in my region: the violence that could fall on anyone who asserted the hidden life of things; the fear of everything that had been violently suppressed, so that this young boy could not bear to hear a young girl speak of a secret self, even that of stones.

About fifteen years before I ever heard the word *lesbian*, much less wondered if I was one, as I sat outside under the hickory tree one steamy hot afternoon, the summer I was thirteen, I was surprised to see a rattling car pull up in our driveway with grownups and a dark-haired girl about my age. I'd never seen her before, but she was company and I had to be nice to her. When she walked over to me, I suppose I said something polite but I don't remember what. She clearly expected something *more*, something to *happen*. We moped around the yard for a while, then her folks came out and took her away.

For years I remembered her, this stranger, because we hardly ever had company at my house, in our isolation with my father's drinking. I thought for years that she was the bootlegger's daughter. I thought she was waiting while her father made a delivery to my father. I didn't think she had anything to do with *me*.

I saw her again twenty years later when I had returned to Alabama to read my poetry and speak about my life as a lesbian. Introducing herself as Marcia, asking if I recalled her, she revealed the real reason for her long-ago, sudden appearance in my yard. While visiting her Aunt Bertha for the summer, she had begun going off to see another girl, with whom she'd become very close. But this girl she spent all her time with lived near the lumberyard by the sawmill. Some of you understand what that means—she was the poorest you could be in a little Southern town and still be white. Marcia was playing all day in the piles of sawdust and stacks of raw pine boards with a girl her aunt considered white trash, and they were happy, wildly happy.

So her aunt decided to get Marcia together with the right kind of girl: me. Quiet, feminine, reading books all the time, safely middle-class, a good influence. If Marcia would just be friends with me, maybe she would be less what she was: less active, less adventurous, less working-class and forthright, less unconventional, less butchy, less dykey, less passionate about women. Did her aunt, by bringing Marcia to my house that hot summer afternoon, implicitly acknowledge some suspicion of hers about the secret lesbian selves of both Marcia and me? Was it so obvious, even then, that we belonged together, were the "same kind," were different from the others? Yet the difference was denied even as those around us sought to save us, correct us, improve us into "nice girls."

But there we were twenty years later, two lesbians looking at each other, and at our shared, hidden past with great interest, wondering about what had happened since that day we met as girls and did *not* recognize the lesbian in us.

Since the day I stood in my yard with Marcia, I had lived much of my life moving farther and farther away from being that "low-class thing," a lesbian. For though at thirteen, in that place and time, I had no word, not even the concept, for *lesbian,* I knew what *outcast* meant; I could see how the Black folks in our community were treated by white folks. I knew, without knowing, the danger in differing from my people; I kept my self hidden, even from my self. I dated boys in high school, married a poet, had two children, earned a Ph.D. in English literature—all respectable, suitably middle-class doings, all taking me away from the girl I was in a little backward town, and the young women I had known there.

But when I began to live as a lesbian, and remember myself as a girl, when I wondered not just "who else?" of the other girls, but "who was I?" then, I also began to ask how, *exactly* how, had we been kept from ourselves and each other? I knew that we had not seen each other as lesbians because we had no language for ourselves, no place of our own for that reality; certainly we had no public space in which our families, friends, teachers welcomed us as lesbians. Yet we were separated from each other as lesbians by more than a lack of language or the failure of communal imagination. And when the friends of my girlhood found me, as Marcia had, through my writing, because I was living openly as a lesbian, then I began to understand something of how our lives and our love for each other had been lost, and could be regained.

I was browsing at Lodestar Books in Birmingham, just before a poetry reading, when I noticed that on the bulletin board was tacked an old photograph of me, from the sixth grade, the ugliest I'd ever had taken, my eyes sullen in thick glasses, my cowlick untamed. And then, at my side, Cathy reappeared with a laugh, the photograph her doing, saved from the last year we exchanged school pictures. She lived in the city, part of a community of women who had created a bookstore, concerts, lives together; this was the first gathering for a lesbian poet, and she was astonished that it was me.

She was as debonair and handsomely butch as ever, in her slacks and crisp white shirt, her cowboy boots. I hadn't seen her since the night we graduated from high school, but what I remembered was the two of us, running through an empty lot across from her house on Depot Street; we were a little older than we were in the garage, and I was still fighting with her, this time because she was insisting on flying my kite *for* me, because I hadn't managed to get it up in the air. We were butch and femme even then.

I had often wondered about her in my speculation about my girlfriends, because in our class she was the only girl that I knew of who had not married, who had always supported herself. But she said she had *never* wondered about *me*, said that she'd "almost dropped her teeth" when she heard I was a lesbian. Why? Because I was always the good girl, the nice girl; she'd never thought of me as the bad girl, the lesbian, certainly not as a femme who was passing, who might eventually decide to break with the privileges and safeties I got from passing, and begin to live publicly as a lesbian, as a dyke.

So I was hidden from Cathy, in part, because of a very basic lesbian fact: There are some of us who, from an early age, look, act, identify (maybe without words but in some conscious way) as lesbians, who are connected early to their rebellious dykeyness (in my experience, these are usually butches), women for whom passing as heterosexual is more difficult. As teenagers they are likely to suffer, in the words of one butch friend, "years of jeering and exclusion," years that are "excruciatingly lonely and self-hating." And then there are those of us who, for whatever reason, get socialized more into "femininity," who can get heterosexual privilege, even as lesbians, by passing. We can, more easily, get a step ahead, into safety, apart from the others, if we choose; and if we choose to present ourselves as *lesbian* to others, we have to work at being visible. We look back at our sexual past and wonder, "Was I *really* a lesbian when I was thirteen?" We are more likely to spend those years as I did, not as an outcast, but in numbness and alienation from self.

So though Cathy and I were both white, middle-class, church-going girls, we were separated as lesbians, based on what I could hide and what Cathy, in some ways, could not: a difference based on body image, physical mannerisms, and sexual style, based on whether other people saw us, and whether we thought of ourselves, as "good girls." It is a difference that still divides lesbians, a difference based on the fear of looking "too much like a lesbian," and so becoming an outcast. I'm not sure I will ever look too dykey, though my lover Joan tells me that my years of heterosexual training are wearing off, and that no woman who is not a lesbian walks, talks, or dresses like I do. Nevertheless, taking no chances, trying to subvert divisive privilege where I can, I persist, as I did that evening in Birmingham, in standing up and naming myself *lesbian*.

After the reading, Cathy told me something of the pain and self-doubt of her early years, the mental anguish of thinking herself less than others, all that time we'd lived almost side by side but unknown to each other. Then she and her lover drove me home through the dark and fragrant streets of the city. When we said good-bye, we exchanged a kiss, a sweet kiss on the lips, the first I ever remembered us sharing since I'd known her, though surely we had kissed as little, little girls.

Late one night the phone rang and I answered, to hear a precise, rapid voice, that of someone I thought gone from my life: Alice, who had been my best friend at the beginning of high school. She had been reading an anthology of coming-out stories and had found the one I had written ("No one else could have *that* name"), had called Information for my phone number in the city described in my narrative, and now was on the phone with me after almost twenty years. She was the one person I shared a mysterious difference with, in the shadowy days before we traveled into heterosexual dating.

And as we talked, I saw her—the tense, plain, outspoken, brilliant girl: the first woman I knew in my life who questioned authority; the first woman I ever danced with, a wild polka one afternoon across the cement band-room floor. We were in the band together, where many of the other oddities and misfits of our school were: the boys who couldn't or wouldn't try out for football, the girls like me who disdained to show off our legs as cheerleaders or baton twirlers at the games. Instead, Alice and I were drummers; she was the first woman I made art with. In fact, we had an all-girl percussion section (except for the bass drummer), but Alice and I were most serious about the music. We practiced for hours together and performed duets of riveting, passionate intricacy. We sat together on road trips, in the bus or the car, companionable in the darkness, our shoulders bumping together. She held my hand once, or perhaps I just *wished* she would touch me in that early darkness. (Later, I asked her, "Did we ever hold hands?" And Alice said with satisfaction, "Yes, we did," and how she remembered my long, slender fingers.)

Our friendship ended in my junior year, with my turning away from her. In the winter she had run away from home, and her family had had her locked up in a state mental institution, as so many young gay people were, and are. And she was locked up because she was poor—she was, in fact, what Marcia had not been, the bootlegger's daughter. There was no money to send her off a year early to college, which she could have managed intellectually with ease; there was no money for discreet visits to a private psychologist, a process that could have been as damning, but less public.

Then I had only my town's definition that you didn't get sent to Bryce's unless you were crazy. Somewhere deep down I felt but never spoke to myself: Alice is my friend, I am *like* her; if she is crazy, I might be too. So I turned away from her; we were physically separated by her poverty and her institutionalization, and emotionally divided by my fear.

But we were first separated, before her running away, by the increasing pressures on us at fifteen and sixteen to be heterosexual. I was profoundly betrayed when she told me that she was beginning to hang out with, and kiss, boys. She had gone without me into some dangerous field of sex, leaving me behind, in the place where we had been together: the secret, powerful place, never spoken of, but filled with the knowledge of the drumming we had done together, the place where we were different, and where, as Alice said later, "The music didn't judge us."

In the complications of her path to her own sexuality, I saw only that she was going off and leaving me. I believed I had better be heterosexual, or I'd be left behind, all alone. In my journal from those months I wrote:

> *I've been thinking about social life—I'm not* femme fatale *but I can dress neatly and look nice. I think I'll experiment with make-up. . . . I seem to be getting along better with all our boys now. Frank said to Martha, "I sure do like M.B. She's changed a lot. She's gotten so sweet.*

So I turned away from that place of difference, feeling betrayed.

But, in one of our many conversations after that first reuniting phone call, Alice told me that betrayal was what she felt when, after her flight, I had turned aside from her, had ended our friendship without ever talking to her, and then had gone off to a college where she enrolled a year later, where I greeted her briefly and superficially as she came through my house during sorority rush. She felt betrayal as she saw me absorbed in the man I was to marry, in my academic work, in my planned career, as I never turned to her to acknowledge her as a friend of my secret self.

We lost each other first in the unrelenting pressure to be heterosexual: there was *no place* for us as lesbians in 1962, in the middle of almost-rural Alabama. And then we lost each other through differences based on money, on what our families could do for us, as I turned away from her, the lesbian who was "low-class," who was "crazy."

And though we have found each other again as lesbians, the divisions of privilege are still painful between us. When I wrote and published a passage, in a long poem, about our friendship, Alice was furious, in part because I had told what she believed was only hers to tell, but mostly because I had written of one moment in our secret life together, a winter afternoon clandestinely spent picnicking in an abandoned house, the glimmer there of us together, a new reality, in the ruins of what had been a home. I had never told anyone of that afternoon and, it turned out, neither had she: "It was our secret, and you did not ask before you told it." She said that in her fury she had wanted to buy every copy of the book that the poem appeared in and burn them all, the fire of her fury that, with my writer's privilege, I had the power to leave her behind again, even in the telling of our shared story.

But this time, as I promised, she has seen the writing before others have read it, and we have talked it over; this time I hope the telling is more like the furious energy of the drumming we did together.

Looking back through my yearbook, I never wondered about Peggy being a lesbian. She was a skinny, funny girl in my high school class, a girl with freckles and long, straight brown hair. But Cathy told me that the year after we graduated, Peggy had had an affair with our gym teacher. The teacher had been let go, or pressured to leave; Peggy had later turned to a heterosexual relationship.

I never knew Peggy well, though I had worked with her older sister in the garment factory; I was earning summer money for college, and Peggy's sister was doing it for life. Cathy told me that Peggy developed cancer in her early thirties; her boyfriend abandoned her, but

Cathy used to visit her and bring her things she needed, as she lay dying in the hospital in Birmingham with not enough money for a pack of gum. I never knew Peggy as a lesbian; we never met again because of death, her very possibly needless death from lack of adequate health care, because she had never had enough money for it. Around her life is a silence broken by the only sound of hers I remember, her hasty, brazen laugh.

I met Mabel at a party given by the Women's Studies Program in Tuscaloosa, after a poetry reading I'd done there. She was sitting quietly in a loud, convivial group of women, a dark woman, dapperly dressed, sitting beside another woman she was clearly "with." We discovered that we were the same age and we'd both grown up in the same town, Centreville, only thirty miles away. But I had never heard of or met Mabel, though there were probably no more than three thousand people in the town when we were growing up; I had assumed, until that moment of meeting Mabel, that I had known everyone my age there, and their brothers and sisters.

But she was a Black woman, and had been kept from knowing me, as I was kept from knowing her, by segregation: we grew up when the bathrooms and water fountains were still marked by signs, *Colored* and *White,* and when the schools were still divided by law into Black and white. Even though Cathy and Marcia and Alice and Peggy and I had been separated, we were all white and we all had *known* each other. I had even met Marcia who had only *visited* in Centreville. I had some memory of the others to use in looking back at those years, to use in finding what had been hidden from us then.

But we were white, and Mabel was Black, and none of us had ever met her or talked to her. We had no shared moments from which to glean the details that would explain what it meant that we were girls together then and lesbians together now. She had grown up in a ramshackle house near a funeral home run by the father of a classmate. We all knew the house; we all knew the boy and his family; none of us knew Mabel, except, perhaps, as a vague impression of a tall girl in a group of Black children hanging on a tire swing at the falling-down house.

At that time and in that place (as, in general, is still true in this country), skin color was what had separated us most thoroughly, most devastatingly, as lesbians: as if we had posed for a photograph, us white girls in the front, giggling and talking together, not looking back, with Mabel a blur behind us. Yet, twenty years later, I can see myself as I sat on the floor by Mabel at a party as she talked to me, for a few brief moments, about her hopes for herself and the woman she was with.

My high-school graduating class had fifty-eight people. By the well-known 10 percent rule (based on the *Kinsey Report*), we should have had 5.8 gay people. Cathy, Alice, and I are three women of that six, and maybe Peggy would have made four of us. Perhaps there are even more women from our class who are now lesbians that I don't know: I've always thought that 10 percent was a low estimate, and glancing at the pictures in the yearbook, I see several girls I still wonder about.

When I talked at the women's music festival in Georgia about using my senior yearbook to recall the lesbians in my class, a white woman shouted out angrily, "Some of us didn't *finish* high school." So I wonder what girl I have no picture of at all, the dyke who had to quit school to support herself or her family, or who quit to leave behind the harassment of her heterosexual classmates.

Of the photographs in my book, I don't know any of the boys to be gay, although I have heard that a boy I had a crush on, who was a year ahead of me in school, is editing the gay newspaper in Birmingham. I've run into none of the gay men I *know* I must have grown up with: we haven't turned up at a party together; they haven't called me because they've read something I've written. This is a sad reminder of how rigid sexual segregation is between boys and girls, men and women, then and now, the powerful division of class and culture based in gender.

I don't know any gay Black men nor, except for Mabel, any other Black lesbians of my generation from my town; race segregation is still a hard barrier between us. I don't know, for certain, any woman older than me in Centreville who is a lesbian. I think of the long friendship between the English teacher who lived for years with her woman friend, the music professor; but I can only speculate about their secret lives and grieve what has been lost in the wordless chasm between the generations of lesbians. I think of lesbians I've come to know in other places, who I never had a chance to grow up with because their folks weren't welcome in my town: the Creek lesbian poet from Oklahoma whose home this might have been if her people had not been attacked and driven out by white folks a few generations back; the Jewish lesbian antiwar activist whose mother was a Communist and atheist, who would have been anathema in this Christian community.

And I look at where we each are materially, me and these other lesbians from my home town who I know today: we are very close to being in the same place in the hierarchy of class as when we started out, over forty years ago. I'm the lesbian who was the most middle-class, the most femme of our group, the blonde, the one who could pass the easiest. Now I'm the one who has the most formal education and, even though I don't make a lot of money, the most status in the lesbian community because of my writing. Cathy, who also started middle-class, has an excellent white-collar job; but her career was slowed, when she was in her early twenties, by anguish and difficulties about her sexual identity.

Both Marcia and Alice are completing master's degrees in social work, with an emphasis on women's issues; both started their advanced work about two years after I *finished* mine. Marcia was delayed in part because of years trapped in an abusive heterosexual marriage and in dead-end clerical "women's work." Alice was delayed by many things, not just poverty or oppression as a lesbian, but lack of family support, community support, by isolation, abandonment. (And reading this essay, she said about her girlhood, "It's as if everything I've had to do, I've had to invent myself. Life has been a circuitous route; it's taken more time. Minnie Bruce, it's as if *you* had to travel from Washington, D.C., to Winnipeg, Canada, and you didn't have a map.")

Peggy, smart Peggy, who might have spent her life in the garment plant if she'd lived, is dead. When last I heard, Mabel was working at a chicken processing plant near Tuscaloosa and planning to move in with her woman lover.

Within our lives as lesbians, there has been a painful duplication of the structure of the larger world, a wedge driven between us. But despite the fact that the world taught us we would lead despised and secret lives, we have found and loved each other as lesbians. How do we find in our love the power to imagine some rhythm not yet heard between us?

I have hope from the sound of Alice's voice on the phone as she tells me that, reading in the library in a search for her first job as a social worker, she has stumbled on an essay I had written about work and class issues. The essay begins with a recollection of my mother, a social worker, and Alice tells me how much my mother meant to her when she was a teenager, how my mother's work offered the possibility of doing *something* about the despair of poverty around us. She tells me about her own struggle for meaningful work now, and I ask questions and try to listen carefully, carefully, her voice in syncopation against all our conversations and our silences. Months later, I listen as she describes sitting in her office in a huge state hospital, on an island in the middle of Galveston Bay, how her job is the vital work of providing help to poor people who straggle in there, like refugees, from all over the state.

I have hope, months later, when I tell her of a bitter desolation in my life, my work, she says to me, "You have my love. That's all I can offer you, but you have always had my love."

Notes

For their friendship, and for their willingness to be included in this essay, and to read and talk to me about it, I thank Alice, Cathy, and Marcia, some of whom are named pseudonymously. For their comments and insights on the issues of this essay, I thank Joan E. Biren, Elly Bulkin, Beth Karbe, Judy Keathly, and Ruth Segal.

Books in the Closet, in the Attic, Boxes, Secrets

When I was growing up, my bedroom had two narrow closets. One was for my clothes, with high shelves I had to climb on a chair to reach; there I kept my books. The other closet held quilts, blankets, and boxes of

This essay was first presented, in an earlier version, as a talk to the Students for Women's Concerns at Vanderbilt University, February 23, 1989.

books from Papa's house, my grandfathers books. Since I read all the time I was growing up, I was always rummaging around in these closets, and those in the dining room and in the hall where books were double-shelved, unseen, forgotten by my mother and father. I learned that a book I'd found meaningless a year before could interest me later, so about every six months I unpacked the boxes of Papa's books, leafing through the blotched, thin pages of Alexander H. Stephens' *War Between the States,* a copy of the Koran, odd volumes of an edition of Scott's *Works* including *Ivanhoe,* and all of Agnes Strickland's *Lives of the English Queens* in red leatherette binding that rubbed off on my sweaty, eager hands. Mixed in with these books were others more recent, of this century—old grammars, serious bestsellers from the thirties, and some paperbacks.

One day when I was eleven or twelve, I came upon a paperback I'd set aside many times before, a cheap edition with a picture on the cover in lurid colors, a desperate looking woman in a white Puritan's cap, the red letter *A* enormous on her breast. It was a book I'd never heard of, but it looked like a story in which something happened, where there was a secret, something hidden in that letter to be found out.

As I held the book in my hand, my mother came into the room and, seeing the cover, said she didn't want me to read that book, not yet anyway: would I promise her not to read it? Her request was rare, momentous; she was a mother who almost never *asked* for obedience; and so I agreed.

I know now the book was hardly scandalous. It was *The Scarlet Letter,* by then, 1958, over a hundred years old, written about a time three hundred years before, and written in a style that would have been stilted, archaic, to my twentieth-century ears. But my mother did not want me to read this book. What was its secret that I was not supposed to know? Was the secret the power of sex? Or the hypocrisy of Christianity, the preacher who taught an ideal and then sneaked off into the woods to do the opposite? Was the secret the vulnerability of a woman alone in the power of a man? Or was the dangerous secret that the story revealed the woman's way of thinking, and that of her child? Was the danger of this book, ultimately, that the secret *is* revealed? That the woman does not suffer alone, the frailty of the man is exposed, and the hidden sin, the thing never talked about, the betrayal of love, is confessed? Why was it dangerous for me to read that book?

I didn't think of reading as dangerous; as a child I read the way people now watch TV or go to the movies. In my tiny Alabama town, Centreville, there was no public library; across the river, in Brent, there was a one-room collection behind the fire station, for white folks only. The school libraries were all even smaller, and locked up during the summers. Most of the books available to me were in closets, attics, or old mahogany glassed-in bookshelves in a back hall, in the homes of my kin or the middle-class folks who belonged to our church. During the long burning summer, I would ride my bike to Robert and Laura Belle's, or to Miz Gwen Kennedy's, or walk down to my Uncle Francis' house, having gotten permission to borrow books any time I wanted. I'd go into the cool hallway or inner porch, through doors that were never locked, to prowl in the shelves and boxes, looking, looking.

What was I looking for as I sat in my uncle's attic, sorting through boxes of books, hundreds of paperbacks bought at the drugstore—mysteries, westerns, historical romances—dusty, crumbly yellow paper, alluring covers? Perhaps I was hunting for escape, some secret hidden in the books about how to get away from this town, my life. I began to read the way the men in my family drank—my father, his brothers—to escape. Sitting in the attic, poring over the cheap hidden books, I felt the intense excitement of their secret: a way to leave behind life as we were living it, which was so sad and unalterable.

And perhaps I was looking for an explanation. The only answer that I'd ever been given for my life was the Bible, the book that told what the past was, what the future would be. This was the only true story, from creation to judgment day, heaven, hell, everything in between. What was written in the Bible (the King James version) was the literal truth, not to be questioned, the truth that justified the world as it was, from who owned the sawmill to who drove the log trucks, from why Black people lived in the Quarters to why we lived on the hill. The only explanation for how I lived was that it had been so ordered by God, and disclosed by the words of his Book.

Almost all the other books I found, searching around town, had stories that existed within this preordained boundary. There was my favorite girls' series, the one I saved my allowance to buy, about the Little Colonel, a granddaughter of the old Confederacy, white, rich, who had houseparties, boarding school escapades. There were the nineteenth-century romances by Augusta Evans Wilson, *The Speckled Bird, St. Elmo,* in which brilliant, intellectual, poor, white heroines surrendered in Christian love and moved up in class status by marrying the rakish, wealthy, but ultimately reformed, white hero. There was

Tennyson, and Margaret Mitchell's *Gone With The Wind*. All lying fictions that distorted history and justified the old patterns of white over Black, money over poverty, man over woman.

Of lesbian and gay existence, I read not a word, except for a passage in Dante's *Inferno*, an old translation from the Harvard Five-Foot-Shelf-of-Books. It was a translation I read with fascination but little comprehension, not knowing what most of the sins people were being punished for *were*, but relishing the punishments, the mesmerizing descriptions, never really understanding what the sodomites of the Third Round of the Seventh Circle had done.

I spent hours, days, years reading, trying to ignore the fearfulness and uncertainty of my own life, in the midst of the anxious contradictions of huge secrets. In a town where people publicly preached that Blacks were close to inhuman, even animal, I was being raised by a Black woman. In a town in which white men prided themselves on protecting their women, at home my father could barely change a light bulb or keep his checking account in order, and my mother was the economic mainstay of our family. In a town in which people emphasized that they treated everyone as *individuals*, we all knew in high school who would definitely go on to college, and who wouldn't, out of our graduating class of fifty-eight people.

None of these hidden contradictions to the public story was ever talked about in the town, that I heard, or written about in the books I read. I continued to escape into romances—Shakespeare, Jane Austen, the Brontes, Book-of-the-Month Club excerpts from popular novels—all the same old story. If about a man, it was his fight with the monster, the god, or nature, some kind of puzzle, some kind of trial; if he won, his reward at the end was heaven, the kingdom, or the girl. If about a woman, the story told of her being good, maybe even a little smart, and waiting for the man to kiss her.

I read the same plot over and over, and found no explanation for why things were the way they were. I found no escape from my life except through fantasy, the thrill of passivity, blotting out my actual life by reading the repetitious fictions, trying to convince myself of the beginning, middle, and end. But two or three times I chanced on a book that gave me a glimpse of other possibilities.

I found an odd volume of Proust, a fragment of *Remembrances of Things Past*, on an aunt's bookshelf next to Gene Stratton Porter. It was the volume with the passage (famous to others, but marvelous and unknown to me) in which the narrator dips a *madeleine* into fragrant tea and, eating it, by taste and scent remembers a place, recreates a village from his past. There I glimpsed how the imagination might do more than escape through fantasy; there I glimpsed how I might be able to stand apart from myself while in myself, and meditate on where I lived and who I was.

In Uncle Francis' attic I uncovered a copy of *Lady Chatterley's Lover*, which I had to sneak home because by then I was fourteen and my cousin Andrea, who sat afternoons in the living room near the bottom of the attic stairs, was checking to see what books with sex in them I might be finding. This edition of Lawrence's novel had an introduction that reviewed court decisions on the book's banning, that justified publication of this writing which certainly was condemned to be a dirty secret in my town. What I heard was not so much the sexual murmurs of the fiction, which were merely more explicit words for what I'd been reading all along. The galvanizing voice was that of the introduction, my first hearing of a contradictory voice, an argumentative voice, one that said that *anything* can be talked about, any secret, a voice that gave me my first belief that what is hidden could be told.

But in the one rickety bookcase in our house, there was a book I looked at and never read, a copy of Lillian Smith's *Strange Fruit*, that novel about secret love, the most forbidden book of the modern South. Perhaps I didn't read it because I couldn't take it from the shelf for long without my mother knowing. Perhaps I glanced through it and was too afraid of what might leap from its pages, the stark punishments for love, and the belief that love could exist across the barrier of Black and white, and, therefore, across all ʼbarriers. Indeed, although I couldn't know this then, Smith portrayed in the novel not just a love affair between a white man and a Black woman, but also, briefly, troublingly, a relationship between two women. Why didn't I read Lillian Smith's novel that sat quietly, openly, on the bookshelf in my own house, where I had read and reread almost every other book? Perhaps because with a glance at even one of the pages, I knew she was going to tell secrets not from three hundred years ago, but from now, near me. Perhaps because the book was only one voice, and there was no other. Perhaps because the only voices I'd heard—the preachers, the governor, other politicians, my teachers, my father—all said the opposite of this one book; and the romances that I'd read said there was only one story that had a happy ending. It was too dangerous to pick up and read that book and be the one alone with the secret: that there was another way to live. And how *could* there be a book written by a human being that contradicted the Bible? If I opened that book, chaos would fly out. I needed a guide through chaos before I was ready to give up predictable romance and distorted history and the literal word of the Bible and everything in my town that was justified by those words, before I was ready for a different kind of book, a different way to live in the world.

In the years after I went off to college at the University of Alabama, I never heard Lillian Smith's name, though we were in the heart of the civil rights years, though people were being shot and blown up all around, though she was the white Southern writer most delving into the secrets of my region and my life. I wasn't taught her work, or that of Dr. King, or any other literature of liberation. Instead, the writers admired by me, and by the students I consorted with, were the Fugitives, who flourished at Vanderbilt from 1922 to 1928, white Southern men, some of whom later went on to establish the groups known as the Agrarians and the New Critics. Of them Smith said: "No writers in literary history have failed their region as completely as they did."[1]

Indeed, they failed me. I was taught by men who had studied under the Fugitives, and by men who shared their beliefs, who were their literary sons, and who handed down their values about writing and its relation to life. And these values were those of my father: love of the land and denial of those who had done the work on the land, despair and a belief in death, a fascination with the past of the old heroes, a failure to understand the new heroes and heroines who were liberating the present.

But the Fugitives wrote the old values so eloquently, so elegantly. I, who had heard the values of the white South articulated only in the furious ravings of my father, in the vitriolic demagoguery of George Wallace, or in the sentimental prose of romances, luxuriated in the beauty of language and the ironic detachment of these writers. I was happy to let them express my relationship to my region, as John Crowe Ransom did in his "Antique Harvesters." I had no understanding of how my identity as a white woman was bound to the idea in his lines on the South as the famous Lady, "the Proud Lady, of the heart of fire, / The look of snow." I had no understanding of the history of lynching, murder, rape against Black folks by white men that was justified and excused by the myth of pure white Southern womanhood.[2]

When my husband wanted to name our first child, a son, after Ransom, I agreed. I didn't understand that my husband—whose father was from Ohio, mother from Tennessee, neither family from the Southern elite, but small shopkeepers, car salesmen, career military—

was trying, with our son's name, to take a place within the long history of white male rule in the South. He would live through this naming some fantasy of being among the elite, among the poets who were still "fighting in retreat" for the Confederacy, fighting for "the land we dreamed to save."[3]

The time of my marriage and early motherhood was a time when Vietnam shriveled beneath defoliants, and the people of Vietnam burned with napalm; when the streets of Washington, Chicago, Pittsburgh burned after the assassination of Dr. King. I, and my husband, and our friends John Finlay and Rette Maddox, and most of the other young writers I knew, turned our backs on this burning landscape; and like other writers all over the country we lived out the heritage of the Fugitives, turning away from the cruel, fertile present to retreat into a tidy boxed structure of words. We bent ourselves to a closer and closer examination of words, making of writing a world in itself, applying what we understood of the New Criticism by escaping into art, into the story, into the poem. We shut out the feelings, thoughts, and histories of people who lived in another dimension of the world than ours; we shut ourselves up, solitary, with our art.

From the Fugitives, the closest comment on what was happening around us in the sixties were some lines of Allen Tate's at the end of "The Swimmers," his poem about how a child meets up with a lynch mob and how the child follows the corpse being dragged back into town: "I could not run / Or walk, but stood. Alone in the public clearing / This private thing was owned by all the town, / Though never claimed by us within my hearing." With a momentary flash, finally Tate reveals one of the secrets; he claims the murdered body, he announces or confesses the sin. Yet at the same time, he denies the humanity and the life of the Black man killed by white men: "This private thing." In the chaos of those days, I had this flash from Tate, but no more, nothing else to go on.[4] In a continuation of this silence, there was no sustained public discussion by my teachers or my classmates about the contemporary challenge to the supremacy of white men in the South, to their social system, their economic system, to the way in which everything, especially love between people, had been rigidly ordered by them.

Of the name *Fugitive*, Ransom had said, "It seemed to be a secret among us, though no one knew what the secret was."[5] Sidney Hirsch, who was Jewish and a member of the original group, named them Fugitive. But there were no poems from him explaining his meaning of that need to escape. Instead, Tate appropriated his point of view by writing: "A Fugitive was quite simply a Poet: the Wanderer, or even the Wandering Jew, the Outcast, the man who carries the secret wisdom of the world."[6] Of course, Tate and Ransom, Davidson and Penn Warren, and others of the group, white and Christian, were never outcast. They became the literary establishment; they collected Guggenheims, Bollingers, Pulitzers, by writing as refugees from a pastoral South that had never existed.[7] They perpetuated this self-delusive romance, this glorification of the old hierarchy, as "secret wisdom." Of the buried lives of the South, the secrets from which they fled, there was no word from them, at least not within my hearing.

The house that I've just moved to has an attic, which is where I work, read, and write. Every day that I climb up the narrow angle-twisted stairs, I feel the rush of anticipation that I used to feel when I climbed up into somebody's attic to find a new book: going up to a secret place, a hide-out, away from the grownups. Now I shiver with anticipation and also from fear, because what I mostly do up in this attic is to write about the secret between me and the world, my lesbian self. The secret is myself and I'm going up, not to escape her, but to meet her.

My attic is lined with rows of books, and boxes of them sit around, not yet unpacked: books about all sorts of folks, especially lesbians; books with startling titles and lurid covers, the kind a mother might snatch from a daughter's hand; books that might provoke a discussion between two women sharing a house and a bedroom when, just before family is to come for a visit, they debate if the books should be moved to a higher shelf, if they should be boxed up and put in the closet.

It's true our books give our secrets away. During the time that I was falling in love with a woman and coming out as a lesbian, my mother arrived for a visit. I had her stay in my tiny bedroom-study, and left my books out as they were, *Lesbian Nation* stacked on top of *Sisterhood Is Powerful*, clues about who I was becoming. Now, years later, strange as it sometimes seems, I am someone who writes such books. I've been imagining with satisfaction how the book I am working on, *Crime Against Nature*,[8] will be the subject of debates on whether it should be hidden, as the kind of book a visitor, browsing in the shelves, would immediately pull down in order to see what secrets were disclosed.

Breaking silence/coming out/becoming visible/speaking out: all themes common not just to me but to much of contemporary lesbian writing.[9]

Certainly this emphasis is to be expected in a literature springing from our experience: in order to live fully as lesbians we have to be able to *find* each other. And since we don't grow up grouped together as a people by skin or religion or family; since, despite all the stereotypes, there is, in fact, no way to identify a lesbian just by looking at her; we have to make ourselves known to one another somehow, by glance, by code, by words.

But I didn't find myself as a writer, or a lesbian, or a person who had something to say, because of words that I read in a book. During the years of my so-called education, both undergraduate and graduate, I continued to escape my daily life as a wife and mother by reading books into which I could flee as an imaginary participant. I also perfected the kind of escape I had learned from the Fugitives and New Critics: I stood back and looked at literature as an artifact to be commented on; I learned to build my own closed space as a critic by constructing narrow theories about what I read. Even when writing was clearly immediate and present, as, for instance, in a poem my husband was writing about *me,* I still refused to see the words as connected to my life. I accepted Tate's pronouncement of a poem as a thing of "perfect inutility."[10] I managed to forget that, in the year before I married, I also, briefly, wrote poetry. I remained trapped in someone else's version of my life; I existed as if I were reading my own life as a badly written novel, which I called "reality."

My ability to imagine another reality for myself came not from something that I read, but from meeting up with people who were living a hidden reality out in the open. I met a group of women in the small Southern university town where I was in graduate school, a group of women emerging in the Second Wave of Women's Liberation during the 1970s in the United States. With them came *talk,* the subversive talk of one woman with another, me talking to the women who were like me but different, my other selves.

The connection between hidden life and literature was something I glimpsed when I began having conversations with another graduate student, Elizabeth, a feminist who had been very kind to me during the time of my second pregnancy. One day during lunch I recounted to her something that had occurred in the class I'd taught that morning on Chaucer's *Canterbury Tales.* I had made a joke about the Pardoner, who is described as having long, yellow, shoulder-length hair, and a high voice "like a goat"; he is beardless and never shaves; Chaucer declares him either "a geldyng or a mare," either a eunuch or a queer.[11]

Suddenly, in the middle of joking to the class, I had wondered if there were any gay men or women there at that moment, enduring this humiliation from me. And, later, as I talked to Elizabeth, I remembered, and mentioned, that I had learned this joke from my husband, who used it in his teaching, and he had learned it from what teacher of his? I was mouthing his words like a ventriloquist's dummy.

When I finished this story, Elizabeth looked at me and said, with some hesitation, "I should tell you that I am having a relationship with Linda." She did not, at that moment, use the word *lesbian*, but we both heard it resonate in the room. This was the first time I heard one of the hidden truths spoken, not as they had been, in whispers, one person gossiping to another about *someone else*, voyeuristic talk, but, instead, the secret truth spoken to me by the one living this truth, someone outside boxed-in life as I had known it, outside literature as I had learned it. I was suddenly, momentarily, on the outside thinking, *Anything can be said, anything can be done,* and I meant, *In my life.*

From my journal at that time (which I began keeping because of these conversations, after long years of silence), I noted of myself in relation to my husband:

> *Fear to question M.—facade will fold, crash—real hatred, fear, despair underneath...I, of course, deeply silent —fear.''*

Of my talks with Elizabeth:

> *Why am I friends with Elizabeth?—I feel she is* honest *with me—and cares about me—even if that feeling is only a principled one toward women—but is friendship with her a retreat from reality?...I am spending* too much time *with Elizabeth.*

But I was spending time not in unreality, but in *another* reality, where there was another way to look at my life. My husband and I had dinner with Elizabeth and her feminist housemate:

> *M. saying tactless male things while trying to be conciliatory—strain—his assumptions bristled at—I have ignored these assumptions or accepted them—it's almost as hard to see your husband as others see him as it is to see yourself.*

But seeing with lesbian eyes I managed to separate myself from my husband. I began the process of contradicting the plots of all the romances I'd read. Instead of merging my perspective, my thoughts, and my feelings with the hero, instead of waiting around for him to do something, I began to live as myself, as some unknown heroine in some unknown story. Even in my journals I began to sound like I was talking to and for myself, and not, as I had been, writing to impress someone who might overhear me, some god I had to convince. I began to summon up my life in myself, a new world, through this writing.

I was able to do this because I was not alone. I knew that there were other women to talk to, and there was more than one book to read. There was the enticing sound of one woman talking to another, conversations that went beyond Virginia Woolf's imagination of a book with the sentence: "Chloe liked Olivia. They shared a laboratory together. . . ."[12] Because Elizabeth had read Isabel Miller's *Patience and Sarah* and recommended it, I read it too; it was my first lesbian book, a historical romance in which I overheard the heroines during their lovemaking, their quarrels, and their discussions about work and money. Elaine gave me Judy Grahn's *Common Woman* poems; Starling gave me Audre Lorde's *New York Head Shop and Museum:* in these poems I heard the voices of women who had not been present at all in the literature I'd been taught, women who were present in my life but not acknowledged by me, poor white women, Black women, women passionately loving other women. Someone told me about June Arnold's *The Cook and the Carpenter* and *Sister Gin,* and about Bertha Harris' *Lover,* all quintessentially lesbian novels by women born and raised in the South, who came to the university during those years and talked about their writing, their politics, their loves.[13]

I began to want to hear *all* the hidden conversations, all the writings that defied the prearranged endings of heaven or hell based on gender or race or class or who we loved. I was able to find many of these voices because political movements in the U.S. have nourished subversive traditions of literature: the movements for abolition of slavery, for suffrage and for women's rights, the trade union movement for working people, the civil rights movement, the efforts of people who had come to this country as slaves or as immigrants to honor themselves and their people, the efforts of women to honor ourselves. All these movements engendered narratives of liberation, community schools to teach literacy and history, small publishing houses and newspapers, self-published authors, independent bookstores—many stubborn efforts by oppressed peoples.

The feminist and lesbian movement into which I emerged embodied this subversive tradition in hundreds of national, regional, and community newspapers and newsletters, like the monthly mimeographed newsletter Elizabeth and others began, which I helped with briefly, a newsletter that was eventually given the name *Feminary*. Some years later, Mab Segrest and others, including me, turned *Feminary* into a regional Southern journal for lesbians. We used to joke about how we were the revolutionary answer to the Fugitives, a new literary tradition bent on turning the old values of the South topsy-turvy, a tradition we did our best to create during the years of the magazine, 1978–1983.[14]

We were inspired in our effort by the work of other lesbians in the South who were creating a subversive transformative literature. From 1976–1978 Harriet Ellenberger Desmoines and Catherine Nicholson edited a national lesbian journal, *Sinister Wisdom*, out of their home in Charlotte, North Carolina. There were early lesbian and feminist publishing houses, like Parke Bowman and June Arnold's Daughters, Inc. Though at that time there were no women's or gay bookstores in North Carolina, where I was living, I'd buy books at conferences; and on my way home to Alabama during the summer to see my mother, I'd go through Atlanta and stop by Charis Books, the first women's bookstore I ever set foot in. It was shocking to me that the bookstore was on Moreland Avenue with all the other stores, two rooms about the size of my high school library, but with more books, and such books, the likes of which I'd never seen. Books that had come out of the movement, just as I had, because of the stories that needed to be told, the forbidden, bloody, beautiful, life-and-death stories, springing from just such conversations as were begun by me and Elizabeth, talking on our lunch hour, boxed-in, sitting in a small office, talking back and forth, talking.

Sitting up here in my attic, in the middle of an April thunderstorm, books stacked all around, I still find it hard to be someone who writes the books, instead of someone who just hides out reading them. I still fall into the trap of despair, of acquiescence in the predictable ending, and find myself escaping into the comfortable dead end of murder mysteries, or into the easy fantasies of science fiction. I still struggle to live and to write the open-ended, ever-changing story, a prose and a poetry that is merely, simply, true to the complexity of my own life.

Despite my skills learned at the university, I would not be writing now except for the talk among women, among suppressed peoples, a talk that has yet to receive its due as part of culture and of art. I would not be writing now except for the stubborn underground culture and the political work of lesbians, how we meet, tell stories about our days in the safety of our homes, in our bars, in our self-help groups, how we talk, sometimes, of our lives at a public meeting of women, and how, sometimes, we go out in the world and demand of others that our lives be recognized.

One of the few regrets of my life is from a time when I was doing political organizing in North Carolina, and had helped bring together the first gathering of lesbians, as lesbians, other than at the bar, in my right-wing, military-base town. When that small group of women finally sat down together in the den of the house I shared with two other women, I was thrilled that they were there—and I didn't listen to a thing that they were saying. I thought that I knew what we should be *doing,* and impatiently thought about how I would instruct them in this plan all the while they spoke. And so I did not listen to the Latina who taught Spanish as a second language in the elementary schools and was closeted. Or to the two red-cheeked flannel-shirted self-sufficient white dykes who'd just moved down from Alaska and told everyone they were lesbians. Or to the two quiet, cropped-hair dykes who were in the Army and worried about the military police and confidentiality, or to the physical education teacher at the local church college who was so terrified to be there that she got drunk and threw up the entire time the meeting went on. I didn't listen to them, or to the dyke who was a butcher, or the one who was a social worker, or to the one whose political work had been with the S.P.C.A. and not with battered women. I didn't listen, really, to any of them, so intent was I on my own way; and now I bitterly regret this.

Now I know that in order to keep hoping, and living, and writing, I need work from other women that is rooted in the messy complexity of our daily lives, work in which we upset the predictable ending. I need all the voices of the women who have been destined for despisal, anonymity, or death, but who, defiant, have survived, and lived to tell their triumph.[15]

When I last went home to Alabama to speak and read my poetry, to a town just over the line south of Nashville, I stood in a room glowing with candles and flowers, in front of an audience gathered together by a small group of lesbians organizing in the town. I watched one young woman in particular, her transfigured face, her lips murmuring along with my words. Later, she told me that her throat ached and almost closed as the words came up in her, words that meant so much to her, about loving another woman, passionately.

I like to think that the muscles in her throat were strengthened and made more flexible by her murmuring, that her voice is stronger now, because I need her to tell about her life to me, and to others. Noreen, do you hear? Don't just listen to me and my talking. I need you to tell your own story. And Susan, who was there that night also, I want you to let the world know the power of your voice which was strong enough to bring someone back from the edge of insanity. And the woman whose name I don't remember, you'd just been fired from your job for being a lesbian: everyone should know how you are driving that bus full of problem children, mostly boys, now, and how you've made the seat behind you the place where any child can sit who's had a bad day, so they can talk it over with you, and how the problem children are not being problems on *your* bus anymore. I want everyone to know the power of your voice talking to the world, and I want to know what happens next in your remarkable life.

And I know you've already lost one job (or perhaps your children, your friends, or your family, depending on who you are) because you said you are a lesbian. I haven't forgotten. But you are with the other women there in your town, and all over; we have each other. We know the power of announcing a secret to the world, how word travels fast, and how this is what we fear. But we know also that this is our power.

Notes

This essay was first published in *The American Voice* (Winter, 1989).

1. Lillian Smith in *Killers of the Dream* (New York: Anchor/Doubleday, 1963), p. 199. Michelle Cliff has edited an excellent collection of articles and speeches by Smith, *The Winner Names the Age* (New York: W.W. Norton, 1978).

2. A brief selection of Ransom's work can be found in *The Fugitive Poets*, edited by William Pratt (New York: E.P. Dutton, 1965). For some information on the lynching of Black men, the rape of Black women, and the cult of white womanhood, see Ida B. Wells' autobiography, *Crusade for Justice*, edited by her daughter Alfreda M. Duster (Chicago: University of Chicago Press, 1970) and Jacquelyn Dowd Hall's *Revolt Against Chivalry* (New York: Columbia University Press, 1979).

3. From Donald Davidson's "Lines Written for Allen Tate on His Sixtieth Anniversary," in W. Pratt.

4. "The Swimmers," also in W. Pratt's collection.

5. *The Fugitives Reunion*, ed. R.R. Purdy (Nashville, Tennessee: Vanderbilt University Press, 1959), p. 122.

6. W. Pratt, pp. 34–39.

7. For more on the Fugitives in relation to Southern literature, see Mab Segrest's "Lines I Dare: Southern Lesbian Writing," in *My Mama's Dead Squirrel: Lesbian Essays on Southern Culture* (Ithaca, New York: Firebrand Books, 1985).

8. *Crime Against Nature* (Ithaca, New York: Firebrand Books, 1990).

9. For more on these themes, see Bonnie Zimmerman, "The Politics of Transliteration: Lesbian Personal Narratives," in *The Lesbian Issue: Essays from Signs* (Chicago: University of Chicago Press, 1985), and Audre Lorde, "The Transformation of Silence into Language and Action," in *Sister Outsider* (Trumansburg, New York: The Crossing Press, 1984).

10. Tate quoted in Segrest, p. 112.

11. Geoffrey Chaucer, *Works*, ed. F.N. Robinson (Cambridge, Massachusetts: Riverside Press, 1961), p. 23.

12. Virginia Woolf, *A Room of One's Own* (New York: Harcourt Brace Jovanovich, 1957), p. 87.

13. For bibliographic information about contemporary lesbian literature, see Margaret Cruikshank, *Lesbian Studies* (Old Westbury, New York: The Feminist Press, 1982).

14. *Feminary* began publication in Durham, North Carolina, as a mimeographed newsletter, *The Research Triangle Women's Liberation Newsletter*, in August 1969. Renamed *Feminary* in October 1974, it continued as a newsletter until spring 1977, when it was expanded into a feminist magazine. With a special lesbian issue in spring 1978, *Feminary* became a lesbian journal, published in Durham until 1983, and in San Francisco until 1985. Throughout all of its sixteen years, *Feminary* was edited collectively.

15. I think especially here of Dorothy Allison's recent book of short stories, *Trash* (Ithaca, New York: Firebrand Books, 1988), and her Preface, "Deciding to Live."

Money and the Shape of Things

All this fall my lover was getting pushed out of the apartment she'd lived in for ten years. Not because she is a lesbian, not because I would come over to visit and the neighbors would get offended. No, in the District of Columbia there are, for the moment, a few minimal protections against discrimination on the basis of sexual orientation; legally, she could not have been thrown out of her apartment for being queer. But there was no law to protect her from the forces of capitalism at work in the market for property and land. Because of rising property values and taxes, her apartment building was being sold by its owner; rent control would no longer apply to the tenants; and Joan, who

This essay was presented originally for the Society of the Humanities at Cornell University, and at Hamilton College, on April 10 and 13, 1989.

could not afford to buy, had to vacate for the new owner.

The neighborhood we lived in had long been a settled, Black, working-class area with only a few white folks, mostly septuagenarians who didn't flee the city after the uprisings of the 1960s. Lately, however, young white singles and couples, middle-class, white-collar, had begun to perceive the city as "safe" and "interesting," after eight years of restrictive Republican administration. They had begun to move onto Capital Hill; property values had gone up; owners with limited incomes were struggling to meet tax payments. Suddenly, *For Sale* signs clanked and clanged on every street, new glossy oak doors appeared, and more bars on the windows, lots of fresh paint; the old-fashioned yards were dug up to be replanted in a day with hostas or pampas grass bought at the nursery, like no other plants seen on the block.

All fall we worried about how to find another apartment Joan could afford, with rent as low as hers had been under rent control, and with room enough for her to live and run her business in. I would walk back and forth between her place and my apartment building and look bitterly, enviously, angrily at the houses along the three blocks. Where I used to examine people's yards with interest, to investigate whatever new leaf or bloom had appeared, to appreciate the way brick details on the old houses shifted into different angles with the changing sun, now I found that the shape of everything had changed.

The world I walked in was more hollow. Sunlight fell on the facades of the houses beautifully, and coldly. I was outside; and inside were the people who were safe, who had money enough to pay their rent, money enough to buy their houses. A huge distance spread between me on the sidewalk, and the front of the houses, and the people inside them, a menacing distance.

Though, of course, not everyone inside *could* pay their rent. Usually around the second week of the month, after the late-rent period had expired, I'd be walking or driving around the neighborhood, and there'd be piles of furniture heaped up like garbage on the sidewalks. Except the garbage was someone's laboriously accumulated possessions, all of their possessions: clothes, furniture, plastic dishes with a rosebud design, a blue maternity smock, sagging mattresses, a shaky fake-wood TV cart, a red velour chair. If people were lucky, when they got back from work or wherever and found their life spread out on the street, no one had taken anything. If they were lucky.

But why was I being so upset? I still had my apartment, big and cheap for the city, protected by rent control, heat included. At least, I had it for the moment, after the two campaigns we had fought as tenants to limit (though not eliminate) exorbitant rent increases. Nevertheless, the sound of money rustled around us all the time, like steam escaping from our radiators: how long before the landlord would try again for his profits, the ones allowed by law? The machine of profits clanked and turned somewhere constantly in the background.

People were beginning to talk of the District as a city under siege, because of drugs and the resulting violence. But what about the folks living in the street or shelters like displaced persons because they couldn't pay their rent? Over the years, whole neighborhoods had been uprooted and dispersed as part of "development," and the frail ties that had been established so tentatively between people who were not blood kin had been broken. Yet no one was talking about the despair behind the drugs, despair at being caught in the inexorable turning of higher rents, and fixed or no incomes, and no skills to get jobs or higher-paying jobs, and no place to go.

Though I still had my apartment, I realized I was feeling like someone who would have nowhere to go if Joan lost hers. I lived in three rooms on the fifth floor, a long way from the ground. But her apartment had a front yard with a huge, sweet-smelling abelia bush just like the one outside my back door at home in Alabama. I'd planted her front yard with daylilies dug up from home, and from a roadside in Georgia—orange, yellow, red. And in her enormous backyard were mulberry trees, hawthorne bushes, a crabapple, a native holly tree; and a shady little garden of coleus and caladiums, with a blue witches' ball on a pedestal, with redbirds, doves, blue jays, and the liquid syllables of wood thrushes, all the bird sounds from home.

When I thought about Joan's moving, I realized myself to be *in* the city in a way I had not before. She had been family only three blocks away, a presence that kept me from being alone in a town where I had no kin, and where no one but her and one other person had known me longer than four years. The yard outside her apartment had been like the dirt of home. When she moved, I wouldn't have a place I could go to dig and plant; I'd have no land, not even a tiny bit of land.

Walking back and forth past the yards of others, I thought bitterly that at home I didn't envy people so much. I had less desire for *things* because things mattered less in the country than in the city; I could always go out my door and in five minutes be in the woods; I didn't need to own things, and there weren't these fences every two steps, everything marked off into little squares of ownership.

What I was remembering about home was my sense of freedom in walking after my father through the sweetbay thickets, poplar trees, sweetgums, and magnolias, on land that he owned. He walked the land with an assurance he lacked in so many other ways; a confidence from his childhood, him walking the land his father owned up by River Bend; the confidence of the landowner, who knows no one can order him off the land. Or, at least the confidence of the white land-owner in the South, who has never had someone try to frighten him off his land. I was remembering this, and forgetting that *his* land was fenced.

Now I wonder how much of my bitterness, my envy, walking in the city, was from my expectation that I would be the owner, I would own the land. Instead, I find myself an immigrant in the city, like so many others here, but different from them also: The Black folks from North and South Carolina, Virginia, the folks who came up the coast away from towns where no one would hire them, or there weren't enough jobs, or they would be hired for only the most menial jobs, cleaning white people's houses or stemming tobacco for the women, the sawmill or nothing for the men. The immigrants from Honduras, Guatemala, El Salvador, fleeing from the wars being fought in their homes over whether the land would be redistributed from the plan-tation owners to those folks who worked for them for starvation wages. The Koreans at the corner store, the Eritreans at the Seven-Eleven, all the other refugees and immigrants fleeing from war, op-pression, poverty in their homes, come to "the capital of the free world," to a land made rich from their countries' despair. The people looking for some work, in construction, in a restaurant, maybe open-ing a store of their own, maybe living in a house no one can throw them out of.

And me coming up from the country, needing to live my life as a lesbian, looking for work where I wouldn't have to hide that life, a real possibility here in the city; for the first time living in a place that was not my land, not the land of my father. Someone else owned this land.

Christmas Eve, about three years after I moved to the city, I heard a radio interview with a homeless man living in Lafayette Park, across from the White House: Benjamin Franklin Johnson, from Kentucky. Asked how he felt about so many people walking through where he lived, he said: "At home, when Bradley was alive—me and Bradley would go hunting. We'd look and walk and listen, and if a twig snapped, it wasn't us. Bradley Howard, my blood brother. Me and Bradley could go in the woods, and Bradley did not talk." Showed a picture of himself peering out from his plastic shelter, he laughed when asked if folks at home would recognize him: "Not likely. I look like I'm looking past things, not like I'm looking two steps ahead. At home I was an independent person. Here I'm not in control of my life." Midway through his talking I began to cry, and cried wildly, inconsolably, for maybe an hour, the tears of an exile. Yes, at home you could just walk out in the woods; and in the pastures there were blackberries if you wanted to dare the copperheads; and someone at home was always trying to give you their extra squash or corn.

But here you had to have money to get food. In the Safeway, I had stood looking at apples, and the woman next to me rummaged in the pears, $1.99 a pound, late in the year. She was scornful, snorting at the price. "At home," she said, "I could just go out and pick as many of these as I wanted up off the ground." The man with her got very still and quiet, and said, "Yes. But you are not back home *now.*"

I cried because, here, money seems like everything. I wasn't out of control of my life like Mr. Johnson, but I was in the presence of the inexorable necessity to have money.

Yet I was remembering my past, at home, as if money wasn't a problem, and that wasn't true, that was not a true memory at all, but a longing for something that really had never existed, or had existed only for brief moments, like the afternoons I walked in the woods behind my father. Yes, there was land, and there were neighbors and friends, but, in the true memory:

My uncle, who as the only son had inherited the family farmhouse my mother grew up in, had a garden, but we didn't. For my father, white skin was not enough to hold onto the family land, lost in economic crises during the 1920s and 1930s. Perhaps one of the crises, at least, was precipitated by my grandfather's drinking; there were vague stories that he'd get drunk and strip and run naked outside, going too far even in a town where alcoholism was accepted as a fact of life, too far even for someone who, like him, was probate judge of the county. (And how much did his drinking have to do with despair at what he saw at that job?) He finally lost an election, and his job; perhaps that's when he had to sell the family land.

Another version was that my grandfather was staunchly anti-Klan in the 1920s when the Democratic party machinery was run by pro-

Klan forces; that he refused to prosecute Black men who used guns to defend their land, houses, and families against white terrorists at the time; that he actually registered some Black men to vote. Perhaps he lost his job and the family land because of skin, his disloyalty to white skin. In any case, my father spent his adult life traveling, living in cities, and in my home town, tiny, not like the city I live in now, but, nevertheless, a town where he yearned for the land, the country; and felt out of control of his life; and drank. He hated being an alcoholic. His drinking made him improvident and careless with money; he missed weeks of work often during my childhood; and probably kept his job because he was a white man from a good family, and what else could they do with him?

My mother worked all the time, all the time, during the day as a social worker, at night and on weekends with canning and cooking and sewing and knitting my clothes. She made all my clothes herself, because, I always assumed, that was the least expensive way to dress me. I worried, underneath, about money constantly. I can remember thinking, after Christmas Day one year, that my mother had spent too much money on presents for me, an only child, small presents of a few books, a doll, and some clothes.

I worried about money, yet I knew how secure we were compared to most others in the town, and out in the countryside; I saw the houses that poor white and Black folk lived in, when I drove my mother in the summer to see her clients. We had a bathroom, running water, a gas floor heater; I had my own room. But ours was a boxy little house with my twelve-foot-by-twelve-foot room at one end of a narrow hall, and at the other, my parents' equally small room. Next to my room was the cramped kitchen, with no door between it and a dining room with seldom-used matching table and chairs and an old upright piano. No door between here and the living room, shabby until after I went off to college and got married; I can remember my mother saving money in a glass jar for years to get a new couch. A very small house, in which every word said in one room could be heard in all the others; a house that, in another region, or in the city, would have been seen as a modest working-class home. But in my town it was a middle-class house, a very nice house, with mostly good furniture, a home that my mother made for us only through incessant work.

But I worried about money. On Sundays I would read the *Birmingham News*, and stare resentfully at the pictures of the debutantes, curled and frilled and white, who, in season, would go to swim parties, dance parties, roller-skating parties. I didn't resent the parties, which seemed to always have the same people at them, the same names mentioned over and over, and the same refreshments, pink-and-green mints and sugary cake. I think I resented those girls because they had all the money they needed; I thought they did not worry about money. And I did say to myself, even then: They are *ahead* of me. I'll never catch up. I'll never get to be easy about money the way these girls are.

A middle-class child anxious about money, with the terror of sliding back somewhere—where was it? A place where you "couldn't take care of yourself." A child with a resentment of the others ahead of her; no matter how hard she worked, she'd never catch up. A child one generation away from the family farm, whose father (so far as I can tell from the perspective of years later) held a job mostly on the strength of family, skin, and charm; whose mother held her job partly because she was a white woman from a respectable family, and partly through great tenacity and competence in her work.

A child whose parents managed enough money to shape her in crucial ways: braces for her buckteeth to make them straight and shining, so she wouldn't look poor and ugly; contact lenses for her terrible near-sightedness, so she'd be an attractive marriageable woman; nice new clothes twice a year, handmade, but at least not from chicken-feed sacks, like the clothes some cousins had to wear some years. And, finally, an education, the best in the state, at the state university. Never a discussion about sending her out of state, despite her exceptional grades; only the wealthiest families did this for their daughters, sent them to Radcliffe or Sweet Briar.

A middle-class child, with her own particular understanding of, and experience of, money, who years later still feels irritated when a reviewer of her poetry persists in identifying her as "working-class," presumably because she was from the Deep South and wrote about dirt and trees. Was the irritation because of the ignorance of a critic who would not see the nuances of Southern reality, a reader who could not imagine a rural small-town middle-class existence, though the poems gave enough clues—mention of her silver napkin ring on the table, the fact that a Black woman worked for the family? Or was her irritation because she was afraid of sliding back, afraid her poetry hadn't gotten her far enough up and out, away from her precarious existence in that town?

A middle-class child angry and resentful about the impossibility of catching up, who, as an adult, becomes angry when another writer, also from the South, implies that their lives have been quite similar. The child's rage because she knows this woman was raised in a family where the mother had "culture," the father a professional job, parents who read and talked about ideas, a mother (she thought) who did not have to sit at the sewing machine all night, a father who didn't sit drunk watching the Friday night boxing matches. The rage of the child knowing she'll never catch up to this woman who started ahead of her.

Her rage at the way that money and the insecurities of class position make her life into a place where she will always be running to keep from losing ground, like some hidden treadmill in an old Hollywood movie. Or like the assembly line she worked on one summer in high school, earning money for college, trapped on the line putting grippers on children's sportswear, doing the same motions over and over, day after day, working frantically so the garments wouldn't pile up by her, so they would move smoothly down the line to the other women. She swore then she'd never do that kind of work again; that's why she was going to college.

The middle-class child who doesn't understand that no matter what kind of work she ends up doing she will still be caught in the flow of money in this country, in the world; caught in the process of how money is made, and how money is spent. The child who wants to be a professional somebody, not a worker. The child who early has a huge rage for those ahead of her. She imagines that they will become secure, will be able to stop working to sit down by the pool sipping lemonade while she still steps repetitively on the treadmill, the assembly line, the line that she, at the same time, denies she is part of.

As for the people behind her, the ones she sees working, working, but who have less than she does, for these she is allowed to feel pity. From her mother, and from her Christian religion, she has learned to have sympathetic feelings for those "less fortunate," and not judge a person's value by whether or not they have money. She is taught clearly: Money corrupts; it is not possible to be a good person with a lot of money; how you act is what determines goodness, not how much money you have. She is not allowed to despise those with less money than she, but she can feel sorry for them.

But if she feels sorry for them, that must mean she is better off, better *than* them in some way. Perhaps she thinks they suffer more than she does; there *is* a suffering that comes with no money; she's seen that clearly enough through her mother's eyes, and her mother's work. Perhaps she allows the people an existence only as poor suffering people, somewhere behind her, so that then she can continue to feel she is better, better off than them, better off than *somebody*.

She doesn't consider the contradiction between being taught to respect someone if they have no money, and being taught to feel sorry for them if they have no money, until many years later, after her girlhood. Nor does she, then, want to think of how, somewhere, there are people who think they are better than *she* is, better off, and that they, from their distance, sit pitying her. Yet, for years, whenever she travels outside her home, she dreads to meet, and prepares to meet, those people. She has no way of talking about the huge reservoir of fear, anger, resentment, dread, false pity, and guilt that she carries about money and people.

This was the child I was growing up in the South just after the Great Depression and World War II, a South in which the Depression still existed. A child growing up less than ten years after Southern tenant farmers, Black and white, met to organize a radical union to protect themselves from farm mechanization, especially the cotton-picking machine, whose introduction threatened to wipe out even such a precarious hand-to-mouth living as they then led; there was a militant branch of the Southern Tenant Farmers Union in Tallapoosa County, three counties east of where I lived.[1] The principles of the union included land for the landless, full and decent employment, the holding in common of all natural resources and all scientific processes, and the liberation of all workers from enslavement to the machine.[2]

While the tenant farmers' organizing was being broken up by threats, physical violence, and lynchings arranged by the large landowners, the steel companies in Birmingham were forming a committee to keep labor organizers out of the mills. The owners had the organizers, many of whom were young men connected to the Communist party, beaten up, or arrested and held incommunicado in jail.[3] When the mills closed during the Depression, Tennessee Coal and Iron allowed workers to stay in the company houses, but shut off the electricity, water, and heat; Republic Steel drove people from the houses with armed guards and posted men to shoot people if they came back to their homes. Many folks began to live in the coke ovens, the brick beehive-shaped ovens where coal was turned into coke for smelting iron ore into steel. To get out of the rain and cold, people began living in the ovens like caves.[4]

When the cotton-picking machine was put into mass production by the Rust family of Memphis, and World War II started, and the steel mills went back into production, another migration of workers from the land to the city began, one of many such in the history of the U.S.[5] Sometimes the migratory shift was huge, sometimes slight, like the one that happened in my home county. The women who were working as housewives on farms that were five-to-ten miles outside my town—women used to working in the family garden, canning, sewing the family clothes, keeping chickens—became women working in the garment plant, clocking in and out every day, and at the end of the week being handed, for the first time in their lives, a pay envelope.

This particular shift came to my town in the 1950s when the garment plant, run by some people from up North, got built. At the time I thought they were locating in Centreville because it was such a nice place, a good location, and we were a pleasant people. I thought, really, that they were doing it for us, as an opportunity. Later I figured out it was a runaway factory from the North, brought down South where the owners could pay lower wages. I don't know what happened to the people who had worked in the plant before it came to our town, whether they lost their houses when they had no jobs, whether they ended up with nowhere to live.

When I worked at the garment plant, I was saving money for my college education, and I'm not sure I would have let myself care about those people if I had known. Because I needed the money: if I worked eight hours a day, five days a week on the assembly line, I could earn about $60 a week, $700 in a summer of work, a large part of my year's tuition.

To get a job in the plant, we had to pass a dexterity test, which was held in the county courthouse. Tables were set up in the courtroom itself, on the platform where the judge and jury usually sat. The day I took the test a Black woman was also taking it, an occurrence explicable only by the fact that the owners were from up North, since everything in my town was segregated—water fountains, schools, doctor's and dentist's waiting rooms, everything. We both worked away at putting pegs into holes, and I never thought about why we were taking this test watched by three white men in the courtroom; never thought about whether the site of the test had been chosen deliberately to intimidate Black women from coming to take the test; or whether this arrangement had been demanded by the white businessmen of the town in some compromise with the Northern owners, who, for reasons of their own, probably not having much to do with civil rights and more to do with keeping wages low, wanted to be sure they could hire Black women as well as white.

Both the Black woman and I were hired; we were part of two new assembly lines of women who had never done factory work before. We were very slow. Whenever the plant ran out of work, middle of the summer, one of the two new lines would get laid off. However, I don't remember being laid off myself; I'd get sent to work in the warehouse until my line got called back. I think management tried to keep the few college-bound kids working, since we were the children of the middle-class men who'd arranged for the plant to come to town. The women I worked with grumbled about the plant, yet were glad of the money, since the other jobs for women in town were white-collar: social worker, teacher, clerk at the shoestore or drugstore. When they got laid off, the women would stalk down the aisles between the lint-covered machines, through the air acrid with the smell of dyed cloth; the women would march toward the door, saying loudly they were going down to the unemployment office *right away*, going to go down to apply for their "pennies."

The first time I lined up for unemployment was the day after I slept with my first woman lover. I was married and had no job, though I'd been trying to get one. After I told my husband that I was going ahead with my love affair, it became clear I'd better arrange to have some money of my own coming in, somehow. Since I wasn't doing the job of being his wife satisfactorily, I couldn't count on his money.

I didn't quite have my Ph.D. then; I had to finish writing my dissertation. But I had had years of graduate classes and was certainly qualified to teach at the college level. This was the education that was supposed to make me independent, the education that was supposed to be the equivalent of having land of my own, something valuable and permanent to draw an income from, and, unlike land, something that would be mobile, flexible, something I could travel with, useful for a woman in the modern world.

But married, with two children and a husband when I began my life as a lesbian, I had not yet been able to get a university job. Not even after two years with scores of letters and resumés sent out, after interviews at several professional conferences with male interviewers asking me who would take care of my children, and staring at my legs, and admiring my pleasant voice, just what they needed around the department. Even though by then I had learned some feminist analysis from women in my graduate school who were involved with women's liberation, at the end of the two years I believed that I couldn't get a teaching job because something was wrong with me: I was be-

ing lazy and procrastinating too much about sending my letters out;
I didn't give a good enough job interview, or have a good enough
resumé; I wasn't working hard enough to finish my dissertation; if I
had it finished, I would certainly get a job (but meanwhile, my male
peers were being hired without having finished their degrees); I wasn't
being aggressive enough about pursuing opportunities (but none of
the professors in my field, all men, referred me to their connections
at other schools).

Now it seems obvious: I simply wasn't acceptable in the upper
ranks of teaching, a woman with two children in such apparent control of her husband that he intended to follow her to her new job. I
was not the kind of woman to admit into the upper academic bracket,
the place reserved for themselves by men who imagined that they had
stepped out of the production line, and were standing on the side, ob-
serving and commenting ironically, amusedly, on the striving world,
while others did the dirty work. College was the place for *ideas,* which
they developed individually, gracefully, the beautiful golden apples
of thought, grown in their secluded garden. Women didn't belong in
the grove; women belonged somewhere else, at home doing the laun-
dry, or at the lower levels, in the schools with the children, or with
the lesser minds of junior colleges.

That was fifteen years ago, but when I was reading through my
journals of that time in order to write this essay, only a few days ago,
I realized: *I* was *not* the one who was wrong; I could not have worked
harder; I was not lazy. I was denied work because I was a woman. The
realization has taken me this long because, with some part of me, I
still must have believed that ideas weren't like other kinds of work;
that eventually the men would acknowledge and admit me because
of my *mind;* that my education would make me independent of the
fact that I was a woman. I must have believed that people with ability *always* get hired in this country to the job they deserve, and if we
don't, why it must be our fault: we must be lazy and unqualified, just
like all the people without jobs. I didn't get hired, therefore I believed
that I was inferior.

I had not connected my life to the lives of the women I observed
the summer I worked on the line: Only men were allowed at the cutting table, slashing out the patterns through brilliant thick layers of
cloth, cutting out a hundred, a thousand shapes, the inalterable pieces
that then we women sewed into finished form, each woman perform-
ing one tiny isolated task, over and over. Women were never hired onto
the cutting table, nor men onto the line, and, of course, the men were

paid much more for their dangerous, important work, the making of the shapes. (But the men at the cutting table, white working-class men, did not decide or design the patterns they spent their days following. Others, higher, unseen, more distant, made those shapes.)

The job I finally got, the one that enabled me to leave my husband and be financially independent, was at a historically Black four-year college. I was hired by a woman, the head of the English Department, who asked not a single question about my personal life. It was no accident that I was hired by this school, an institution that was part of a long tradition of Black families educating their daughters best as they could, in order to qualify them for jobs that would get them out of domestic positions in white households, or factory positions under white bosses. Dr. Elaine Newsome did not seem to think that there was a *thing* peculiar about my being a woman who needed to earn her own living.

But she wasn't in a position to promote me; in the end I suppose I was lucky to keep my job at all. When I came back in the fall of the fourth year I taught at the school, another English teacher gossiped to me that all the Black lesbians on campus, some at the very highest positions in the school administration, had been fired or demoted. I was already in the lowest teaching position that I could be; I was not fired, perhaps because I was white, since I certainly had been outspoken about my feminism, and my students had hinted that they knew I was a lesbian. I had not spoken about this to my colleagues, nor did I know as lesbians any of the women who were named; we were all hidden from each other, trying to survive.

The college was dependent on the state university system of North Carolina for money; on good relations with the hierarchy of the nearby military base to get nonscholarship white students; and on acceptance by the white businessmen in the area, one of the most conservative in the state, in order to place its students in jobs. The mostly Black men in the administration, struggling for the survival of the school, perhaps thought that they could not afford to have too many women in positions of power, especially women who weren't attached to any men, women who allied themselves with other women; these women could not be trusted at a high level with shaping the plan for the students, for the school. Always there was immense pressure coming down from the white authorities above to run the university like a cost-effective assembly line; or like a plantation, by growing ideas of only one kind, in orderly, endless rows, like cotton; pressure to produce students from our classes year in and out, in huge numbers, prolifically, mindlessly, like women producing babies.

Just the other day I got a flyer from the school; I saw that the white man who was hired after me, and promoted the year that I finished my degree but did *not* get promoted, is now head of the English Department. Once, when we were at our desks in the English faculty office, he spoke to me about the baby he and his wife were expecting. She would stay at home with the child, he said to me, and added violently: "She'll stay at home, not like the women *here* who just drop their children, and get up again and go back to work, like animals." He is now chair of the department, but, so far as I know, none of the Black lesbians I taught with are still employed by that school.

I've been sitting up in the attic that's now my work place, doing my taxes this week. Since I moved to Washington and began to work as a lesbian and a writer, I've patched together an income from part-time teaching in women's studies, creative writing residencies, lecture fees and poetry readings, royalties, money back from my income taxes. I haven't stepped outside the economic system or off the line, but sometimes I feel like I'm hiding out in crevices and chinks in the system, the way raccoons and possums live in the middle of the city and no one ever knows or sees them.

This year my income was three thousand dollars over the official poverty line—or at least according to the D.C. government I'm in the bracket of the almost-poor. But I am not poor, I don't feel poor, and I certainly do not live in poverty in relation to poor folks who live in the District. I have a car, a Ph.D., middle-class skills, and arrangements for work that give me time to travel, meet people, do my own writing.

Partly I don't feel poor because I'm teaching some classes right now and know where my money will come from. When I have money in the bank it's easy to forget when I was so worried about my finances that I would spend only the change I had in the house on daily errands. It's easy to forget how I stood at the Seven-Eleven laboriously counting out pennies for a loaf of bread. But with just a little money in the bank, I recover my confidence quickly. I still carry the middle-class child around with me, the child who has never been hungry a day in her life, who knows she can still turn to her mother for help, the child who is the adult who glimpses, and then forgets, the stark fact of money needed for survival in the world.

Partly I don't feel even close to poor right now because of the house I'm living in, with Joan, a huge house with an attic for me, a basement for Joan's darkroom, a ground floor for her office space, a big kitchen and a back porch, a second floor with living space for us and for company. An enormous house, twice, maybe three times as big as the house I grew up in. The rent is low for its size, but we could never manage it individually. We're able to be here by sharing the rent, and because the man and woman who own it, a Black couple perhaps only a little older than we are, wanted tenants who would keep the yard up. When the landlord interviewed us, I knew the names of the bushes and shrubs the woman before us had planted, snow-on-the-mountain, crown-of-thorns, rose of Sharon. This, and the fact the owners were happy that we were not a couple with several children and many pets, got us the house.

Before we moved in, I worked three days transplanting bulbs and plants from Joan's yard, shifting the round yellow rocks that marked the flowerbed borders in the new yard, weeding, mulching, twelve-hour days for three days. At the end of the third day, my neighbor, Miz Harris, came out of her back door, beckoned me over, introduced herself. An African-American woman in her eighties, a hairdresser for years, she now gives a home in her big house to teenaged boys and young men who need a place to live. She looked at me, filthy with dirt, hands too muddy to shake hers, and nodded approvingly, and said, "You work hard. I like that," waving me through some test that I hadn't even known I was taking. She and most of the others on the block are working folk who own their houses; she approves when she sees me, a renter and a white person, on her knees, cleaning up the yard of a house I don't even own, a house, in fact, owned by Black people. Miz Harris' house and the one we're renting are as big as the nicest old homes where I grew up, but only white people lived in those houses.

A few days ago, Mr. Keyes, found for me by Miz Harris, came with his Rototiller and turned a patch of dirt at the back of the yard so we could plant tomatoes, squash, okra, beans. He was old enough to be my father, at least, and alternated between calling me *ma'm* and *baby*, sliding me back and forth between being a white woman, and being in the same affectionate category of young person as his grandbaby who had come to help him rake. A Black man who owns an acre and a half of ground somewhere in the District, he told me that morning he'd planted three rows of peas, in rows as long as "from here to that light pole over there." I was comforted by his presence, made at home by him calling me *baby*, and by the fact I'd be able to grow food in my backyard.

Today, looking out at the crabapple tree in rosy bloom—maybe there will be apples for jelly later—I think how being poor is about having possibility closed off to you; and how easy it is to forget this when one has the land or the money or the right clothes or the bus/train/plane fare in hand, or a high school or college diploma. How easy it is to forget that someone without those things cannot *choose* what someone else who has these things can. How glibly I have heard my students and other people say that women not like them could just choose to live differently; they imply that if "those women" don't so choose, why they must just be lazy, not willing to make an effort, something must be wrong with *them.*

The only reason that I can now choose to piece together my financially precarious but deeply satisfying way of making a living is because many women, those in the women's liberation movement, the civil rights movement, the gay and lesbian liberation movement, have made places within the economic system where I can do my work and be paid for it. I can work because folks established women's studies programs, first outside, then inside the universities and colleges; student groups put together cultural programs about women's and lesbian issues; women began feminist and lesbian publishing houses, magazines, newspapers; women started women's bookstores and traveling libraries that operated out of the trunk of someone's car; women in small communities formed production companies to bring visiting artists to town.

Because of their work, I now have a choice. I do not have to kill my feelings and go to work every day to produce some thing or some idea that has no meaning for me. Unlike so many of my students and my friends, I do not have to leave the land of myself, my lesbian self, my woman self, in order to do my work. I do not have to pretend to be someone not myself, to assimilate or disguise myself, and go secretly into a hostile place in order to support myself. Though sometimes I go into hostile places, I at least can do so as myself and survive.

But this place where I work and live, how different is it from the life of the academic men, deluded in thinking they were out of the way of the assembly line of the world? I think of the classes I am teaching in women's studies this semester, how the academic program for women is entrenched in the class hierarchy of the university. There is the salary difference between full-time tenure-track staff and part-time lecturers who may teach as many classes as full-time people for a tenth the money. There are the differences in space allocation, with full-time but lower-level workers placed in cubicles, and higher-ups, who may come in two or three days a week, occupying offices with doors that close. There are the attitudes about who is doing important work and who is not, about whose work can be interrupted at any time and whose cannot; assumptions about what kind of language is acceptable as intellectual and appropriate and what is not; about what should be taught in academic courses and what material isn't really literature or theory worth taking seriously.[6] I ask myself as I work and teach, am I merely making a place to be complacent, thinking I've gotten off the assembly line? Or am I doing work to try to change the shape of things?

When Joan and I moved into this house, we hired a moving company, which sent three men and a supervisor, a foreman, all Black men. The men labored for twelve hours, loading, unloading, up and down the elevator, and then up and down two flights of stairs, boxes, tables, the TV on their backs, repetitively, over and over, without a pause, except briefly for the supper that we brought in. I cringed with discomfort, with shame, as I watched them, which I had to, in order to direct where boxes and furniture went.

I could hardly bear to look at them. I remembered photographs of white men, bosses, overseers, or owners, sitting on their horses in the field, watching Black people work. I remembered my great-aunt, in her eighties, calling in the Black man who oversaw her dwindling farm, a short, stocky, very Black man of great dignity and presence, a laborer all his life; my great-aunt's daughter, who said she valued him, who said she felt affection for him, would laugh and call him her Short-Man, Shortie, calling him into their sitting room to account for work on their land, year after year.

I've known intellectually for a while that the world's economy rests on the backs of people of color; but until the day we moved I had not had to watch that work up close in a long time, and perhaps never for so many hours at a time. I calculated: even if the company was paying the men $10 an hour (which was highly unlikely), they couldn't be making more than $120 for the day; even with the tip of $50 apiece which the foreman had made clear was expected, and which we paid, they wouldn't go away from this long day of literally back-breaking labor with more than about $170 each. On the day we moved in I had a letter waiting from a magazine, accepting a poem of mine with the payment of $150, by far the most money I'd ever been paid for a poem, a very little poem, fourteen lines, $10 a line; I'm not sure if I worked on it as long as twelve hours.

At the end of the day, when I paid the foreman the company fee and the men's tips, and he made out the receipt, I could see he could hardly write. He'd been a mover for seven years, since he got out of the Army, and was so skillful at his trade that he had walked through our houses in the morning and predicted down to the half-hour how long it would take to move us out and into a house he'd never even seen, only heard described. But he said he didn't want to do this his whole life; he hoped his luck would change. I paid him and said good-bye; the men were tired, exhausted, irritably urging him to come on and go home, their muscles tightening up and getting sore already from the day's work.

I kept thinking about how much money the company made that day, how much we'd paid, how little the men got, how I wanted to be paying *them* more money, but the payment had taken everything I had for the move, which I had only because my mother had sent me money. And no matter how large my tip had been, I alone would never have been able to give enough, the money alone would not have been enough, because they still would have had to get up the next day and bend their backs to the same labor.

A couple of weeks ago Joan and I took a weekend vacation, just the two of us for the first time in a year and a half. We drove down to the beach where it rained and rained, and ended up on Friday night, inside, playing bingo at the Chincoteague Fire Department. Across from us were four women, white women who reminded me of the women I'd worked with at the garment plant. They were very friendly and explained the arcane language of bingo to us: what a postage-stamp game was, a crazy seven, a diamond game, a black-out. They laughed and rattled their big magic markers like dice, daubing neon purple, red, blue spots on the numbers in their green paper squares. Only one of them won, and at the end of the night we saw that she divided up her cash between herself and the other three. One of the women, seemingly the oldest, said that they were sisters, at least, three of them were, and the fourth one, the one that had won, who was younger and more blonde, well, she was a neighbor and an honorary sister. The two oldest worked at the beach rental place, a tiny, cramped wooden lean-to next to the pizza place on the boulevard. They came every other Friday, all together, to bingo; and they always split their winnings, no matter how little or how much they won, no matter what their luck. They always shared, the oldest one said smiling, as the youngest parceled out the eight dollars she'd won among the other women.

What do we have yet to learn about sharing our money? How do we figure out the way to do more than share our windfall, the rare winnings? How do we do more than sit and wait for people's luck to change? And how do we learn to change the shape of things so that money is not what determines how people live, or if they die, or whether we live our life out bent to someone else's use, instead of in meaningful work and in joy?

Notes

1. See Theodore Rosengarten's *All God's Dangers: The Life of Nate Shaw* (New York: Knopf, 1974).

2. Anthony P. Dunbar, *Against the Grain: Southern Radicals and Prophets 1929–1959* (Charlottesville: University of Virginia Press, 1981).

3. Virginia Durr, *Outside the Magic Circle* (New York: Simon and Schuster, 1985), p. 110.

4. Durr, p. 79.

5. W. J. Cash, *The Mind of the South* (New York: Vintage/Random House, 1941), p. 422.

6. I think here of Lois Hembold's remarks at the Working Class/Poor Women's Plenary, National Women's Studies Association, Atlanta, June 24, 1987. Also, bell hooks, "keeping close to home: class and education," in *talking back: thinking feminist, thinking black* (Boston: South End Press, 1989), and *Fireweed: A Feminist Quarterly*, #25, "The Issue Is Class," guest-edited by Cy-Thea Sand. An earlier collection, *Class and Feminism*, was edited by Charlotte Bunch and Nancy Myron (Baltimore, Maryland: Diana Press, 1974). A recent collection of stories and poems by working-class women is *Calling Home: An Anthology* (New Brunswick, New Jersey: Rutgers University Press, 1990), edited by Janet Zandy. It has a comprehensive bibliography which lists writing by working-class women as well as historical and theoretical work about class. For a vivid (though male-centered) account of ferocious struggles that have been waged to change the class structure in the U.S. see *Labor's Untold Story* by Richard O. Boyer and Herbert M. Morais (New York: United Electrical, Radio & Machine Workers of America, 1955).

Watching the Door

The gay bar that I went to, in 1975, when I was first coming out as a lesbian, was called The Other Side; it was an old warehouse on Russell Street, in Fayetteville, North Carolina, and was, in fact, located on the other side of the tracks. When I went there with my friends, we'd stand in a clump in the narrow doorway, then squeeze an awkward entrance between the cigarette machine and the counter where we paid our money and someone stamped our hands with black-light ink. No matter how many or how few people were in the bar, everyone always turned around to see who had come in. It took me awhile to understand that every-body looked because it could be the sheriff at the door, or the military police from Ft. Bragg, come on another raid to check I.D.'s, to arrest queers. The entrance was deliber-ately narrow so it could be easily blocked by

This speech, in slightly different form, was given May 16, 1989, in New York City, at the Guggenheim Museum, on the occasion of my second book of poetry being chosen as the 1989 Lamont Poetry Selection by the Academy of American Poets.

one person while we all ran out the big double doors in the next room.

[*And here, I looked around me at the dressed-up crowd in the grand hall where I was standing, and thought, but did not speak, of the one night when a woman and two men, all three dressed elegantly in black and white, slumming for the evening, came to lean smiling and laughing against the cigarette machine while we danced. The three of them looked at us with avid eyes, heterosexuals watching us seek love in the midst of great danger, watching our laughter, our defiance, our erotic intensity, our fear. They never once turned to look when the door opened.*]

I was never arrested in a raid on that bar or any other. Judgment on me as a lesbian came down in another place in my life, when I was told that I was not fit under the General Statutes of the State, not fit under its sodomy law, to be both a lover of women and the mother of my two sons. The poems in the book *Crime Against Nature*, for which I am receiving this award tonight, are a reconciliation of a contradiction that I do not accept, and that I have defied in my life and in my writing.

It is very curious and hard to comprehend that I am here, in this room where no one is turning to watch the door with fear, to accept an award given by judges for poems that at times I was not sure I would survive to write; for poems about being judged in the most bitter, soul-destroying way by my family, my husband, by the law, by the world, because I lived my life as a lesbian. I feel this contradiction especially when I place this award against the fact that I am still potentially a felon under the sodomy law of the District of Columbia where I live, and under sodomy laws in twenty-five states in the U.S. I feel the contradiction between this award and my knowledge, our knowledge, that women are still losing their children because they are lesbians; that we still lose jobs, housing, or families, still are physically attacked or raped because we are *queers* to the world; that gay people are still living, and dying, with AIDS because of discrimination against us as a despised sexual minority.

However, the poems are also about holding on, living through, and continuing to love; and so I hope that is also what this night is about. I thank my sons, Ransom Weaver and Ben Weaver, for being here with me, and for holding onto me with their love for all these years. And I especially thank my lover, Joan E. Biren, and my friends Elly Bulkin, Nanette Gartrell, and Dee Mosbacher for their love and support of my work; and my publisher Nancy Bereano for her energetic confidence in my work.

I would not have begun to live as a lesbian nor have survived to write these poems without the women's liberation and the gay and lesbian liberation movements. Many of the people who made the political and cultural realities that helped me survive are here tonight: Women who've excavated and saved the facts of lesbian history, women who've written the poems, edited the magazines, newspapers, and journals, taken the photographs, taped the radio shows, run the bookstores, and begun the women's studies and gay studies programs, women who have created the places where lesbians can live and think and flourish. Women who've organized to get *homosexual* removed from psychiatry's list of mental illnesses; who've organized to get better health care for gay men and lesbians; who've fought legal battles for gay rights, for lesbian custody of our children. Women who've worked on what it means to live as a lesbian without blunting the joy and terror of that life with drugs or alcohol; who've worked to know how we heal from the sexual abuse that many women, most girls, experience in our lives. Women who've defiantly explored the erotic truths of what it means to be a lesbian; women who've searchingly explored what it means to be lesbian and Native American, Jewish, African-American, to be lesbian and to be poor, to be lesbian and oppose U.S. policies of domination in the rest of the world, to be lesbian in the complex matrix of our lives. These are women whose work has sustained us *all*, whether we know it or not. For myself, I thank you; it makes me very happy that we are here together tonight.

I also thank the judges of the Lamont Selection for reading my poems and for honoring, in the largest sense, what the poems are. And I thank the Academy for materially supporting the publication of the poems.

The only other award I've ever received for my poetry was over twenty years ago, before I was married, before my sons were born: a hundred dollars for a little poem called "The Shell." At that time in Alabama, and in the South, a revolution was under way; all around me, Black people and some white people were giving their lives, being blown up, shotgunned, set upon with dogs, for asking for the simplest needs of human life. But I was oblivious to all this: I was a scholar and a poet. A sorority sister told me I should take the prize money for my poem and buy something that would be a good investment. So I used my hundred dollars to buy a string of pearls, which lies now, unworn for many years, in my bureau drawer.

But when I began to live as a lesbian, what I needed to know to survive despisal, and to do my work, was the knowledge of those who had come before me, who I had not acknowledged, those in the Black civil rights movement, in the women's liberation movement, in our gay and lesbian past. So it gives me much satisfaction to be able to say that, this time, I am returning my award money to those communities, who have given me my life.

I hope that when these poems go out into the world that they will return some of what I learned in my need to others struggling with how to live. I hope that those who read the book will do so not as mere observers, but as readers who see that they live with these poems in a larger political and historical context. I hope the poems will somehow move each reader to act to end the ways in which we are all divided self from self, self from life, self from our human loves.

Notes

This speech was first published in *Gay Community News.* For an account of the events at the Guggenheim ceremony, and their significance in the context of contemporary poetry, see the review of *Crime Against Nature* by Adrienne Rich, "Sliding Stone from the Cave's Mouth," in *The American Poetry Review,* September/October 1990.

The Maps in My Bible

Yesterday evening was the beginning of Rosh Hashanah, the new year for Jews all over the world, including Joan, my lover, the woman I live with. She is spending today in reflection on the back porch, or at least trying to, since all day Jim, our neighbor, has been cutting down bushes along our shared fence, chopping, breaking, making holes in her privacy and serenity; so I went out at one point to ask him to spare some of the vegetation, hoping that he would stop. As I leaned on the chainlink fence, waiting through his explanations for a chance to make my plea, hearing my own anxieties (including the need to work on this essay) louder in my ears than his justifying voice, I found myself wishing him gone, far away. I could hear my cousin Ruth saying, as she so often did of someone who aggravated her, "How I wish that man in Je-*ru*-sa-lem!"

For, in my childhood in Alabama, if you

This essay was originally published in a slightly different form in *Bridges: A Journal for Jewish Feminists and Our Friends,* vol. 2, no. 1 (Spring 1991/5751).

were a Christian, you wouldn't wish another person (especially a fellow-Christian) in Hell, but you could consign them to the most remote, other-side-of-the-world place you could think of; oh yes, you could wish someone in Jerusalem. To us, that was a mythical place, a metaphor, a symbol, not a city mostly of Jews and Arabs, with their own histories, including long histories of Christian hostility, persecution, expulsion, exile.

In the neighborhood where we live now, I have learned, from Joan, that there is a miniature of this mythic place, this idea of Jerusalem. If I go to the corner of my street, to 14th and Franklin, and then turn north the twelve blocks to Quincy, I'll arrive at Jerusalem, in the gardens of the Franciscan Monastery. I've been meaning to walk there almost since we moved here, two years ago. Standing in the September sunshine, trying to shed my exasperation and anxiety, I decide I will go there today, an inverted pilgrimage, a way to reflect on what it has meant to me to be a Christian, to be brought up in Christianity; on what I mean now when I say I am not a Christian; and what I mean when I say I am a woman who struggles to oppose Jew-hating, anti-Semitism, when I say I intend to be an ally of Jews.

The sign in the parking lot reads, *Franciscan Monastery—Holy Land of America.* Across the street, through a cloistered walkway, I come to an iron-fenced garden, brilliant with spidery cleome, lavender crocus. I wander with some confusion among mosaic shrines to St. Francis, and plaster-and-brick pillars that are the last Stations of the Cross, a replica of Christ's walk to his crucifixion. I am at the end before I've started, until I find behind me a steep stair down through ferny limestone rocks. I climb down this entrance, like the mouth of a labyrinth, tracing a spiritual journey, a reminder of the maze pattern inlaid with stones in the floors of some medieval cathedrals, a path marked out for Christians to march on, solemnly, round and round, until they got to the heart of their faith, the center of the maze, the Promised Land, Jerusalem, the Holy Land.

When I was growing up, Protestant, Presbyterian, "The Holy Land" was the only foreign land I ever received any detailed instruction about. In Sunday School I learned that people ate supper on the roof of their houses, under grapevines for shade, just like (I imagined) the muscadine grape arbor at my cousin Ruth's house. When I was seven-and-a-half, my parents gave me my own Bible, with my name in gold on the leather cover. I found in the back wonderful maps of that Land in pastel yellow, pink, blue: "Canaan, in the Time of the

Patriarchs," "Ancient Jerusalem," "Palestine in the Time of Christ," "Modern Palestine." Looking at these maps, I felt secure yet adventurous. Their details proved what I was learning in my religion, that there was a place whose terrain, cities, buildings, corresponded to the words of a Bible that was to be believed literally and absolutely. The place existed and it was *mine:* mine to imagine being in, traveling to; mine to experience the blood, wars, and drama of; mine, because Christ had given it to me through the sacrifice of his life.

Even now, when I hold this heavy Bible and sift the flimsy pages through my hands until I come to the maps, I feel the fascination with which I stared at "Modern Jerusalem": the pastel green of the Jewish quarter, the yellow of the Armenian quarter, the pink Mohammedan section, the lavender Christian quarter, the unnamed yellow section to the east, all marked with grand, exotic names: "Gate of the Chain, the Eternal Gate, Gate of the Tribes, the Dome of the Rock, the Mosque tel Aksa." Poring over the maps in the late 1950s, I wished I could travel to this Land I felt so connected to, unaware that my maps were a hundred years out-of-date, unaware of my enmeshment in a history that had drawn, and redrawn them. Poring over the maps, I wished with the self that wanted fiercely to be free of the miseries of childhood, of human existence, to be there, like the spiritual I sang at school: "I want to be ready / I want to be ready / I want to be ready / To walk in Jerusalem, just like John."

As I climb down between the limestone rocks, I discover that they are fake, a pile of concrete smoothed over with a veneer of cement to simulate limestone, with ferns and wisteria camouflaging the deception. At the bottom of the stairs, I suddenly come on an enormous cave, also man-made, fenced off by iron bars in its mouth. The sign tells me that this is a replica of the *Grotto of Gethsemane in the Holy Land,* commemorating *the agony of Christ in the Garden.* The cave is cluttered with dusty prayer benches, blackened glass prayer candles, galvanized tin buckets with plastic palm trees. An unseen overhead opening lets in a flood of light in a corner; I imagine people standing at the fence who watch as their inner image of Christ prays, like a flickering hologram, in the conveniently arranged light.

Around the corner, there is a shallow indentation in the rock, with, left and right, stone benches, and a rectangular door etched in the back wall; the sign says that here is a replica of *a Jewish tomb during the time of Christ.* I realize that the path is leading me along the main points of Jesus' life after his "Last Supper" with his disciples. I note how the sign carefully does not admit that Jesus was a Jew; the tomb might be Jewish but the man laid down in the sepulchre was not really Jewish; he was God, and had blue eyes and gently waving golden-brown hair, like the Jesus pictured on the back of the paper fans we once waved in church.

When I attended my first Seder, I was surprised to learn it was a Jewish family ritual celebrating the liberation of Jews from slavery in Egypt and the journey, for forty years, to the Promised Land. When I participated in the ceremony of drinking wine and breaking matzoh, I realized that this was the origin of our Christian communion ritual; the Last Supper, which I had thought of as simply another meal, so named because it was Christ's last, was in actuality a Seder which Jesus had celebrated as a Jewish rabbi with his Jewish friends and disciples. With an almost physical shock I realized that I, as a young woman, had studied in detail the divergence of Protestantism from Catholicism, the political entanglements of Christianity with European national history, endless theological fine points, and yet I knew almost nothing about the historical reality of Jesus' life *as a Jew,* nor of Jewish history, nor anything of the distinctions between Judaism and Christianity or the history of oppression which has marked Christianity's relation to Judaism.

But why should I have been taught these things? The attitude toward Judaism that I learned through my church is clear in some notes I made as part of my systematic Bible study between the ages of seven and seventeen. In my notes on the Old Testament I wrote: "How can you tell if an Old Testament book is really important? By how much Jesus quotes from it." (Even with the phrase *Old Testament* I encompassed as Christian, and thus obscured, the holiest scriptures of Judaism, the Torah.) To me, to other Christians, these books were significant only as they prepared for the New Testament, for Christianity; valuable in the way that Jews, as "the Hebrews" of history, were important only as they foreshadowed Jesus and Christianity.

But after Jesus, "the Hebrews" turned into "the Jews," their destiny essentially fulfilled, their *usefulness* finished, except for a limited, though crucial, role in the Last Days before the Second Coming of Christ. Jews were a people who might have survived into modern times, but as a curious relic, as an anachronism, now that history, time, reality, belonged to Christ. What more proof did I need of triumphant Christian reality that each year was claimed as Anno Domini, the Year of Our Lord?[1]

The path emerges into a big clearing. To the left is a replica of the Tomb of the Virgin Mary as constructed by Crusaders in the twelfth century C.E., with a note that the original is located *just east of Jerusalem.* To the right is another enormous artificial cave, a replica of the Grotto of Lourdes in France, a place of legendary cures for Catholics. All pretense at duplicating the geography of Jerusalem has been abandoned: place is real here only as reality is conferred by Christian significance. Of course, there are no replicas of places particularly meaningful to Jews or to Moslems: there is no Temple Mount/Haram al-Sharif, no Dome of the Rock.

But I am noticing not just what has been omitted, but what has been added: a celebration of Mary, statues of her, one over the Lourdes cavern, a figure in a white plaster robe with a red plastic rose in her hand. In our Protestant church, I was taught religious statues were idolatry, a violation of the Fourth Commandment; that Catholicism was a straying from the path, marked out first by the Jews, that led to Christ; that Protestantism was a return to a purified Christianity, stripped of suspect ritual. So there were certain anti-Semitic Catholic beliefs, rooted in ritual, that my Protestant anti-Semitism lacked: the blood libel of ritual murder, for instance, an accusation by Christians, dating from at least 1144 C.E. in England, that Jews killed a Christian child every year during Passover and used his blood to make the matzoh for the Seder ritual.[2]

But I was taught something else quite as insidious: that unlike Catholics who lived by myth and legend, we Protestants lived our faith rationally, grounded by grace in the inerrant Bible, to be taken as the literal and infallible word of God. By the facts in that Bible, Jews were undoubtedly guilty, Jews undoubtedly killed Christ. There *were* the verses in the Bible: how Herod wanted to release him, and the chief priests—the Pharisees and Sadducees—and the crowd shouted, "Crucify him." So was "proved" a Protestant version of the Catholic blood libel, the Jew as ultimate disbeliever, allied with the Devil, witness to the truth of Jesus' life and still rejecting this Truth, the "bad Jew" who, with malice and hostility, is out to get Christians.

But in contrast to these "bad Jews," the infallible Bible offered a few exceptions: the "good Jews" who followed Jesus before he had proved he was God; Jews like Zacchaeus, a rich publican who gave half his money away in response to a command from Jesus, or Nicodemus, "a man of the Pharisees, a ruler of the Jews," who came to learn from Jesus by night, calling him Rabbi. "Good Jews" listened to, and accepted, Christian truth as Truth.

As I learned from the New Testament, and interpretations of it in the preacher's sermons, what a good Jew was—one who bowed to our ways, Christian ways, acknowledging our superiority—I was offered one example from the secular history of Confederate legend that paralleled religious myth in our small town. In the books I read to prepare history essays on The War, in addition to the praises of Robert E. Lee (such a "Christian gentlemen"), there were occasional references to Judah P. Benjamin, the "brains of the Confederacy," a slave-owning Sephardic Jew, originally from Charleston, who served as attorney general, secretary of war, and secretary of state.

Of course, none of the history I read or was taught included the origins of Benjamin's family in the mass killing, forced baptism, and expulsion of Jews from Spain and Portugal centuries earlier, or the story of Jews like Rabbi David Einhorn, living in Baltimore, whose condemnation of slavery from the pulpit was followed by the burning of his printing press and riots by Southern sympathizers, so that he had to flee for his life. Nor do I remember reading about the vilification heaped on Benjamin as a Jew during his years in office, the scapegoating of him, along with other Jews, for the South's problems, the letter-writer to the *Richmond Enquirer* who said the "prayers of the Confederacy would have more effect" if Benjamin were dismissed from public office.[3] (A remark echoed a hundred years later by the president of the Southern Baptist Convention when he joked that God doesn't hear the prayers of a Jew.)[4] I read nothing of the Civil War Associated Press reporter who stated, "The Jews of New Orleans and all the South ought to be exterminated. They run the blockade and are always to be found at the bottom of every new villainy."[5] (And, a hundred years later, I lived in, but was in no way taught how to recognize or analyze, the anti-Semitism of post–World War II United States, the Jew-baiting of the McCarthy era, the execution of Julius and Ethel Rosenberg to prove the myth of the inevitably disloyal Jew who "runs the blockade," crosses national boundaries for profit, the traitor Jew.)[6]

Now I try to remember if I learned of any historical Jew other than Judah Benjamin, the slave-owning Jew. In all my years of reading on my own, in high school, or English and European history and literature in college and graduate school, I can't remember *one person* being named as Jewish, except Anne Frank, though I know, now, that many writers and public figures whom I studied must have been Jews. But they had become one kind of "good Jew," those who had been appropriated by Christian culture and denied the name of Jew at all, or another kind, those who had assimilated, been intimidated into hiding or giving up their identity, and thus were invisible as Jews to me.

I suspect that Anne Frank was acceptable as a visible Jew because she was popularized as a victim—a young girl with a quiet voice, no longer threatening because she, and her story, were over. There was nothing in my cheap mass-produced paperback edition of the *Diary* that detailed the genocidal proportions of the Holocaust, that gave a historical context for Christian persecution of Jews, or that told of young Jewish women, and men, resistance fighters like Hannah Senesh.[7] I heard nothing but the individual voice, slender and, no matter how determined, dead, as irrelevant to my life as "the ancient Hebrews" were.

As a teenager and well into adulthood, I did not think of my sympathetic ignorance about Judaism and Jews as anti-Semitic; after all, I *did* feel positively toward *some* Jews. I had some concept of anti-Semitism, though not by that name, as being hatred and fear like my father's ravings about Jews during the civil rights era. When I wrote, eventually, about this hatred of Jews, my mother, defending my father, asserted that he was not anti-Semitic because one of his very good friends was Mr. Paul Edelman, who hung out with Pa and the other men at Meigs Drugstore, drinking coffee in the mornings before work.

But, in fact, I knew nothing of Mr. Edelman's life except that he *was* a Jew. So thoroughly were he and his family submerged beneath the daily weight of Christian assumptions, however, that years later, describing my home town to Joan, I could say, "There were no Jews there."[8] Of course there were—and other Jews besides Mr. Edelman. Long before my remark to Joan, when I separated from my husband during my late twenties, I chose as my lawyer a Jewish man who at a social gathering had reminded me that he knew me: he had grown up in the little town across the river from mine; his father had run the dry-goods store there in Brent. I met him, I forgot him, I knew him again, and forgot his existence again, from a lifetime of learning to live in my town as if there were no Jews there.

At school we had the Lord's Prayer and daily Bible readings—the latter required under an Alabama law that was declared unconstitutional only in 1971.[9] These rituals were so habitual that I hardly remember them, except for fourth grade, when Miz Nell Weaver made us memorize twenty-six Bible verses, mostly from the New Testament, each starting with a different letter of the alphabet, to be recited ultimately from *A–Z*, chapter and verse, all at one time. To me this was a mental challenge, a chance to be a bit smug with religious accomplishment: but for the isolated Jewish child, a lesson learned at what emotional cost? A child forced to learn in excruciating detail the culture of her oppressor, while I was taught virtually nothing of hers. (And still the struggle goes on to have a public school system where a child from any religious background will not be discriminated against. The Christian right-wing has damned this movement to remove Christian bias from the schools as "secular humanism.")[10]

Past the replica of Lourdes, I begin walking down the Stations of the Cross, yellow brick markers that represent fourteen moments in Jesus' walk from his sentence of death to his being placed in the sepulchre. This Catholic yellow brick is the same as the brick of the old Baptist church at home, but I don't expect anything else in the Stations to be familiar. Yet, as I go from marker to marker (Jesus takes up the Cross, Jesus falls for the first time, Simon helps carry the Cross), I realize I know each of the moments and something else besides: in the bas-relief plaster friezes I recognize faces and emotions. I see Jesus with an expressionless face, a person beyond human feeling; I see the faces of his persecutors, men laughing, ridiculing, mocking. I think of the old anti-Semitic myth of the Wandering Jew: that Jews are condemned to wander the earth until Christ's Second Coming, because one Jew had mocked and struck Jesus as he walked to his crucifixion, a myth used to rationalize the expulsion and exile of Jews as "foreigners" from many Christian countries.[11] I follow the markers uphill, again a suggestion of the geography of the story, the climb up Mount Calvary, the Stations for the crucifixion, death, interment.

And, at the top, only a few steps away from the last Station, I see the steps leading back down to the Grotto of Gethsemane. Just a few steps, and I could return to the ritual circle, its very form a repetition of the idea I was raised with, the security of leading a righteous life, a Christ-centered life. The logical circle of learning that Jesus was "the Way, the Truth, and the Life," that my Christian belief *was* the Truth, and those who disagreed or differed from that truth were the equivalent of the mockers and crucifiers of Christ.

There was only One Truth, and the world was shaped around it. Even the seasons of the year were marked; in spring, as proof of the Resurrection, the dogwood flower petals were stained with rust-red dots, like blood from the Cross. History and the future were shaped around this Truth. I knew Christ would come again, there would be a Judgment Day, Christians would be saved and the rest trampled like grapes in the great winepress of the wrath of God: the good would be saved, the bad who had not listened, had not converted, would be doomed.

But there was a place for Jews within this God-ordained sequence of events. Just as the ancient Hebrews existed as a symbol, the root of the tree of God that blossomed forth with Jesus, so contemporary Jews existed to fulfill the Second Coming. Before Judgment Day and Christ's rule, before the Last Days, the final catastrophes of earthquake, fire, the darkening of sun and stars, and the battle Armageddon, Jews must be "gathered in" to the Holy Land to live, and there must be the sealing of 144,000 Jews, 12,000 from each tribe of Israel. These "good Jews" would be saved as a sign that God acknowledged their special place in the Christian scheme of salvation, part of completing the divine circle begun when God selected them as His chosen people. And the other Jews, the ones not chosen for the final "sealing"? Damned, of course, like all Jews after the time of Christ who did not convert, like all heathen who had not accepted the Truth.

Standing in the garden, between the end of this story and the steps down to its beginning again, I think of how long it had been since I was caught inside this particular circle of self-enclosed thinking. But the silence of the garden, the fence limiting the intrusion of the world, the fearless squirrels skittering by, all remind me of the protection of that circle, how seductively secure it was for me to think I knew the One Truth and lived in it, the self-righteousness of knowing that I was in God's plan, almost half of my life spent in this belief.

I shiver at moments when some part of that past self is called up, the way I can still sing the words to almost any hymn chimed out by the neighborhood church carillon that plays morning and afternoon, "Blessed Assurance" or "Leaning on the Everlasting Arms," all the words to the hymns still singing away somewhere inside me. Or my confusion while attending Yom Kippur services with Joan, when the scriptural passages read out loud included one used every Sunday in our church: "Let the words of my mouth, and the meditations of my heart. . ." Hearing this phrase in a spiritual setting where I thought I had left behind my entrapping past, I felt with consternation how I would always have to untangle my experience of, my connection to, Judaism from those early memories, from the trap of believing we were the only ones who had the Truth.

I shiver when I think of the thoroughness of my education in this belief: from as early as I can remember until I left for college, Sunday School and church on Sunday morning for two hours; when I was small, Vacation Bible School in the summer for two weeks, memoriz-

ing the catechism; when I was a teenager, by that time the church or-
ganist, evening service on Sunday night for an hour, Wednesday night
prayer service for an hour and then choir practice, and on Saturdays
two hours planning the music for Sundays; every night I read my Bible. I remember the warmth and affection given to me by the older
people of our small church, their kindness; and how also I was their
emissary into the next generation, carrying on their Truth.

And I remember how quickly, in my last year of high school, I began to doubt, having read several paperback books on comparative
religion, newly donated to our two-shelf church library by a slightly
more liberal than usual preacher. I read some of the historical
challenges to the infallibility of the Bible, and began to question. It was
a doubt fueled by the discrepancy between what I was taught—
Christian love as an ideal—and what I observed in my own town—
grinding poverty and racial segregation accepted by my church. But
I had no way, theological or political, to use this discrepancy to amend
my Christian belief and to live a religious life that would challenge the
social assumptions of my culture. Instead, what I had was a religion
that taught me either I believed *completely* or I was no longer a Christian: Christianity was not contingent on how many years I had gone
to church, nor on my good deeds, nor on the fact that all of my family
had been Christians for as far back as we could trace; I would be
judged only on whether I *believed*. But the new facts, the information,
the other point of view in those cheap paperback books began to shift
my belief in the truth of the Bible, and thus shook the foundation
stones of my faith.

Leaving through the cloistered walk, I notice that the walls are covered with words, translations of the "Ave Maria" and the "Lord's
Prayer" into languages labeled Assyrian, Assiboin Indian, Arabic,
Quiche Indian, Esperanto, Ethiopic, Xosa-Cape Colony, Urdu, Korean,
Mayan, 150 languages, a monument to the Christian belief that the
Gospel must be carried to all people, so everyone will at least have the
chance of salvation after hearing the Truth. As a teenager, I thrilled
at a *Reader's Digest* account of missionaries who went into remote areas
of the Amazon Basin, risking death to learn the language of "hostile
Indian tribes" so Christians could begin translating the New Testament
into that language and "save" the Indians. Later I discovered that the
heroes I admired were the Wycliffe Bible Translators, who have served
as adjuncts to the CIA and other repressive forces; an organization that

in 1960, for instance, provided air and radio support for the Colombian national police as they crushed a revolt by the Guahibo Indians, one of the Wycliffe "language groups"; an organization that selectively edits language, preparing dictionaries that omit the indigenous words for *oppression, revolution, community, rebellion.*[12] I think again of how Christianity has been used as an excuse and a tool of conquest, of how Christian-based thinking, at its most fundamental, holds the fates of all peoples, all cultures, as subject to the will of its living God.

I turn the last corner of the cloister and see a bronze plaque designating this monastery as the *Commissariat of the Holy Land,* dedicated to *the preservation of the Holy Places* and to missionary activities. (*Commissariat:* a branch of an army that provides food and supplies for the troops.) Another plaque commemorates Father Charles Vissani, *founder of the cause of the Holy Land in the U.S.,* the first person to lead an American Catholic pilgrimage there, in 1889, and *to place the stars and stripes of our glorious republic on the Holy Sepulchre of Our Lord Jesus Christ in Jerusalem* (the inscription an echo of the boasts of the European Crusaders).

I imagine Father Vissani on a sunny day in Jerusalem, proud as a conqueror by his flagpole, standing there in counterpoint to the Russian Interior Minister of that day who said, "We would very much like to see the creation of an independent Jewish state capable of absorbing several million Jews. We should like to keep the very intelligent ones. . . . But we should like to rid ouselves of the weak-minded and those with little property." In counterpoint to the Kaiser who said, "I am all in favour of the kikes going to Palestine. The sooner they take off the better." In counterpoint to British Prime Minister Lloyd George who backed a Jewish state in Palestine to keep "the agnostic, atheist *French* out of the Holy Places" during the European carving-up of the remains of the Ottoman Empire. In counterpoint to the British War Minister, Lord Kitchener, who rejected Theodor Herzl's plan for a Jewish homeland, since "Palestine would be of no value to us whatsover," assuming that a Jewish state backed by Britain would be under English control, assuming that Jewish lives existed for his use.[13]

In the next weeks, after Rosh Hashanah, after Yom Kippur, into the weeks toward Succoth, I drive past the monastery several times. As the days go by, and grim news continues from the Middle East, I pass the neatly clipped boxwoods, the serene cloister, the Holy Land of America, and begin to see this place more and more as a dangerous illusion.

I think how little I have concerned myself with the history of the Middle East, how facilely the *Washington Post* has reported Arab leadership as the work of madmen or fanatics, and Israeli leadership as an extension of U.S. policy. Now, as our former ally, Iraq, takes over Kuwait and threatens U.S. interests in other oil fields of the Gulf States, now with massive U.S. intervention and presence in Saudi Arabia, the *Post*'s reporting begins to turn. Arch-conservative columnist Pat Buchanan, an advocate in past years of military aid to Israel, accuses Israel of being the main instigator urging the United States into war with Iraq.[14] Though the editor of the *New York Times* accurately challenges Buchanan's remarks as anti-Semitic, no one questions to what extent Buchanan's previous support, based in new-right Christianity, was also anti-Semitic.

For, in addition to strategists who assess U.S. support for Israel by how best we can use Israel for our own economic or political reasons, there are politically influential religious groups in this country who see Israel not as a refuge for Jews, not as a land torn by the needs of both Palestinians and Jews to have a homeland, but as a foreign policy battleground for Christian spiritual warfare. A crude example: Ronald Reagan's comment, made while he was running for president in 1980, on Pat Robertson's PTL (Praise the Lord) television network, that "We may be the generation that sees Armageddon," and Reagan's later justification of his anti-Soviet/anti-Communist policy as preparing for the Final Battle which will come when Russia (as Magog) invades Israel.[15]

Reagan might be dismissed as simply parroting lines for the benefit of a PTL campaign audience. And it is tempting to dismiss as the writings of a fringe fanatic someone like Hal Lindsey, with his *The 1980s: Countdown to Armageddon*. For the 1990s, Lindsey has updated his timetable to mark the beginning of the Final Days with Israel's military capture, in 1967, of the city of Jerusalem and the occupation of the West Bank and Gaza; this capture fulfills the Biblical prophecy that Israel would return to its ancient boundaries of Judea and Samaria, an occurrence necessary for Christ's return.[16] In Lindsey's universe, Israel's "security" becomes a Christian concern; but only as part of a Christian eschatology that sees a Jewish homeland as a place for Jews to gather for final tribulation and "purification" before the Second Coming.

Lindsey seems a crackpot, yet his ideas are simply an extension of the scriptures of my childhood, the belief that history has a sacred shape. Meanwhile, right-wing Christians describing themselves as

Christian Zionists have organized, since the 1980 elections, a yearly International Christian Celebration of Succoth—the Feast of Tabernacles in Jerusalem, as a way of "fulfilling a prophetic sign pointing toward the coming of Christ." (Here, suddenly, I think of the Christian Seders some churches have begun to celebrate.) These Christian Zionists also established the International Christian Embassy of Jerusalem (ICEJ) to intensify the "theo-political commitment to Israel" of evangelicals worldwide; ICEJ publishes a newsletter, encourages the "ingathering" of Soviet Jews, runs Holy Land tours, sells Israeli bonds, and helps sponsor the National Religious Broadcasters annual Israel "prayer breakfast."

Finally, the ICEJ has been linked to some efforts to "hasten the coming of the Messiah" through reestablishment of the Third Temple on the site of the First and Second Temples, sacred to Judaism, of which nothing now remains but the Western Wall. For this reestablishment to happen, the Moslem mosque, al-Aqsa, second holiest shrine of Islam, located on the Dome of the Rock, on Haram al-Sharif/the Temple Mount, would have to be destroyed. There was one attempt to bomb the mosque in 1988; a small group of Christian Zionists raised funds for the legal defense of right-wing Jews involved in this bombing, and one of the men of this "Temple Mount plot" admitted that he received money from the ICEJ.[17]

Succoth comes, the Feast of Tabernacles. The days continue sunny. In Jerusalem, The Movement of the Faithful to the Temple Mount and the Land of Israel, a right-wing Jewish group that has marched for years in attempts to lay the new Temple foundation stone on the Dome of the Rock, in preparation for the coming of their Messiah, marches again. Before the contingent reaches the Western Wall and the approach to al-Aqsa, Palestinian protesters, gathered chaotically on the Dome, are fired on by Israeli police. At least nineteen Palestinians are killed; over a hundred people, Jews and Arabs, are injured in the rock-throwing, tear-gassing, and shooting. The *Washington Post* runs a picture of a Palestinian woman kissing bloody handprints left by wounded protesters on Haram al-Sharif. In an unusual move, the U.S. agrees to a United Nations resolution condemning Israel, a move explained in news coverage as necessary because "the main goal this week [for the U.S. is] not to serve as Israel's protector in the Security Council but to prevent damage to the anti-Iraq alliance."[18]

And in all the outcry in the news coverage, not one word is said about the role of U.S. right-wing Christians in promoting a politics of religious fanaticism in relation to Israel. Nothing is said about the U.S. policy that actively discouraged a peaceful settlement of the Israeli-Palestinian conflict. And, of course, no word is said of the efforts of Jewish or Arab peace activists in Israel or in this country.[19]

We are left with the image of bloody handprints on a bullet-scarred wall, instead of a picture of the Stars and Stripes flapping on a flag-pole with a cross on top. But I have another memory, from a TV broadcast months earlier: a huge crowd of women marching for peace in Jerusalem, Israeli Jewish and Arab women, Palestinian women, Jewish women from the U.S. I searched for the faces of women I knew, Irena, Melanie, in the crowd; I did not expect to see gentile women I knew in the march. I think of my two boys, now men, and how war in the Middle East could be the war of their generation. I see, again, the river of women in the streets of Jerusalem, and feel myself trying to shift the weight of religious fatalism that I have been given about this place, its history. I am trying to shift the stone boundaries of the Christian way I was taught into new thinking, into action.

At the back of the Bible my parents gave me there is a map of "The Ancient World" showing "The Probable Settlements of the Descendants of Noah." Africa all in yellow for the children of Ham, the disobedient son cursed by Noah so that "a servant of servants shall he be unto his brethren." The Arabian peninsula in green, the rest of the Middle East in orange, both colors denoting the children of Shem, but separating Arabs and Jews, definitively. All of Europe, stretching far east toward China, in pink, for the descendants of Japheth, the gentiles, my people.

The map was proof to me of what I had been taught, the God-ordained separation of people into separate races, by blood. To me as a child, the map justified the history of slavery and existing segregation in the South. It justified thinking of Jews as people of a different race, a different blood, ultimately strangers. Yet not so foreign that intermarriage was impossible; there *was* the shared white skin, the shared (Old Testament) history. All that was required was conversion, a purification of Jewish blood through Christianity, the purification we sang of in our hymns about the "wonder-working blood of the Lamb."

But when I sang of this miraculous cleansing, I knew only mythic history and time sacred to Christianity. I had no map showing the path of the Crusaders through Europe over hundreds of years, and the thousands of Jews left dead behind them, thousands dragged to the baptismal font, the choice either massacre or forcible conversion. I had no map that showed the travels of Franciscan friars of the thirteenth century, their missions set up outside the Jewish quarters of towns, their policy to convert the Jews or throw them out, purification or expulsion, the monks working to set royal policies, like the exile of all Jews from England. And I had no map that showed the history of Jews in Spain, the intensifying persecution after the fourteenth century, the growing conversions for safety, the *marranos* who practiced their Jewish faith secretly, the riots and massacres of these *conversos,* and the development of racial, as well as religious, tests to discover "secret Jews."[20]

There was no map given to me that showed the spread of the idea of race-hatred as expressed toward Jews in Europe: The popularity in the mid-nineteenth century of Gobineau's *Essai sur l'inegalité des races humaines,* which became a handbook for anti-Semites. The growth of race-stereotypes of Jewish men as rapists, Jewish women as promiscuous and animalistic, Jews as sexually impure. The assignment of school exercises for German children on "How We Can Learn to Recognize a Person's Race: Observe the Jew—his way of walking, his bearing, gestures, and movements when talking. What are the occupations in which Jews are not to be found? Explain this phenomenon on the basis of the character of the Jew's soul." The intensification of anti-Semitic propaganda in the twentieth century, with articles like the German essay, "The Earth-Centered Jew Lacks a Soul."[21]

There was no map to show me that I was living in a place and a time, Alabama in the deep South of the 1950s and 1960s, which was marked by the convergence of racial and anti-Semitic theories developed in Europe and a specific racism practiced by white people in the United States against African Americans. Buttressed by the Christian religious myth of Ham's eternal servitude, the white folks around me admitted no possibility of purification of the Black people living among us, almost all of whom were raised Christian. No amount of cleansing could make them *white* enough to permit social interaction or love between Blacks and whites as equals, or intermarriage. The deepest racial fear I heard verbalized by those around me, mostly white men, was that of "miscegenation," the mixing of Black and white.

When I heard my father muttering about the mongrelization of the white race and the Jewish conspiracy, as he sat watching on TV the distorted reports on Black people fighting for basic civil rights, I was hearing the echoes of other men who saw Jews, the "ultimate outsiders," as being behind the uprising of Blacks in the South, as part of a malicious conspiracy against whites. First Northern Jews were

blamed, not "our Jews," but some always held that all Jews were responsible, and synagogues were bombed in Charlotte, Miami, Nashville, Birmingham, and Jackson, Mississippi, no matter what the stand
of the congregation on integration.[22]

The idea that Jews were instigating racial rebellion was still current in the early 1980s. Bill Wilkinson, head of the Invisible Empire,
Knights of the Ku Klux Klan, expressed it succinctly when he said that
"The American Jewish community is using vast sums of money to
mongrelize the white race." U.S. Nazi propaganda of the 1980s relied
on the same assumption: "Should we cut off, root and branch, the
satanic Jews and all their lackies [sic] who are stirring up the niggers
against us? After all, they're trying to kill us. The Jews have secretly
wanted to exterminate the White man for centuries. What's 'integration' but the slow mass murder of our race?"[23]

This anti-Semitic myth continues. David Duke, who won the
Republican primary for the Senate in Louisiana in 1990, has denied
the racial persecution of Jews by denying the historical fact of the Holocaust; he asserts that Jews are still backing Blacks in order to perse-
cute whites and destroy white culture. In the recent general election,
clean-cut, smooth-talking Duke polled 44 percent of all votes in the
Senate race, and 60 percent of the "white vote."[24]

But even with this substantial endorsement, Duke is talked of as
an aberration, someone from a far-off, isolated state in the South, at
the edge of everything, on the map but peripheral, unimportant. Considered equally aberrant, if not heretical, is a form of Christianity gain-
ing popularity among right-wing extremists and activists like Duke:
Identity Christianity gives a theological foundation to an anti-Semitism
based in racism. An extension in the U.S. of an older fabrication, British Israelism, this theology holds that Anglo-Saxons are the true Jews,
that the "Nordic people" of Europe are the Ten Tribes of Israel; that
Jews are imposters, posing as children of God, but really children of
Satan, offspring of Eve seduced by the Devil; that all races other than
the "white" race are mongrelized or subhuman; and that the Bible
(Old and New Testaments) was written for white people only.[25]

Aberration, hallucination, lines on a fantasy map with no relation
to history, and yet—I have sat in meetings, often progressive, left-
political, or women's meetings, and heard Jewish lives obliterated, Jewish existence made to fit into one racial category or another, because
of the ideological agenda of a person who spoke without acknowledging the specific race-hatred that gentiles have turned on Jews in the
nineteenth and twentieth centuries, a race-hatred used to justify the

Nazi's genocide of Jews.

I have sat in a forum on Israel and Palestine, where speakers characterized Israeli abuses of power not as racist or anti-Arab, but as part of a system of white supremacy. Somewhat prepared to speak, because I had been meeting with an informal group of white gentile and Jewish women to discuss racism and anti-Semitism, I fumblingly talked about my experience, that the white supremacy I was raised in was the ideology of Christian white men determined to keep control, through state power, of both Black people and Jews (as well as women and gay folks), all for different reasons. I tried to say that a place created by an oppressed people, even when power may be viciously abused in that place, still cannot be equated absolutely with the structures of their oppressor. Others with loud voices instructed me that I was wrong, they had the truth: Jews who want a homeland of their own were white supremacists. Literature handed out there exhorted, "Fight Zionism and Worldwide White Supremacy"; Jews are described as a "white minority." I was confounded by this definition in the face of my own experience that Jews who will not convert, assimilate, or pass are hated as a racial minority who are *not* white; and in the face of the attempted annihilation of Jews as a "dark race" in Nazi-dominated Europe.[26]

And yet at a lecture I gave on racism and anti-Semitism, I was also amazed as a Jewish woman, working in coalition with women of color, identified herself as being "of color." Her skin was only slightly more brown than mine. At home, of course she would be treated as "white."

At a women-of-color cultural gathering, an African-American woman read a poem in which she referred to a "Jew bastard," wishing that he'd been killed at Auschwitz. To the poet, later, I said I was very distressed by this statement, asked if she'd say of a Black man with whom she disagreed that she wished him lynched by the Klan. She said, "Yes." Later, another woman from the gathering called me up and shouted that the statement was justified, that of course Jews were in control, that "they control the media, the newspapers." I could not understand, then, how a Black woman could be speaking the same anti-Semitic Jewish conspiracy hatred that I had heard come out of my father's mouth, out of the mouths of white supremacists.

All of us caught on the black-and-white map of the U.S., in the history of white supremacy and slavery, the necessity of being one or the other, slave or free, by blood, by race: White gentiles with our privilege of thinking we always know who we are and what we are in relation to others, never even having to think about it. African Americans and others who we mark out visibly by their darkness for hatred and discrimination, angry at those of us who are white for centuries of oppression and ignorance; angry with the anger of betrayal at Jews with white-skin privilege who retain some economic benefits. Jews with their past of being hated and killed as the "darkest ones" in Europe, a history that few gentiles know or care about in this country; Jews caught in the middle of Black and white, offered a chance to assimilate to safety and to a racist norm, while living with the history that safety has always vanished in past centuries, whether they have lived openly or secretly as Jews.

All of us caught on a map marked off by race, by color, by blood. As I drove South across this landscape one spring, I came to Charleston, where I wandered looking for the birthplace of Sarah and Angelina Grimké, white Southern antislavery activists and women's rights activists. I could not find their house, but came upon a synagogue, Beth Elohim. It was a huge old Greek Revival building, the oldest synagogue in continuous use in the U.S., the birthplace of Reform Judaism in this country, a response to the intense pressures to assimilate in the Christian South.[27] Unsure what part of the synagogue I could visit, I went in a side door to a small gallery, where a traveling exhibit of photographs was assembled, portraits of Jews from all over the world, from Israel, Italy, England—and Argentina, Japan, India, and many other countries. I stood before a portrait of a Jewish woman of Calcutta; in traditional Indian dress, she looked nothing like a Jew, to me. Her presence in India was explained by a typed description of the expulsions, migrations, and struggles for safety that brought her ancestors there. But I remained baffled by her appearance. The landscape of my past, of Black and white and Jews in between, had no place for her. In the folds of her sari were the contours of whole other lands, other centuries, of Jewish life and history not even guessed at by me.

That woman comes back to me when, reading in preparation for this essay, I see in a pamphlet the italicized words: *Jews are not a race.*[28] And I am confronted with her face stark against the deep lessons of my childhood, with how long I have clung, subconsciously, to a belief in a racial definition of Jewishness developed by white supremacists; how that definition has hindered me from understanding what it means for Jews to define themselves *as a people*, that they have been hated and oppressed simply as *Jews*, as themselves. That they have survived as a people through building cultures of their own, through religion, family tradition and lineage, literature, music, food, philosophy and economics, language, ritual and history. That all or any of these aspects of Jewish life may be chosen as a focus for the hatred or fear of others, gentiles, those outside Jewish life. We, outside, see a people surviving as themselves, separate but still present after millenia of persecution, and, in reaction, doubt ourselves, and, in retribution, blame our doubts and fears on "the Jew," the projected image of our unresolved fears or desires, our secret selves.[29]

I think of how my father's friends down at the drugstore used to tease him about his supposedly Jewish features, his big nose, his long fleshy ears; they'd joke and call him Mr. Ginsberg. I think of how when he was in his last illness, barely coherent, he would rouse enough to joke in a sweetly self-deprecating way that, of course, he knew who he was: he'd smile and say, "Mr. Ginsberg." What it meant to him, I don't know; but to me this memory brings enormous grief, the tragedy of my father estranged from himself all his life, a conflict that he attempted to resolve through whiskey, through theories of Blacks and Jews who were "trying to take over," and, finally, through some small knowledge that he held of a secret other self, a self he could not name as his own, but had to name as "Jew," the one forever apart.

In my century, in my home, we marked out Jews as dangerously *other* by race and religion. But in the ancient world, where the Greeks advocated oneness of all peoples, pagan anti-Semites castigated Jews as inhuman barbarians, people of "strangeness" with their dietary laws and their custom of circumcision, an antisocial people who set themselves apart from the rest of humanity.[30] I have learned that the shape of anti-Semitism has shifted over the map of the world, with gentiles of each century, country, placing on Jews the qualities of whatever was most marked off or despised as otherness in the culture of the majority. We live now in what is only the most recent form of anti-Semitism, a fear always based on shifting religious, economic, sexual fears, and on the making of a symbol for our fears out of the Jew, the Other.[31]

As a teacher, I have watched this shift in my own classroom, during sessions in feminist theory in which I focus on anti-Semitism. For one of these sessions, students read a handbook on "recognizing and resisting anti-Semitism," co-authored by Melanie Kaye/Kantrowitz and Irena Klepfisz. The handbook, written specifically for Jews, gives concrete examples and exercises that are also extremely useful for general discussion.[32] But when I ask students, after this reading, to give examples of anti-Semitism that they themselves have committed or witnessed, their answer, almost overwhelmingly, is this: Some gentile students begin, with complaint and with anger, to tell anecdotes of how Jews have excluded *them*, of how Jews have, in some way, injured *them* by asserting Jewish identity. Often these anecdotes focus on dating and marriage; one Protestant woman dating a Jewish man gave a scathing catalog of his mother's unwelcoming behavior toward her, the pain that she felt at not being made part of his Jewish family. I asked her and the class: What does it mean that when I ask you to talk about *your* anti-Semitism, what we get instead is your anger at Jews?

In the discussion that follows it becomes clear that many students perceive Jewish cultural separateness as a kind of discrimination, like racism, and have little understanding of Jews as an historically oppressed people. I attempt to explain the difference between separatism and ghettoization. I tell them of how I've learned that the word *ghetto* came from the segregated part of Venice to which Jews were confined by law, beginning in 1515, to live walled, guarded by Christian watchmen at night, all expenses paid by special taxes on the Jews within.[33] I say that when a hostile majority (by numbers or by power) designates another group as despised, and forcibly separates them from the majority culture, that is ghettoization. But when an oppressed group separates itself, to build cultural pride, to reflect on its own values, to make decisions without undue influence from the oppressor, that is cultural separatism. It is necessary for the spiritual and physical survival of an oppressed group; and it is always feared and objected to angrily by folks in the majority culture who wish to retain control.

I have seen this failure to understand the affirmation of a separate Jewish identity in women other than my students. I think of myself at the 1981 Women-In-Print Conference, where we discussed angrily, lovingly, passionately, issues of race and identity. At the end of the conference, a Jewish woman asked the other Jewish women to rise, since Jewish identity had been unspoken and invisible at the gathering. There were many Jewish women there, and I remember thinking, with a kind of panic: What if they were not here? What if their work was not part of ours? What if they withdraw, or what (a memory of the Holocaust) if they were taken from us? And, with a flicker of fear, the thought that others there would see in this very visibility the conspiracy my father raved of, always the possibility that "the Jews are taking over." (And, in fact, "jokes" were later made about how feminist publishing was being taken over by "Jewish working-class lesbians.") This simple act of self-declaration raised within me yet again all the issues of exclusion, longing, fear. Once again I saw Jewish existence from the outside only in relation to, as part of, to be used by, the larger entity, in this instance, for me, the women's movement.[34]

Sometimes I have seen anti-Semitism shift from gentiles' anger and fear at feeling excluded to a longing to be "inside." I have heard gentile women speak of abuse, coldness, and dislocation in their birth families, of childhood fantasies of being Jewish and being part of a "warm" Jewish family. Longing, without reflection on what it has meant to create a Jewish home, century after century, in hostile and inhospitable surroundings. The labor of sustaining Jewish culture reduced to a metaphor for *family,* a substitute for what is lacked.[35]

I've seen in myself this lack of understanding about what it means to nourish Jewish identity in a gentile world. Over the last ten years I have watched, often with little comprehension, as my lover Joan, my friends Elly, Evi, Nancy, Lauren, Helen, many other friends and acquaintances, have labored arduously to create or maintain a foundation of Jewish identity in their lives. They have produced cultural events, written essays and poetry, created historic photographs of feminist and lesbian Jewish life, edited anthologies and pamphlets, organized within New Jewish Agenda and within mainstream Jewish organizations; they have taken and taught classes, read, talked, researched, to understand what being Jewish is for them; they have created their own rituals; they have created *Bridges.*[36] Only now, ten years after I began to reflect on anti-Semitism, feminism, and Jewish existence, have I begun to understand the enormous effort made by them to create, and to go on creating, a place to exist as Jews. I have learned from them, have been welcomed by women in this movement, have tried to support them. And I have felt the appeal of taking as my "home" the circle they have created, taking refuge in the friendships, the parties, the holiday rituals.

But I know it is irresponsible fantasy, an escape to some land on a map not yet drawn, to think that I can live, *as one of them,* with people whom I and my people have oppressed. It would be another act of oppression to use what they have created as mine, their work, their place as mine.

So, instead, I have faced the necessity of going back into my own home, my childhood, my Christian upbringing, the anti-Semitism of my culture. How is it possible to change the old pattern of seeing "the Jew" as metaphor, symbol, a shifting emblem of fear, desire? Seeking guidance, I have read stories of some who have tried to understand the anti-Semitism they were raised with as Christians. I followed the narrator of one autobiography as she traced, with agony and insight, the role of her parents in Nazi Germany; only to find her, at the end, abruptly and without explanation, merrily drinking champagne with her mother in Vienna, as if everything that had happened belonged to the past and could be exorcised with the smashing of wine glasses on the pavement below their hotel window.[37] But we cannot smash the past and pretend that it never existed. We live with the loves and hatreds of the past shifted into new forms in our lives, in our generation.

I have turned to a lesbian friend who identifies herself as a Christian now; I wanted to know what liberation she had come to, what she had done with the lessons and the images of her childhood. She said that she did not feel she was theologically a Christian, but that she clung emotionally to the power of Christian images, given to her as a child, which open like gates into her adult spiritual life.

But I fear those images, embedded in me with the words of the hymns, the scriptures, the images of sacrifice and purification, of power and dominion. I am skeptical of attempts to redeem the images, the system of belief contaminated by centuries of misuse. And, indeed, Christian feminist theologians who have found a revolutionary gender equality in the teachings of a "feminist" Jesus, and thus in Christianity, have sometimes done so by assigning an overwhelming patriarchal oppression to Judaism. Jewish feminist scholars, such as Judith Plaskow, have challenged this anti-Semitic bias, and some Christian feminists have responded by looking at the hatred of Jews still tangled in the roots of their belief. Liberation theologian Mary Hunt has said of this struggle that "Ideology is praxis": since Christian theology is a guide for Christians in how to live, anti-Semitism in Christian life will cease only if there is no anti-Semitism in Christian theology.[38]

So I remain suspicious of the images of power, domination, submission given to me by Christianity. I gain some hope from reading the meditations of Christian feminist Nelle Morton, who worked against segregation as a white Southerner. Raised, like me, a Presbyterian, she became connected through her church to a belief grounded in equality, freedom, social transformation—a Christianity unimaginable to me in my growing-up years, but the faith of most Black, and a few white, Southerners at that time.[39] Morton interprets God, and the images and words used for that concept, as simply metaphor, a way to express a dynamic relation between us and another; she sees patterns of dominance and power as frozen into traditional

Christian metaphor, and seeks for new ways to express sacred relation. She speaks of God as "the hearing one—the one who hears us
to our own responsible word." She asks, "If the images out of which
you live should prove phony (false), would you be willing to have
them shattered in order to let the shining reality of truth come
through?"[40]

I think of these words when I read another Christian feminist,
Carter Heyward, as she wrestles with a theological belief I was raised
with, the doctrine of election, the idea that God has chosen only certain people to be saved, to become part of the "mystical body of
Christ." She refuses to rest her faith on such "exclusivity and special
privilege"; she asserts a theology of liberation. Yet when she says,
"God chose us all, Christians and Jews and Moslems and wicca. . . .
We are the ones who elect. . .how we shall live as members of this
mystical body," I see, once again, Jews (and others) being converted
to Christianity, here through metaphor; I think of the Jews, over thousands of years, who died or were forcibly converted because they did
not want to become part of the Church or the body of Christ.[41]

So I continue to fear the images of God given to me. I have tried
to create new spiritual images for myself, my own, as much as any image can be, through poetry. I meet weekly with a group of others, lesbians and gay men of no one religion or race or ethnic group, seeking to map my own soul, to know my own fears and desires, and not
seek dominion, nor turn another person into gold, iron, or blood, nor
into wheat, lilies, or fire, seeking to give up use, to give up on having
the truth. I cling to the words of my friend Barbara Deming who said,
and lived, "We are all part of one another."[42] I try simply to go in search
of my self, and bring her back as a friend to me and to others.

A month after Rosh Hashanah, the weather still beautiful, Joan
and I go at lunchtime to sit in the sun in the monastery garden and
feed the squirrels stale peanuts and bread scraps they take from our
hands, as they roam fearless in this curious peace, a cloistered place,
apart from, protected from "the world." I was taught as a Christian
to distrust and separate from the things of the world, to doubt the
ownership of possessions, to know a person's worth was not to be
measured by clothes, money, social standing. The one verse I remember from Miz Nell Weaver's Bible alphabet (besides "Jesus wept") was
"Lay not up for yourselves treasures upon earth, where moth and rust
doth corrupt, and where thieves break through and steal: But lay up

for yourselves treasures in heaven...Matthew 6:19." (These words have the power of an incantation which I still believe, not literally, but as a call to the realm of the spirit.)

Yet, to be thus disengaged from the world is easier if your family is securely founded as mine was, on generations of farmers, small plantation owners, doctors, lawyers, school teachers, judges; sometimes we were precariously middle class—my mother's family in her childhood was money-poor, her life as a young woman impoverished by the Depression—but we were always a *respectable* Christian family, as my grandmother Brown asserted, all the way back to the first of us coming to North Carolina.

That immigration was, in part, an exile as we fled as Presbyterians from Catholic persecution in Scotland, yet we came into the U.S. as part of a centuries-long *mission* by Christians of all persuasions to claim a savage, heathen continent for God. The brutal massacres and systematic annihilation of indigenous American peoples were part of the sanctification of the land, a "purification" that continues in other parts of the world even now.[43] But, in the religion I was raised with, as long as one is Christian, one can possess the land, and the people of that land, and still not be "of the world" if one is properly humble, tithes, acknowledges that such possessions are really worthless, are made possible only through the grace of God.

For those who are not Christian, no escape is possible: those who are "not saved" are in the world, and possess the world for the sinful world's sake. To hear my father refer to a Jewish conspiracy during my childhood made sense, for, of course, "Godless" Jews would care about "the world." To have my mother explain years later that my father meant not all Jews, just "Zionists who he thought were trying to take over the world," was even clearer: *Zionists* as a code word for Jews who do not assimilate to self-denial on the Christian model, who seek something for themselves, some part of the world. The image: a Mercator map of the world, dissected and flattened, with everywhere, in every country, invisible secret Jews in cities, families, businesses, working to control everything.

I didn't know as a child that my father was repeating one of the oldest conspiracy theories in the world: that Jews were taking over, had taken over, the workings of a state, a country, a world, through business dealings, for their own use, for their own profit. It was an idea that stretched back at least to the Protestant Martin Luther, who wrote, in 1543 in Germany, that Jewish homes should be "smashed and destroyed"; displaying racism as well as anti-Semitism, he declared that Jewish people should be put in "a stable like gypsies, to teach them they are not master in our land" through their "wealth... extorted usuriously from us." An idea believed by Ukrainian Orthodox peasants in 1648 when they rose to massacre thousands of Jewish middlemen, overseers for Polish and Catholic nobility who were making a fortune in food exports during the European war. An idea argued by the anticlerical and rationalist Voltaire in 1756 when he said, "[The Jews] trained...as a whole in the art of usury...are a totally ignorant nation who for many years have combined contemptible miserliness and the most revolting superstition with a violent hatred of all those nations which have tolerated them." An idea believed by Marx, a baptized, assimilated Jew, who wrote, in an essay in 1844, prior to formulating his theory of communism, that he approved of assertions that "the Jew" determined the destiny of Europe by "his money power"; he also wrote, "Money is the jealous God of Israel, besides which no other god may exist...money is the alienated essence of man's work and existence; this essence dominates him and he worships it. The god of the Jews has been secularized and has become the god of the world." An idea believed in early twentieth-century Germany, where Jews were accused of stealing German culture; even the use of the German language by Jews who were German by birth was considered, according to Kafka, to be "usurpation of an alien property, which had not been acquired but stolen."

In Nazi Germany, hard-hit by the world depression, needing an economic scapegoat, the idea was expanded to justify the seizure of Jewish property as "restitution," and then to justify the murder of millions of Jews, because "the Jews had been engaged for generations in defrauding the German people." It was an idea being publicly stated by Goebbels and Himmler, at the same time that, in the U.S., President Roosevelt was expressing his sympathy with the "understandable complaints which the Germans bore toward the Jews in Germany, namely that while they represented a small part of the population, over 50 percent of the lawyers, doctors, schoolteachers, [and] college professors in Germany were Jews." (The actual percentages were 16.3, 10.9, 2.6, and 0.5.)[45]

The idea did not end with the Nazis or with World War II. In this decade the insidious idea that Jews are somehow innately or inevitably connected to money, power, and the abuse of power has been popular in Japan, where "international Jewish capital" is blamed for Japanese economic problems, and a Japanese author has written *Understanding the Protocols of the Elders of Zion*, reviving as fact a forgery that was originally created to convince Russian Czar Nicholas I that Jews were out to control the world, and that was used in the U.S. in the 1920s as part of Henry Ford's propaganda "war on the Jews." The idea has been revived in the Poland of the 1990s with the fall of communism; there Jews are once again being blamed for a country's economic crisis—this in a nation of ten million gentiles with a population of fewer than ten thousand elderly Jews remaining from a pre-Hitler Jewish population of over three million—in a country with a .001 percent Jewish population.[46]

In the U.S., anti-Semitic flyers were circulated during Carter's presidency, blaring accusations about *President Carter and His Kosher Crowd, Jews Rule America!, Did You Know. . .Jews in America are less than 5% of the total population but hold over 90% of top government jobs?, How Long Can. . .America survive when Jews control the government, the news, the money, and the churches?* In the Midwest in the mid-1980s, farmers in a crisis of foreclosures and bankruptcies turned increasingly to right-wing groups like the Populist Party and the Posse Comitatus which blamed the economic crash on "Jew-run banks and loan agencies. . . Jewish money barons" working "hand in hand" with the federal government.[47]

And during the last decade in the U.S., the idea that Jews have some kind of intrinsic connection to money and power has been perpetuated by people as varied as Black nationalist Minister Louis Farrakhan and white feminist humorist Marilyn Woodsea, who issued a mock certificate to induct "half-Jews" into a "Semi-Semite Society," with one benefit to be "wealth and fame as rewards for the vastly superior talent and intelligence that is ours as a birthright."[48]

And here, as I am listing these examples of anti-Semitism, I fear that someone reading this will simply nod and say, "Well, if so many different people have believed this, over such a long period of time, then it must be true, as I've thought all along, Jews are—" And in her mind begin repeating, all over again, the lies.

I think especially of students at schools where I have taught, the fraternity men at George Washington University who sponsored "No JAPS" parties, with flyers covered with hateful caricatures of the "Jewish American Prince and Princess," a crude sketch of a man and woman with stereotypically "Jewish" big nose and frizzy hair, a set of car keys marked BMW, a sweater labeled Benetton, symbols of "Jewish materialism." I took down the flyer that I saw, as some kind of proof, and brought it to the Women's Studies Department, where we made calls of protest to the administration. The fraternity was eventually reprimanded; but has any one of these young men changed his mind and repudiated the stereotype of "the Jew" as greedy, grasping, materialistic?

Did any of them possess enough history to know that the Nazi co-optation of students began fifteen years before Hitler came to power, with the passage of the Eisenach Resolution by student fraternities, by which Jews were excluded from fraternity membership for racial as well as religious grounds? In this year of German reunification and the glorification of West German economic triumphs, do any of these young men reflect, now, on the historical fact that none of the German industrialists who used Jews as slave-labor in their factories during the Nazi era ever acknowledged any moral responsibility for this act? Industrialist Friedrich Flick, for instance, never paid a single compensation claim to survivors of his slave-labor, and was worth many millions when he died at the age of ninety. Though some companies paid some small compensation to survivors, the families of Jews worked to death in the factories received nothing.[49]

I can imagine these young men saying to me, "Oh, the Holocaust—that was a long time ago, and it's over with," as other gentiles have said when confronted with this history. Perhaps, to some of us, it is far away—not our families, not our country, not our responsibility. Yet I have seen in my teaching how the stereotype of the "greedy" Jew permeates student life, now, in the 1990s. In my introductory women's studies classes, at the University of Maryland, as we talk about the lives of different kinds of women—Native American, Asian-American, African-American—and we come to Jewish women, the anecdotes begin: the tables in the dining hall designated as "JAP" tables, where you don't sit if you don't want to be identified with a certain kind of woman, a bitch, a woman with an attitude, a Daddy's girl who expects to get anything she wants, obsessed with clothes, with flamboyant style and a certain kind of hair, with a Long Island accent.

Many students say that, before they came to college, they had no vocabulary for this concept, the JAP, the Jewish American Princess; but within a few days at school they had learned the word and who to avoid—and the young Jewish students had begun to experience despisal and contempt on an even wider scale in their lives.[50]

When I speak of this as anti-Semitism, often students, both gentile and Jewish, will protest that it can't be: women who *aren't Jewish* are called JAP's. A Black middle-class woman who is assertive and stylishly dressed recounts how *she* has been called a JAP for those reasons. In their first days on campus, some think *JAP* is a racial epithet aimed at Japanese; some don't know that the *J* in *JAP* stands for *Jewish*. But many do, and the Jewish students always know. Still, many deny the anti-Semitism of the term and the way young women are stereotyped. I ask them why the concept of Jewishness is embedded in this negative slang word if it is not connected to anti-Semitism? I have them read articles on JAP-baiting on college campuses. And I try to talk to them of history, of the making of stereotypes.[51]

I speak of the occupations from which Jews were systematically excluded in different Catholic countries from the Middle Ages through the nineteenth century, so that often the only work possible for them outside the Jewish community was that of ragpicker, shopkeeper, itinerant peddler, or money lender. I speak of the fact that some Jews, in the grip of this history, did develop skills in finance, in business, and of the way in which this part of Jewish culture is exaggerated in the stereotype of the Greedy Jew.[52] I ask: Is this a guilty reaction on the part of the gentile community for the centuries in which gentiles extorted money from Jews, granted them safety in a Christian nation, a Christian community, only if Jews paid exorbitant fines, fees, taxes?

I speak to my students of how difficult it is to see what place, what class, what struggles, any one person has come from; of the invisibility of Jews who don't fit the stereotype of the Rich Jew. I talk about the poverty of Jewish immigrants in the U.S., about the restrictions and quotas once imposed here on hiring Jews and on the admission of Jews to universities.[53] I use the example of an anthology of working-class women's writings that I've recently read: out of fifty-two writers, Anzia Yezierska, who wrote in the earlier immigrant years and is dead, is named as Jewish; but, of the living contemporary writers, only one, Pat Wynne, is identified as Jewish in the biographical comments. Even though I know that at least four of the others, all prominent writers, are Jewish, and doubtless so are others unknown to me, only one is clearly named as Jewish and working-class.[54]

I speak of the power of stereotype, caricature, ridicule, omission, hatred, how these have their own history, down into our lives now. And here I come to the center of the problem: Why do we need this image, the greedy Jew, the materialistic Jewish woman? I ask them to think about what I have been struggling with in myself: What is our place, as *ourselves*, in the complications of money, class, the oppressive uses of capitalism, as we live these? What are our fears that we will be lost, will not be able to make it, will end up wandering the streets as a bag lady? (And many talk about this as their fear.) What of our belief that we must be able to use and command others to find *our* way through to economic survival, the necessity (we think) to have others behind us in the rat race? What of our guilt over this? What of our hostility and jealousy toward those who we see as ahead of us in this maze, the ones who drive their way with fancier cars, fly first class? And how much do we understand of the economic and class boundaries that shape us, of the men who shape those boundaries? What analysis, what history, what map have we studied of these? Do we take the easy way prepared for us, for centuries, and blame "the Jews," in our need to be quit of responsibility for understanding, acting, and unwinding our relation to money and to power?

We are almost to winter, but the warm days continue. I go to sit in the monastery garden to edit and revise this essay, which I think of as a kind of sequel to "Identity: Skin Blood Heart," an earlier piece that I wrote about racism and anti-Semitism in my life, but in which I emphasized what I was learning about racism. That essay was written at a time shortly after anti-Semitism was being raised as an issue within the women's movement by Jewish women. Some women, including other Jewish women, expressed concern at this; one 1983 letter to *Ms.* magazine spoke of the "current. . .disproportionate concern with anti-Semitism in the Women's Movement," which the writers interpreted as a move by "many white feminists, defensive about constant charges of racism," who "may be seeking to restore their sense of political rectitude by identifying an oppression of their own." The letter deplored an emphasis on the "politics of identity," which the writers defined as a replacement for a "politics of issues."[55]

These comments remind me, now, of the times when my students, surrounded by new complexities of women's lives and cultures, by the intersection of oppressions and privileges in our lives, say to me: "But where do I *start*? What do I *begin* with? What is the *right* way to do this work?" The answer I give is: We start with ourselves; we stand at the beginning of the maze, in our own bodies, our own lives, and begin to unwind all from there. This is a politics of identity, but I understand *identity* to include *all* of our identities, our multiple selves, the one who has been hurt, the one who has worked hurt on another, the one who has despised, the one who has gloried in another and in her self.

For me, what this has meant is that I started feeling, thinking, and writing first about my own life as a lesbian, from the place that has been the center of oppression and liberation for me. And, then, as a white Southerner whose physical, visible reality was defined earliest by race, by Black and white, I came to feeling, thinking, and writing about race, as I began to try to understand how I have oppressed others. Yet, in understanding how my emotional and intellectual life must change to be rid of my race prejudice, I came to understand that a change in attitude was not enough; for the practice of racism to end, for sexism to end, material change must happen. Thus, I began to think about class, as well as race, to understand my place in this system I live in. My path to change became a material as well as a psychological and spiritual journey.[56]

Part of this path has been a circling back to try again to understand more of what hatred of Jews has meant in my life, how false praise and blame of Jews has been used to punish for religious reasons, to hold in place racial and class structures. And I was able to begin this circling back, to understand more about the intersection of oppressions, only because Jewish women, including friends, political colleagues, and my lover Joan, have raised anti-Semitism as an issue in their lives, and I have felt their lives as part of my life.

There are many ways that I have sought to understand anti-Semitism, and I've named some of these throughout this essay: I have read, asked questions, studied history; gone to cultural events, religious services, museums; listened to my Jewish lover and my Jewish friends; met with others to analyze racism and anti-Semitism; or interrupted when others were being anti-Semitic by offering my own struggles with prejudice and misconceptions. These things can be done, and many others: In Washington, D.C., community Seders have been organized by Christian and Jewish women working together through W.A.T.E.R., the Women's Alliance for Ethics, Theology and Ritual. At the Equity Institute, formerly located in Massachusetts, Jewish women and Christian allies have developed a workshop for middle and high school educators on recognizing, and intervening in, anti-Semitism and on Jewish history and tradition.[57]

But why do we undertake actions like these at all? I remind myself with words from the poet Rilke, himself German, Catholic-raised, who lived the end of his life during the rise of Hitler. Of his attempt as a man, the outsider, the oppressor, to understand the lives of women, he says:

> *Work of the eyes is done, now*
> *go and do heart-work*

on all the images imprisoned within you; for you
overpowered them: but even now you don't know them.[58]

To wind through my self has been to come to a place where the deepest images of my childhood distort and condemn Jews; to come to a place where, as an adult, I have denied the reality and existence of Jews, as a people, as individuals, simply because of who they were, no other reason.

Recently I read a newspaper story that told how Gypsies, in order to flee disastrous poverty in Rumania, had entered prosperous areas of Germany; several thousand Gypsies had been placed in a camp surrounded by barbed wire. The article mentioned discrimination against other "non-German" ethnic groups, including Turks, Yemenites, Cubans; quoted the mayor of Berlin as saying, "We are just *not* a multiracial and multicultural society. We are a really pure, good German society. . . ." But the story only briefly acknowledged the half-million Gypsies annihilated in Nazi concentration camps. As I read I shivered at what seemed a stark repetition, today, of that time, and at the telling of new atrocities as if they were happening in a place with no history. Then I realized that the article, which documented the tenacity of racist hatred, had not mentioned Jews, nor the central place that the elimination of millions of Jews occupied in the not-so-long-ago German plan to become a "pure, good" homogeneous society.[59]

In this story I recognized the place within me that has obliterated lives, particularly Jewish lives, by assuming their nonexistence, the place that is then used to *justify* nonexistence. But in my recognition I also saw the place I have made, within me, with my work, to acquire new information, experience, ability to act, through a journey to the imprisoning and imprisoned images, and, finally, to a place where I have puzzled over, admitted, welcomed Jewish lives, the place where new images overlay the old:

In the spring past, and, I hope, in the spring to come, Joan and me seated side-by-side at the Seder table with her Jewish-lesbian family, candles, cups of grape juice and wine, the *haggadah*, the telling of the story of liberation from slavery, the inclusion of meditations and prayers on our contemporary imprisonments, homophobia, racism, the prayer for peace in the Middle East with homelands for both Jews and Palestinians, the prayers for liberation from our own inner bondages of prejudice and hatred, and my own voice, after years of listening and learning, steady in singing: *"Hineh ma tove u'mana'yim / Shevet achyot gam yachad.* Oh, how wonderful it is, for women to dwell together."

Notes

I give many thanks to Joan E. Biren and to the editors of *Bridges*, especially Elly Bulkin and Adrienne Rich, for their guidance, support, and comments on this essay. Also I thank Ruth Eisenberg for her responses to the final draft, and Ransom Weaver for his help with the Arabic spellings.

1. The A.D. of Anno Domini can easily be changed to C.E., Common Era; B.C.E. is Before Common Era, rather than using B.C., Before Christ.

2. Paul Johnson, *A History of the Jews* (New York: Harper & Row, 1987), pp. 332–333.

3. Eli Evans, *The Provincials: A Personal History of Jews in the South* (New York: Atheneum, 1980), pp. 64–65, 300, 303.

4. Jack Adams, "Anti-Semitism," *Durham Morning Herald*, February 28, 1982, p. 7A.

5. Evans, p. 65.

6. Books on anti-Semitism in the U.S. that I have found helpful include Nathan Belth's *A Promise to Keep: A Narrative of the American Encounter with Anti-Semitism* (New York: Quadrangle, 1979), and Melvin Tumin's *An Inventory and Appraisal of Research in American Anti-Semitism* (New York: Freedom Books, 1961). For insights on anti-Semitism within the women's movement and elsewhere, I have found invaluable *Nice Jewish Girls: A Lesbian Anthology*, ed. Evelyn Torton Beck (Boston: Beacon, 1989; revised and updated from the original); and also writings by Irena Klepfisz in her collected essays, *Dreams of an Insomniac: Jewish Feminist Essays, Speeches and Diatribes* (Portland, Oregon: Eighth Mountain Press, 1990).

7. Some of my ignorance was remedied by the section on "Jewish Foremothers" in Melanie Kaye/Kantrowitz's essay, "Some Notes on Jewish Lesbian Identity" in *Nice Jewish Girls*, pp. 134–50. But I began to take in the significance of the naming only when this passage was read out loud as part of a cultural event celebrating *Nice Jewish Girls*, which was organized by a group of lesbian-feminists in Washington, D.C., in 1981.

8. I wrote of this in "Identity: Skin Blood Heart," in *Yours in Struggle: Three Feminist Perspectives on Anti-Semitism and Racism*, co-authored with Elly Bulkin and Barbara Smith (Ithaca, New York: Firebrand Books, 1988; reprinted from the 1984 original Long Haul Press edition), pp. 17–18.

9. *New York Times*, October 5, 1971.

10. Sara Diamond, *Spiritual Warfare: The Politics of the Christian Right* (Boston: South End Press, 1989), pp. 84–87.

11. Johnson, p. 323.

12. Diamond, pp. 216–219.

13. Johnson, pp. 400, 426–427.

14. Eleanor Randolph, "Rosenthal Attacks Buchanan Column, *Washington Post*, September 15, 1990, p. D1.

15. Diamond, p. 32.

16. Diamond, p. 134.

17. Diamond, pp. 202–204.

18. Jackson Diehl, "The Battle at Temple Mount," *Washington Post*, October 14, 1990, pp. A1, A28; John M. Goshko, "Despite Allies' Warning," *Washington Post*, October 14, 1990, p. A27.

19. Some accounts of these organizing efforts can be found in *The Tribe of Dina: A Jewish Women's Anthology*, ed. Melanie Kaye/Kantrowitz and Irena Klepfisz (Montpelier, Vermont: Sinister Wisdom, 1986; recently reissued by Beacon). More recent efforts are given in *Jewish Women's Call for Peace: A Handbook for Jewish Women on the Israeli/Palestinian Conflict*, ed. Rita Falbel, Irena Klepfisz, and Donna Nevel (Ithaca, New York: Firebrand Books, 1990). The *Jewish Women's Peace Bulletin* can be obtained from JWCEO (Jewish Women's Committee to End the Occupation), Room 1100, 64 Fulton Street, New York, New York 10038, (212) 227-5912.

20. Johnson, pp. 208, 216, 217–229.

21. Johnson, p. 382; Andrea Dworkin, *Right-Wing Women* (New York: Perigee/Putnam, 1983), pp. 122–123; *Nazi Culture: Intellectual, Cultural, and Social Life in the Third Reich*, ed. George L. Mosse (New York: Grosset & Dunlap, 1966), pp. 80–81, 75.

22. Evans, pp. 341–343.

23. Kirk Loggins and Susan Thomas, *The New Klan: A Report from the Pages of the Tennessean* (Nashville, n.d.), p. 11; documents from the National Socialist White People's Party, 2507 North Franklin Road, Arlington, Virginia 22202.

24. Loggins and Thomas, p. 18.

25. Loggins and Thomas, pp. 14–15; Diamond, pp. 139–141; Herbert W. Armstrong, *The United States and Britain in Prophecy* (n.p.: Worldwide Church of God, 1980) is an example of British Israelism transplanted to the U.S.; I picked up my copy at Washington National Airport where it was displayed, for free, along with copies of *The Plain Truth* magazine.

26. The John Brown Anti-Klan Committee, *The Dividing Line of the 80's: Take a Stand Against the Klan*, xeroxed pamphlet handout.

27. Evans, pp. 50–60.

28. "Jewish Liberation Policy Statement," draft policy #4 from Re-evaluation Counseling (RC), undated xerox.

29. I found eloquent and useful thought on how my culture defines Jewish life as alien in Hannah Arendt, *The Origins of Totalitarianism* (New York: Harcourt Brace, 1951), Pt. II, pp. 296–298.

30. J.N. Sevenster, *The Roots of Pagan Anti-Semitism in the Ancient World* (London: E.T. Brill, 1975); also, see Johnson, pp. 133, 314, 178, 216, 242.

31. Klepfisz, *Dreams*, p. 104.

32. "In *Gerangl*/In Struggle," in *The Tribe of Dina*, pp. 304–316.

33. Johnson, p. 235.

34. Evelyn Beck discusses this incident in her introduction to *Nice Jewish Girls* within the context of anti-Semitism in the women's movement.

35. A more complex meditation on what it means to be part of a Jewish family is Adrienne Rich's long poem "Sources," pp. 3–27 in *Your Native Land, Your Life* (New York: W.W. Norton, 1986), and her essay, "Split at the Root," pp. 73–90, in *Nice Jewish Girls*.

36. *Bridges*, vol. 1, no. 1 (Spring 1990/5750) has a moving photographic essay, "A Decade of Jewish Feminism" by Joan E. Biren (JEB), on pp. 57–66, and an overview, "The Rise of Jewish Lesbian Feminism," by Faith Rogow, pp. 67–79. The address for *Bridges* is P.O. Box 18437, Seattle, Washington 98118.

37. Ingeborg Day, *Ghost Waltz* (New York: Viking, 1980).

38. On criticism of anti-Semitism in Christian feminist theology, see Judith Plaskow's essay, "Blaming the Jews for the Birth of Patriarchy," pp. 298–302 in *Nice Jewish Girls;* Plaskow's most recent work is *Standing Again at Sinai: Judaism from a Feminist Perspective* (New York: Harper & Row, 1990). For an example of a Christian feminist examining anti-Semitism in her work and revising that work, see Elisabeth Schüssler Fiorenza, "The Jesus Movement as Renewal Movement within Judaism," in *In Memory of Her: A Feminist Theological Reconstruction of Christian Origins* (New York: Crossroads, 1983). Mary Hunt's comments were in a personal conversation with me on November 24, 1990; her most recent work is *Fierce Tenderness: A Feminist Theology of Friendship* (New York: Crossroads, 1991).

39. Nelle Morton's book of essays is *The Journey Is Home* (Boston: Beacon, 1985); her brief autobiographical statement on pp. 183–194 was most meaningful to me. For the revolutionary potential of Christianity for white Southerners in resisting slavery, segregation, racism, and sexism, see, among many sources, Angelina E. Grimké's *Appeal to the Christian Women of the South* (New York, 1836) and Sara Evans' *Personal Politics: The Roots*

   of *Women's Liberation in the Civil Rights Movement and the New Left* (New York: Vintage/Random House, 1979), pp. 24–59.

40. Morton, pp. 129, 221.

41. Carter Heyward writes on her work in reconciling her Christian faith with her recognition of a multicultural, multifaith world in her *Speaking of Christ: A Lesbian Feminist Voice* (New York: Pilgrim Press, 1989); the passage I cite is from p. 61.

42. Barbara Deming, *We Are All Part of One Another*, ed. Jane Meyerding (Philadelphia: New Society Press, 1984), p. 167. I have found helpful some thoughts on metaphors for God from a Jewish perspective in Yoel H. Kahn's "How We Talk About God," *Bridges*, vol. 1, no. 2 (Fall 1990/5751), pp. 25–29.

43. The role of right-wing Christianity in possessing the land is exemplified recently by the actions of evangelical Christian General Rios Montt and his supervision of the massacres of Guatemalan indigenous peoples; Diamond, pp. 164–169.

44. Johnson, pp. 242, 258–259, 309, 350–351.

45. Johnson, pp. 477, 504.

46. John Burgess, "Japan Discovers the Jews," *Washington Post*, May 17, 1987, p. G5; Belth, pp. 75–86; George G. Higgins, "Polish Anti-Semitism, *Washington Post*, January 1, 1982, editorial page; "Report on the Polish Elections," National Public Radio, November 24, 1990.

47. Pamphlet from the San Diego area, January 26, 1981 (Los Angeles: World Service, n.d.); Frank Hornstein, "Anti-Semitism and the Farm Crisis," *Genesis 2*, May/June 1985—Iyyar/Sivan 5745, p. 4.

48. Nathan McCall, "Facing the Farrakhan Factor," *Washington Post*, November 4, 1990, p. C5; Marilyn Woodsea, "Semi-Semite Certificate," dated 1980.

49. Johnson, pp. 474, 515–516.

50. Evelyn Torton Beck's "From 'Kike' to 'JAP'," *Sojourner*, vol. 14, no. 1 (September 1988), pp. 18–23, gives a history and context to the development of these stereotypes of Jewish women. Her "Therapy's Double Dilemma: Anti-Semitism and Misogyny" gives a more extensive analysis of anti-Semitism that focuses on Jewish women; this article is in *Jewish Women and Therapy: Seen But Not Heard*, eds. Ellen Cole and Rachel Josephowitz Siegel (New York: The Haworth Press, 1990; vol. 10, no. 4 of *The Journal of Women and Therapy*).

51. A special issue of *Lilith*, no. 17 (Fall 1987/5748) featured several articles on JAP-baiting on college campuses.

52. See entries in Johnson under *money, finance, banking, and money lending.*

53. Donna Ippolito, *The Uprising of the 20,000* (Pittsburg, Pennsylvania: Motheroot Publications, 1979); also, *The Jewish Woman in America,* eds. Charlotte Baum, Paula Hyman, Sonya Michel (New York: NAL, 1975).

54. *Calling Home: Working Class Women's Writings,* ed. Janet Zandy (New Brunswick, New Jersey: Rutgers University Press, 1990).

55. "Letters to the Editors," *Ms.,* February 1983, p. 13; "Identity: Skin Blood Heart," in *Yours in Struggle.*

56. I've explored my thinking on class, work, and money issues in several essays. One, "My Mother's Question," was published in *Frontiers,* vol. 10, no. 2 (1988), pp. 1–5; others, as well as this essay, are included in this collection of my writing.

57. For more information about the joint Seders, including the new *haggadah* written for the occasion, contact W.A.T.E.R., 8035 13th Street, Silver Spring, Maryland 20910, (301) 589-2509. The Equity Institute has brochures and materials available. Contact them at 6400 Hollis Street, Suite 15, Emeryville, California 94608, (415) 658-4577.

58. From "Turning Point," in *The Selected Poetry of Rainer Maria Rilke,* ed. and trans. Stephen Mitchell (New York: Vintage, 1989).

59. Marc Fisher, "Gypsies Add to German Ethnic Upheaval," *Washington Post,* October 22, 1990, p. A18. I thank Susanna Smith for drawing my attention to how I erased the oppression of Gypsies in the earlier version of this essay; see her Letter to the Editors of *Bridges,* vol. 2, no. 2 (Fall 1991/5752).

60. I have found the handouts on Alliance-Building developed by the late Ricky Sherover-Marcuse to be extremely helpful; for information on her life and work, contact: The Ricky Sherover-Marcuse Liberation Fund, 6501 Dana, Oakland, California 94609. The *haggadah* of the Jewish-lesbian group of Washington, D.C., has been in the process of creation since their first Seder in 1982; this *haggadah* transforms the traditional *brothers* of the *"Hineh ma tove"* into *sisters,* which is translated into English as *women.*

Poetry in Time of War

On the Saturday before the war starts, driving to the protest vigil in front of the White House, I begin to cry as I listen on the car radio to the Congressional roll call vote, the patriotic yesses, with which the legislators authorize U.S. military force against Iraq. Standing with the somber and angry crowd, I let the tears roll down my face, tears of despair, wordless prayers.

Four young people kneel on the sidewalk, three white boys and a white girl perhaps not out of their teens. They hold up replicas of body bags, white garbage bags with magic-marker slogans, long passionate messages staggering across the plastic. We all begin to chant, "NO BLOOD FOR OIL." The police push us back behind a line on the sidewalk which they declare illegal to cross. They bring out the dogs, German shepherds straining on the leash, and stand

This essay was originally presented in a slightly different form at the lesbian and gay Publishing Triangle forum on Censorship, November 29, 1990, New York City, and at the Folger Poetry Series, January 28, 1991, Georgetown University.

over the four young folks, then jerk them up, one by one, handcuff
them, shove them into a paddywagon. All the while the young woman is shouting, shouting her reasons for opposing the war.

In the crowd, folks pass out leaflets, pink flyers for the march next
week, white flyers for the march in two weeks, scraps of paper detail-
ing the connection of the war to money, to homelessness, to invasions
of other small countries by the United States. No one is passing out
poems.

I wander, looking for leaflets for my sons on how to resist a possible draft. During the Vietnam War, I was pregnant with my first son;
before it was over, I had delivered my second son; unbelievably, a new
war is beginning just as they reach the age of soldiers. I have written
poems for them, years before this day, poems of resistance to war, of
the connection between war and other dominations offered to them
as men. But my words have not even slowed this war down.

I stand alone on the street, with the crowd, in the anguish of how
it is happening again, the domination and the violence justified by
law. And I watch the resistance begin again, and remember that in my
own life poetry has been more to me than a gun or a knife, more than
the will to resist.

In the second week of the war, I speak at a local university, part
of a poetry series with a theme from Shelley's statement: "Poets are
the unacknowledged legislators of the world." I look out over the half-
filled auditorium and see friends, former students, and, lining the back
rows, uniformed young men and women from the Naval Academy,
sent by an English instructor to get an evening's worth of culture. This
evening they get me. I say to them:

*As a lesbian poet, I have been contemplating Shelley's words. To be a poet
who is a lesbian is to be a potential felon in half the states of this country* and
*the District of Columbia, where I live. In some countries of the world, to be
a lesbian poet is to be subject, by law, to imprisonment or even execution. How
I love is outside the law. And when I write and speak of my life as a lesbian,
my poems have also been seen as outside the bounds of poetry.*

*It has taken me years to call myself a poet. I am a woman who stopped
writing in her early twenties, when my imagination faltered before the poets
my teachers offered for emulation—the white male writers of my region, the
poets who glorified the values of the Old South; who gave, in the lyric beauty
of their poems, the literary equivalent of laws that kept women in their place,
Blacks in their place, and those of us with perverted love entirely hidden. To
me, then,* poets *looked and acted very much like* legislators: *two sets of upper-*

class white men, the legislators in control of public communal space, the poets
endorsing their world or (some few) locked in isolated reaction to it.

When I began living as a lesbian, I had no place in that world of legisla-
tors and poets except as a criminal. I had to create a new reality, find in hid-
den lives the bittersweet kernel of possibility, and bring that in my hands, on
my tongue, to being. I was able to emerge as a poet and a lesbian only because
a place had been opened to me through creative organizing and acts of in-
dividual courage by lesbian and gay people over the last twenty years, as well
as through the larger civil rights and liberation movements in this country.

In those movements, there has been a vision and a dream of a place with-
out domination, without injustice authorized by law. I can say because of that
dream I have become a poet, not one who offers alternative legislation, but one
who offers possibility, threatening to some, desired by others, but possibility.

The audience is very quiet. I read some poems, one based on the
laws used against lesbians to take our children away from us, as had
happened to me. I say I am worried about my children being taken
away from me, now, by the war. I read a poem in which the father asks
his son not to go to war: "The father who says to the son: *It is time /*
to rebel, but do not leave alone. Talk / to the others." A poem written because of how, in the father's world, the voice of the mother, the
woman, the lesbian, is almost never heard, or if heard, is dismissed
as "unrealistic, hysterical, irrational."[1] I read a prayer poem for my sons,
a wish for blessings on them. I say that I believe my greatest gift to
my children has been my decision to live openly as a lesbian, an example of personal integrity, the possibility that they can decide to live
differently as men.

I fold my papers, people clap, some come to talk; but the uniformed students disappear quickly, back to the Naval Academy. This
is the day when the U.S. command announces that allied bombers
and warships have sunk eighteen Iraqi ships; this is the night when,
from bombed pipelines, oil flows down the waters of the Persian Gulf,
a thirty-mile-long slick, smothering the sound of the waves.

Now in the morning I open the front door, pick the *Washington
Post* up off the porch, and unfold it with the dread that has become
usual. Today, besides the chronicle of "successful" bombings, there
is a buried headline: "Rights Suffer in Wartime, ACLU Warns." The
FBI is questioning Arab Americans about their political beliefs in an
uneasy parallel to government actions preceding the roundup of Japanese Americans during World War II. Students have been denied the
right to protest the war on university campuses; conscientious objec-

tors have been shipped out to the Gulf before their appeals are reviewed; government workers are afraid their antiwar protests could cause them to be fired. ACLU spokesman Morton Halperin says, "In short, we are seeing once again that the first casualty of war is the civil liberties of Americans."[2]

Elsewhere in the paper are strong protests from print and network news reporters about censorship and manipulation by the U.S. government of information on the war. It appears, for instance, that *successful bombing* means only that the bombs were dropped, not whether they hit a military target, or someone's house. But the newspapers are practicing their own form of selective reporting. From friends I have heard of dramatic protests all over the country, students taking over the legislative chambers of the state of Washington, African Americans arrested at gas station "pump protests" throughout the deep South. However, a TV news report on a march of 150,000 people against the war gives more time to a pro-war counterprotest of 200.

On most days nothing in the newspaper shows that anyone opposes this war; instead the *Post* runs educational charts to teach us military terminology—what a *battalion* of soldiers is, a *flight* of warplanes. One day there is a photograph of U.S. soldiers practicing how to kill in hand-to-hand combat: one man kneels on the prone body of another, his arm raised, the long knife visible, ready to descend.

Stunned by the picture of one man preparing to kill another, I remember other photographs that many people in this town had not considered acceptable for public viewing: the erotic pictures by gay male photographer Robert Mapplethorpe, work that had been scheduled for a showing at the prestigious Corcoran Gallery of Art, and then cancelled by its directors out of fear of Congressional disapproval. Nevertheless, there ensued a two-year legislative battle in which right-wing senators and representatives passed legislation, originally sponsored by Sen. Jesse Helms, that excluded from federal funding any art that was "obscene," especially art about gay and lesbian life, "homoerotic" art, which was held by them to be obscene by definition.[3]

But in the current talk about censorship and First Amendment rights in war, nothing is said of this last debate and its relation to the individual's struggle with the arbitrary power of the state. Even though Congress fought over the censorship of lesbian and gay art only weeks before its vote on the Gulf war, nothing is said in the news about the importance of legally guaranteeing a place for the dissent and imagination of lesbian and gay people as a protection integral to the freedom of all in this country. Nothing is said of the connection between

some legislators' fear of art that explores love and sex, and their rous-
ing approval of hate and war, and how this might be connected to the
loss of civil rights and liberty.

Yet, during the last year, I have opened my newspaper many
mornings with a nauseated dread like that with which I now face the
war news. I have scanned the stories to see if *my* life was being attacked, *my* poetry vilified by some lawmaker on the floor of the House
or Senate. Not a paranoid fantasy: at the beginning of the year I had
received a grant from the National Endowment for the Arts, for poems
I had written that dealt explicitly with my life as a lesbian, as a mother,
as a sexual being. These poems took as a text for variation the sodomy statute, the crime-against-nature law of North Carolina, where
I was living when I came out as a lesbian and lost custody of my two
young sons because I was defined by law to be a person unfit to love
them.[4]

I lived through punishment for my rejection of male authority over
my life and my children; lived on to reclaim my relationship with my
sons, and to write poetry about those years of struggle and triumph;
lived to see my work and that of others create some widening in the
public space where we could live as a lesbian and gay people. And
then, ironically, or inevitably, I watched that space, and my art, threatened by censorship forces led by a senator from North Carolina, Jesse
Helms.

At first I felt disbelief when Helms began to attack my writing
directly, along with the work of Chrystos of the Menominee Nation
and Audre Lorde, two lesbians of color who had also received NEA
grants. In a letter to the General Accounting Office, he named us by
name, together with several performance artists and some arts organizations, as examples of the misuse of federal money in funding "obscene" art. His request for an investigation by the Comptroller General
began: "First of all, because of the nature of the enclosed material, I
urge that great care be taken to assure that your women associates not
be exposed to the material." It seemed that the only reason Chrystos,
Audre, and I were included in this investigation was that we publicly
acknowledged ourselves to be lesbians and poets. According to the
right-wing promoters of "traditional values," our love was obscene, our
very being was obscene, therefore our writing must be obscene.[5]

My disbelief at Helms' attack came in part because I had written
the very poems he pointed at exactly to answer and turn inside-out
such lying logic. I wondered with some desperation if I were going
to have to write the poems *all over again*? How could I say, more ir-

refutably, that which I had already said in the truthful complexity of poetry?

But more than disbelief, I felt fear. I was seized by a terrible fear, like that I'd lived with for years in North Carolina. In this battle over censorship, I was struck back into the isolation and helplessness I'd felt as a lesbian mother, my knowledge that the social and judicial system was designed to punish me, was based on values that held me to be despicable. For months after Helms pointed his accusing finger at me and my work, I was surrounded by fear and unable to write.

I realized that the fear deep in my bones, dragging me down, was also the fear I carried from having lived in a South run by demagogues such as Helms. I should not have been surprised at his attack for I knew him well: A man who'd had an English instructor fired from the university, when I was in graduate school there, for teaching a seventeenth-century "poem of seduction"—Marvell's "To His Coy Mistress"; and who had organized a university ban on speakers opposed to the Vietnam War, because they were "Communistic." A man who, as "my" senator, mobilized praying and shouting antiabortion and anti–Equal Rights Amendment church groups, while I was losing my children in the town next to his. A man so prejudiced against women and sex that he stated that abortion for a pregnancy caused by rape was not needed as a legal option, because a woman who *really* was raped *could not* get pregnant.[6]

In his most recent senatorial campaign, Helms had shifted back and forth between viciously homophobic advertisements and blatantly racist ads. He had won by feeding people fear, the kind of fear that I had drunk and eaten as a child growing up in the deep South, where I had lived in what was, literally, an authoritarian state, a place where African-American people were protected by *no* legal, *no* Constitutional guarantees. There was not even lip service given to democracy where Black folks were concerned. But the violence done to Black people by white people laid on the white community a paralyzing fear, a silence, a deadly conformity of thought and of feeling. The violence set strict taboos in the *white* community against any voicing of dissident opinions, against any kind of loving that might challenge the belief that some people should not talk to others, and some could not lie down with those others except in degradation, and someone had to be on top in love and someone underneath. We lived in a fear that was meant to kill the imagination, any yearning in us toward what was different from ourselves.[7]

Yet enough of my imagination survived so that, offered the possibility, I eventually imagined myself living as a lesbian, and then, writing as a poet, my voice raised against the voice of the demagogue. I decided to accept my federal grant although the Helms-sponsored law threatened punishment, disgrace, if I used public money to produce "obscene" work. I declared that I would not censor myself, as a lesbian, as a poet. If challenged by the government, I knew I would fight to defend my writing as a lesbian; and believed that I had some theoretical protection through my Constitutional right to "freedom of speech."[8] I also needed the money, needed the time off from teaching to do my work; but I had no legal protection for *this* reason since there is yet no way, through the Constitution of this country, to plead economic necessity, take the money, and then refuse to kill my words, my imagination.

When I go, in the middle of the war, to a demonstration across from the White House, in Lafayette Park, "Peace Park," I hear the *thud-thud* of the drum a group of protestors have been beating there for days. The federal money budgeted yearly for the arts in the U.S. is less than the amount spent on military bands alone, the drums beating to war.[9] In the midst of brutal budget cuts on human services, Congress found billions to fund the war; and Jesse Helms fund-raised millions for himself as a defender of this country's "morals" against "homosexuality." I imagine Helms on the campaign trail in Fayetteville, enjoying a Ft. Bragg band pounding out "The Stars and Stripes Forever," just before he begins his usual rant about government money being wasted on art that is really "smut" and "pornography"; just before he begins his pitch for campaign funds to fight that menace; just before everybody digs into the barbeque and he leads the men aside, again, to show them his portfolio of Mapplethorpe photographs, simultaneously warning them they may throw up and urging them to look.[10]

And the voice of Helms echoes that of Anthony Comstock who, over a hundred years ago, seized so-called pornographic materials and put them in a room in Congress for members to view, horrifying "indecencies" which, by the 1872 federal law instigated by Comstock, included any "obscene" books, pamphlets, photographs, or devices that gave information about birth control, abortion, sex education, or sexual pleasure. Then, with a mechanism set up under the Comstock laws, the U.S. Post Office, from 1873 until 1957, operated virtually as an independent censor on what materials could be mailed, and therefore be widely accessible, within the U.S. The freedom of the mails, supposedly guaranteed by the Constitution, was denied to thousands and tens of thousands, exactly for the reason being offered now by opponents of NEA grant awards: U.S. tax money shouldn't be used to support "immoral," "indecent," or "obscene" material.[11]

The case that broke this censorship was brought by the gay publication *One*. Banned from the mails because of a short story about two lesbians that it had published, *One* sued the Postmaster General and won in a 1957 Supreme Court ruling.[12] I imagine that General sitting at his desk, feet propped up, reading "the homosexual magazine," outraged, his voiced raised against the obscenity of it, his power extended to wipe out the simple fact of two women together.

I suspect my imaginary shouting General was roaring for the same reasons those in power roar now over lesbian art: maddened at the portrayal of two women together within their own culture, and therefore momentarily outside the state's control of production and reproduction, outside capitalism's control by commodification. Two women existing, if only on the page of our imagination, simply for each other, existing for no other use, as dangerous as other "useless" things like sexual pleasure, like poetry, dangerous, full of possibility.

I stand in the park near the statue of another General, Lafayette, hero of a revolutionary struggle that continues today with this antiwar demonstration. A struggle against a tyranny of worth based solely on economics. A struggle for a country in which a Black person's value cannot be given by law as three-fifths of a white person; a country where a woman's earning power cannot be set by the "free" market at three-quarters or less than a man's; the struggle for a country where lesbians and gay men are not despised for having sex for pleasure, nonprocreative, "nonproductive" sex. I have learned in this struggle that there is no "free" speech: we pay, in money or blood, time or pain, to assert our human dignity, to assert that we are even human. The power of our art, the making of a blood-and-bones representation of our lives, is the triumph of our imagination in a world that does not want us to believe that we *can* live, here, now, for ourselves.[13]

People passing the demonstration scream out: "SHUT UP, SHUT UP, SHUT YOUR FUCKING MOUTHS!" Their voices merge with that of a white man watching an earlier antiwar rally who yelled at an African-American woman: "Why don't you go back to Africa?" Merging with the voice I heard on the street in Dupont Circle only a month ago, a young white man, held down by other men, screaming, "I want to kill the faggots. I'm going to kill the faggots." The two men he had assaulted for walking down the street stood before him on a sunny

Monday afternoon, one with blood streaming down his face, hands bloody from trying to staunch the flow.

The drum beats beside me, against war, against power-over-others. I watch the hands of the drummers. I have seen how we have held our lives up, bloody and beautiful, in the grim face of assaults on us, held out to others our lives in poetry, in art, showing the possibility, how we have imagined another way to live.

On the night the U.S. begins its ground war against Iraq, I listen to news reports in my hotel room. I've been staying there for two days while I teach an intensive course on Women's Needs, Women's Theories. Now, suddenly, the TV men in my room are vehemently defending our attack with talk of Iraqi atrocities; how their invasion was a "rape of Kuwait"; how "we" had no choice but to come to the aid of that helpless little country, "the most Westernized" in the Middle East, now sexually assaulted by an Arab and his brutal men.[14] Furious, I leave the room, go down to the hotel basement and parking lot to get some books for my students from my car.

Downstairs, waiting for the up elevator, I hear again the voices glibly using rape as a convenient justification for violence. I hear other voices also: The cries of Black men lynched, burned alive, castrated while alive, accused by white men of raping white women. The screams of Black women raped by white men for hundreds of years, but no outcry raised by those in power over their fate. I reflect, bitterly, that for a month, because of the "rape of Kuwait," U.S. planes have been bombing Iraqi positions unmercifully, and that lying in these trenches, dying, are thousands of brown-skinned men, from the countryside or from the city, conscripted into the army, now rotting in the desert sun. And making this killing possible are the men and women of our volunteer army, the ones who joined because they could get no work, or had no skills, or could not afford to pay for college or medical school or computer training and so signed up for the reserves, ROTC, National Guard, the Armed Services.

Standing at the elevator, I hear, in the snack room behind me, an ominous crackling, a slamming thud, and a metallic male voice grunts out: "Uphold the Law. Protect the Innocent." More thuds, the whining zing of a fired weapon. The voice again: "I'm Robo-Cop. Uphold the Law. Protect the Innocent."

I jump, flinch. Relieved that I'm not actually being fired at, I begin to think about protection, about innocence. How protection, in order to exist, needs helplessness to exist. How protection places perversion outside itself, in others, in order to justify throwing a strong arm around innocent helplessness, in order to justify strong-arming the "guilty" ones outside "the law."

How often I hear the problem defined as perversion; how seldom I hear it described as domination. Tonight, the pilots dropping their bombs on people will be called heroes. A man who strangled his wife to death in the wholesome American Midwest was judged a fit father for his two daughters. But I am someone from whom children should be protected; even my own children should be protected from their deviant mother, the lesbian.

The U.S. Supreme Court decided a few years ago to protect the country from the "corruption" of lesbians and gay men by declaring sodomy laws Constitutional and us criminals; those of us engaged in loving consensual sex with each other, as adults, were left by that decision with no fundamental legal protection to live *as ourselves*, without hiding, in this country.[15] This criminalization of our love has traditionally been justified as protection for children from supposedly sexually predatory lesbians and gay men. Yet I have listened for many years to women who have told me of being raped by their heterosexual fathers, uncles, cousins, brothers, some abused by their heterosexual mothers. By all accounts, sexually abused children are assaulted overwhelmingly by heterosexual men. The abuse does not spring from sexual orientation or gender, but from the abuse of power, with children at the mercy of those adults, most usually heterosexual men, who have the greatest power over them.

Within the system of this father-state I am someone who is a danger to children. And now the Rev. Donald Wildmon, of the American Family Association, preaches that the *country* should be protected from poets like me. His Christian organization "promotes the Biblical ethic of decency in American society with primary emphasis on TV and other media." Through mass mail campaigns the AFA rallies right-wing and fundamentalist Christians against any public visibility of lesbians and gay men.[16]

One result of this kind of hate is that, not long ago, invited to be interviewed on a Los Angeles public radio station, I discovered that I couldn't read certain passages in some of my poems without endangering the station's broadcast license. The interviewer explained that right-wing monitors had complained to the Federal Communications Commission about a radio play designed to teach safe sex to gay men, the sexually explicit *Jerker,* which the station had aired. The FCC had threatened to cancel their license, so they were having to be cautious about what they broadcast. I wondered how we could teach people about practicing safer sex without using sexual words? And I wondered how I could write about the full range of human existence, which, despite opinions to the contrary, *does* include gay and lesbian existence, without using sexual words?

FCC head Albert Sikes has rationalized a new twenty-four-hour-a-day radio ban on all "indecent language" as necessary to "protect the children." Meanwhile, suicide is the leading cause of death among lesbian, gay, and sexual minority youth, in large part because they have no positive reflections of themselves in the world, on radio and TV. The Task Force on Youth Suicide, a report ordered by the U.S. Secretary of Health and Human Services, urged more factual information about "homosexuality" be given to teenagers to overcome their isolation and self-hate. But HHS Secretary Sullivan repudiated the report's recommendations meant to prevent the deaths of lesbian and gay young people. His explanation? That he was "strongly committed to strengthening traditional family values," which presumably excludes helping lesbian and gay children stay alive.[17]

There are other examples of "better dead than gay" thinking in how limits have been placed on information that can be given by federally funded projects. For instance, a Helms amendment on AIDS-specific funding during the 101st Congress directed that "no educational material that promotes homosexuality" could be financed with federal money. The legislation originally was written by Helms and Rep. William Dannemeyer in response to a safe-sex comic book produced by a gay men's health clinic; the depiction of two men demonstrating life-saving sex techniques was declared by Dannemeyer to be "pornographic," by Helms to be "obscene."[18]

Behind me the Robo-Cop game grunts and rattles. I imagine there are many young men in the desert who fired their first gun in a video arcade, relieved to be executioner and defender instead of target, victim, woman, queer. Now they have real guns in their hands to protect and defend an American way that has no place for people like me, queers whose very existence is a questioning of authority, a refusal of the right of some to dominate, the duty of others to submit.

Some of those attacking lesbian and gay art link the fate of this country to their success in protecting the United States from "the queers." But the current governmental and social panic about lesbian and gay people has happened before, in the 1950s, the era of McCarthyism, when we were condemned as the sexual equivalent of Communists, our love for each other not seen as a possibility for human connection, but as a threat. Just as lesbians and gay men are now banned from military service because of fears that our boundary-crossing love will compromise national security, so, too, in the 1950s there were purges to banish gay men and lesbians from government payrolls, university faculties, all public places.[19]

When I talked to Audre about the attacks on our writing and my fears, she said yes, that events now reminded her of living through the 1950s, but we must keep doing our work. What the censors wanted was to keep us from our work.

My work: to question out loud, to write the not-yet-spoken words. Shifting back and forth, waiting for the elevator so I can go back to my students, I think about protection, domination, perversion, poetry. The metallic voice repeats over and over, "Uphold the Law. Protect the Innocent."

In the middle of the war, Joan and I drive out one starry night, over the darkly glittering Potomac River, while I try to imagine bombs falling here out of the sky, the criss-cross of Scud and Patriot missiles like Fourth of July fireworks, the fairytale sparkle of antiaircraft tracers, the explosions, the death. Instead, we are going quietly to a party, a lesbian housewarming given by a writer and a lawyer, which also celebrates a case that the lawyer's organization has just won challenging the NEA restrictions on obscene art.

Bella Lewitsky, a dancer and choreographer whose company had been awarded money from the NEA, had refused to accept it if the "obscene art" prohibition was attached to the grant. She then announced a lawsuit against the U.S. government at the same Hollywood hotel where she had refused to answer the questions of the House Un-American Activities Committee in the 1950s. She said, "Sen. Joe McCarthy, after damaging endless lives, was. . .declared a madman. I am witness to Jesse Helm's destructive attacks. . . . How many times must history repeat itself? We must act. Having been witness, I must act."[20] Now, in a strong opinion in Lewitsky's favor, a federal judge had ruled that the government could not award money contingent on the restriction of the freedom to speak.[21]

At the party, the lawyer talks to me about the case, while around us women are telling gleefully how they had come out as lesbians to perfect strangers: *"When she and I went to pick up the ring that was being sized down, the jeweller said, 'What does it look like?' So I held out my hand with the matching ring, and smiled, 'Why, it looks just like mine.'"* The lawyer tells me the federal government is likely to appeal the Lewitsky ruling because it could easily be used by folks like her to challenge other federal restrictions currently in place, like laws that forbid family planning clinics to give out *any* information about abortions if the clinic receives federal money.[22]

A flash, the dark light of a photograph breaks open in my memory: a woman sprawled half-naked on a bare, dirty floor, her blood pooling around her; Rosie Jimenez, dead from a self-induced abortion, the first victim of a law withholding federal money from poor women who need abortions. Censorship, the denial of information, will kill more than the imagination. Louder than the murmur of the party, I hear my friend Barbara Smith saying to me, months ago, "The NEA is the *least* of it." I remember the cadence of a sentence from the open letter on the NEA written by Chrystos, Audre, and me: "We believe that the current heightened censorship of lesbian and gay artists is an opening salvo in an escalating war against the artists, and cultures, of any group that is dedicated to social change, and dedicated to the overturning of hierarchies of power...."[23]

Behind me a woman is saying angrily, "I wish we could lock George Bush and Saddam Hussein in a room together and let *them* fight it out." Instead, tonight, these men have the power to sacrifice hundreds of thousands of lives, the power to lock others up, make others fight for them. We, as a lesbian and gay people, have been closed up together, threatened with violence if we did not stay huddled, hidden, if we did not submit to power. But, despite the sorrow and pain we have sometimes wreaked on each other, we have made, not war, not despair, but a life, a future for ourselves, a vision of possibility, and passionate art.

Standing in that brightly lit room with laughing, angry, women, I remember two men I once saw dancing, locked fiercely breast to breast. Two men in blood-red costumes, a performance in a bar before hundreds of lesbians and gay men: their embraces, kisses, punches, wordless howls, and seeming nonsense syllables; their attempt to show us a human relationship dancing free of dominance and submission, of victor and vanquished. Two men twisting, bending toward each other in a lit, finite circle.[24]

Suddenly, one morning a hundred days after it started, the war is "over," without ever having been officially declared. The newspapers shift from photographs of exploding buildings to pictures of captured Iraqi troops, to accounts that Iraqi soldiers "have prostrated themselves at the feet of allied soldiers, clung to their legs, kissed their hands."

In this attitude of submission they are now spoken of as "real nice guys. . . just people."[25] As they lie defeated on the ground, it becomes possible for the victors to pity them, love them even.

An image flashes back to me from one antiwar march in D.C.: the queer contingent hugging and kissing, men with men, women with women, all together; the bafflement of onlookers as to the connections between faggots, peace, dykes, war. Our shared assumption that we did not need to humiliate someone who is like us, who is different from us, before we could feel love for them, before we could even begin to think of them as human. As I wandered through that crowd, I saw a man whose sign was a quotation from Shelley: *"War Is: The Statesman's Game, The Priest's Delight, The Lawyer's Jest, The Hired Assassin's Trade—."*

And for the lesbian? The poet? Another flash, from another demonstration: I am walking around and around in front of the National Endowment for the Arts building with the local D.C. group OUT! to protest censorship of gay and lesbian art. Someone has made big signs featuring "homoerotic art": a poem about making love to another woman by Audre Lorde, to another man by Essex Hemphill, a photograph of two women sweetly asleep together by Joan E. Biren (JEB). There is a sign with my poem, "Peach," which is full of flesh, ass, lust.[26] I decide to carry this sign as I circle in front of the tourists, unknown to them as the poet. I chant and hold one of the many poems I have written about love; and remember how some have responded to those poems as poems of hope, and others have vowed to drive me, and others like me, back into silence. I watch the faces of the tourists, especially one blond college-aged group, two men and a woman. They stare, puzzled, as I circle; the third time I pass by, one of the men smiles as if he agrees, raises a fist, says, "All *right!*"

What does he think he understands? Does he know how hard it is to write about sex and love as a woman who has been raised up in a land where men make war on women every day, through sex, and no one calls it war? Does he understand that a kind of war is waged on us daily as a gay people, as we are assaulted in the streets, as our children are taken from us, and the reason given is what we do sexually? And my "homoerotic" poem is considered evidence of our perversity that deserves obliteration.[27]

Does it even occur to him that my poem is between two women? Perhaps not, for though almost every sign we carry says *gay and lesbian, homoerotic,* and we are shouting, "We're here, we're queer, we're fabulous," it is unlikely that he shifted, as he watched, to a queer point of view. In his easy public claiming of the alrightness of sexual desire, does he have any glimmer of how difficult, how dangerous, how forbidden it is for a woman to talk about or write about her sexual life? For me as a lesbian to write about mine, for me to circle on that public sidewalk with words proclaiming desire?

I tremble as I walk by them with my poem, but I walk on, holding it up, claiming with others a momentary fragile public space for myself and my art. Later, a former student of mine, Tracy, steps into the wheeling circle with me; she says she's just been ejected with a group of other protestors from the NEA Council meeting inside, which they had disrupted at the announcement that awards to lesbian and gay artists had been turned down. Her form of disruption? She had begun reciting my "Peach" poem as loudly as she could. I smile as I imagine NEA Chairman Frohnmayer, the other dignitaries, caught in the middle of this battle over what will be allowed as art, as speech, over who will be allowed to *live* in the public spaces of this country. Caught in the room with Tracy chanting: "My tongue, your ass: / the center of a peach, / ripe, soft, pitted, red-fibred flesh, / dissolving toward earth, lust. / *Eat you?* I ask."

I smile now, remembering, even though the *Post* front-page headline today read, "U.S. Tanks Go Deeper Into Iraq," even though we continue to war while saying, "The war is over." Even though, all around, I see domination justified by force and the rule of law, and called "good," and called "decent." Even though the latest Congressional law governing publicly funded art is that it must be "sensitive to the general standards of decency. . .of the American public."[28] Even though I think of the hatred that hides behind the word *decent* in this country, hundreds of years of hatred.

I smile because my imagination has carried me beyond the bounds of law and propriety, into life. I smile because my poem rolled that day, not a bomb, but a peach, through the overcrowded, stuffy room. The poem fragrant, slightly indecent, tender to the touch, ripe with possibility.

Notes

I received much-needed love, support, and thoughtful political analysis from Joan E. Biren (JEB) during the NEA censorship struggle and I am deeply grateful to her. Others who I thank for their support are my co-grantees, Chrystos and Audre Lorde; Elly Bulkin; Dr. Nanette Gartrell and Dr. Dee Mosbacher; and Judith Beth Cohen for her thoughts on "the imagination." And thanks to Ben Weaver for help with Lafayette. For their organizing work against censorship and the information they shared with me, I especially thank Deanna R. Duby of People for the American Way; Peri Jude Radecic of the National Gay and Lesbian Task Force; Liam Rector of the Council of Writing Organizations and the Associated Writing Programs. I thank the Fund for Free Expression for awarding Chrystos, Audre Lorde, and me one of its 1991 grants made to "writers anywhere in the world who have been victimized by political persecution." To my knowledge, this is the first time an international nongay human rights organization has recognized lesbian and gay persecution as political persecution.

1. "On Reading Timerman's *The Longest War*," from my book of poems, *Crime Against Nature* (Ithaca, New York: Firebrand Books, 1990).

2. See Howard Kurtz, "U.S. Lets Some News Filter Through 'Blackout,' " in *Washington Post*, February 25, 1991, p. A18; Tracy Thompson, "Rights Suffer In Wartime, ACLU Warns," in *Washington Post*, January 29, 1991, p. A16.

3. The amendment attached to the NEA FY 1990 appropriations bill (Public Law 101–121) read: "None of the funds authorized to be appropriated for the National Endowment for the Arts...may be used to promote, disseminate, or produce materials which in the judgment of the National Endowment for the Arts...may be considered obscene, including but not limited to, depictions of sadomasochism, homoeroticism, the sexual exploitation of children, or individuals engaged in sex acts and which, when taken as a whole, do not have serious literary, artistic, political or scientific value." A signed compliance form was required from grant recipients before they could receive their money; if "in the judgment of the NEA" the work they produced with the grant was obscene, the NEA could attempt to reclaim the money. For stories about the debate on censorship and art, including "homoerotic art," see the *Washington Post* and the *New York Times*, as well as many other mainstream and alternative publications, beginning in June 1989. For information about censorship in the U.S., I have found helpful Robert W. Haney, *Comstockery in America: Patterns of Censorship and Control* (Boston: Beacon Press, 1960); Felice Flanery Lewis, *Literature, Obscenity, and Law* (Carbondale: Southern Illinois University Press, 1976); James C.N. Paul and Murray L. Schwartz, *Federal Censorship* (New York: The Free Press, 1961).

4. These poems included the title poem of *Crime Against Nature*.

5. Audre Lorde's poetry includes *From A Land Where Other People Live* (Detroit: Broadside Press, 1973), *The New York Head Shop and Museum* (Detroit: Broadside Press, 1974), *Coal* (New York: W.W. Norton, 1976), *The Black Unicorn* (New York: W.W. Norton, 1978), and *Our Dead Behind Us* (New York: W.W. Norton, 1986). Chrystos' poetry includes *Not Vanishing* (Vancouver, Canada: Press Gang Publishers, 1988) and *Dream On* (Vancouver, Canada: Press Gang Publishers, 1991). I have a xerox copy of a letter to the Honorable Charles A. Bosher, Comptroller General, General Accounting Office, dated March 6, 1990, from Senator Jesse Helms, with an attached "Table of Contents" that lists, under "Questionable NEA Activities," eleven items including "D. Three NEA $20,000 Creative Writing Fellowships to Audre Lorde, Minnie Bruce Pratt and Chrystos." See also Lou Chibbaro, Jr., "Despite curb on art funding, Lesbians win NEA grants," *Washington Blade*, January 19, 1990, p. 1; Valerie Richardson, "National Endowment for the Arts helps fund porn star's stage shows," *Washington Times*, February 6, 1990, p. A6.

6. Juan Williams, "Carolina Gothic," *Washington Post Magazine*, October 28, 1990, p. 38.

7. I was born into this town in 1946, two years after the banning of Lillian Smith's *Strange Fruit*, a book that grappled with the reality of love across race, class, and gender in the South; besides the central couple, a white man and a Black woman, there is a lesbian character who meditates on love between women. Smith wrote a letter on censorship to the Civil Liberties Union of Massachusetts in which she said: "There are many people who cannot bear to face a truth that hurts. . . . They fear the book because it has the effect of stirring imagination. . . ." For the full text of this letter, see " 'Old Seeds Bearing a Heavy Crop' " in *Southern Changes*, vol. 12, no. 5 (November 1990), with an introduction by Rose Gladney which refers to the NEA and censorship.

8. William O'Rourke usefully discussed his decision to accept an NEA grant without submitting to obscenity restrictions as analogous to committing civil disobedience; see "Protesting N.E.A.," *Nation*, June 25, 1990, pp. 880–881.

9. John Koch, "The real agenda behind attacks on the NEA," *Boston Globe*, June 3, 1990, p. B33; Robert Hughes, "Whose Art Is It, Anyway?" *Time*, June 4, 1990, pp. 46–48. The Heritage Foundation has released a report, "The National Endowment for the Arts: Misusing Tax Payers' Money," which lists in an appendix "Some Controversial NEA-Funded Works." Most of the works and artists named are feminist and/or lesbian and gay; I am the last person listed, with a "damning" quote from the *Washington Blade* that "the material I sent to the NEA was explicitly lesbian and it was homoerotic." *The Heritage Foundation Backgrounder*, January 18, 1991, no. 803.

10. Charles Babington, "Senator Alms," *New Republic*, May 28, 1990, pp. 15–17. As early as October 1989, Pat Robertson was sending fund-raising letters out from his Christian Coalition that began, "The enclosed red envelope contains graphic descriptions of homosexual erotic photographs that were funded by your tax dollars. I'd never send you the photos, but I did want you to know about the vile contents of your tax funded material."

11. Haney, *Federal Censorship*, pp. 21, 23, 34. This reasoning is revived and endorsed at the highest level by the *Rust v. Sullivan* ruling in which the values of capitalism triumph over the concept of a constitutional democracy. The author of one letter to the editor interpreted the ruling as: "He who pays the piper calls the tune." James M. Dickey, "No Mention of Abortion," *Washington Post*, June 3, 1991, p. A8. See footnote 22.

12. Paul and Schwartz, pp. 115–116.

13. The labels "politically correct" and "thought police" are currently being promoted by President Bush in an attempt to discredit those of us who object to the current hierarchies of power and unjust status quo. Conservative forces have glibly named as "censorship" attempts on college campuses to broaden Eurocentric male-centered curricula and discourage harassment of women, people of color, gay people. In discrediting attempts at cultural and social diversity, this tactic co-opts the issue of free speech to advance a "traditionally correct" political agenda. See Julianne Malveux, "The right wing's forceful fight against liberal 'thought police' " (*San Francisco Examiner*, June 21, 1991, p. A25) on the difference between censorship enforced by those in authority, and criticism. Meanwhile, significant censorship of the voices of minority groups continues. For instance, in one month, June 1991, twenty of the top fifty PBS television stations would not broadcast Marlon Riggs' award-winning film, *Tongues Untied* (Mark Sullivan, "PBS stations refuse to air documentary on Black gays," *Washington Blade*, July 5, 1991, p. 1) and more than 1,000 copies of a book of lesbian erotic photography, Della Grace's *Love Bites*, were seized by U.S. Customs (Wickie Stamps, "Book seized," *Gay Community News*, June 16–22, 1991, p. 3.

14. See Michael Bronski's articles on the sexual language of war in *Gay Community News*, January 27–February 3 and February 4–10, 1991.

15. The Supreme Court decision, no. 85–140 (June 30, 1986) was *Michael J. Bowers, Attorney General of Georgia, v. Michael Hardwick, and John and Mary Doe.* For more on the significance of this case for lesbian and gay people, see my earlier essay, "I Plead Guilty to Being a Lesbian."

16. See *Journal of the American Family Association*, June 1990, for this article in which *homoerotic* was defined as *homosexual pornography*.

17. The twenty-four-hour ban was recently overturned as "unconstitutionally vague" but some "protected" time for children will remain in place;

the decision may be appealed to the U.S. Supreme Court. See Paul Farhi, "FCC Bans All 'Indecent' Broadcasts," *Washington Post*, July 13, 1990, p. A1; "FCC Chairman Sikes Responds," *Washington Post*, July 20, 1990, p. A18; Paul Farhi, " 'Indecency' Ban By FCC Overturned," *Washington Post*, May 18, 1991, p. A1. Information on the Youth Suicide Task Force report from Kevin Berrill, Anti-Violence Coordinator, National Gay and Lesbian Task Force (NGLTF), March 27, 1991. Also Julie Brienza, "New Maryland report focuses on Gay teens' suicide rate," *Washington Blade*, October 5, 1990, p. 1.

18. Belinda Rochelle, Health Issues Advocate of the National Gay and Lesbian Task Force; March 3, 1991, phone conversation. Rick Harding, "House and Senate Approve Anti-Gay Amendment," *Advocate*, November 24, 1987, p. 15.

19. See Jack Lait and Lee Mortimer, *Washington Confidential* (New York: Crown/ Dell, 1951), p. 124. Also "FBI kept gay files for 40 years," *Gay Community News*, March 4–10, 1991, p. 2.

20. Allan Parachini, "Choreographer Rejects NEA's $72,000 Grant," *Los Angeles Times*, June 15, 1990.

21. *Bella Lewitzky Dance Foundation v. John E. Frohnmayer et al.*, U.S. District Court, Central District of California, Case No. CV 90–3616 JGD, CV 90–5142 JGD, filed Jan. 9, 1991.

22. Nat Hentoff, "Gag Rule in Family Planning Clinics," *Washington Post*, October 20, 1990, p. A23. An appeal of the Lewitsky case seems unlikely given the 1991 U.S. Supreme Court ruling in *Rust v. Sullivan*, which upheld a ban on federally funded family planning clinics offering information about abortion. See Elizabeth Ukins, "High Courts Bans Abortion Advice," *Gay Community News*, June 2–8, 1991, p. 1; Kim Masters, "The Abortion Ruling's Impact," *Washington Post*, June 3, 1991, p. C7. See also footnote 11.

23. For Rosie Jimenez' story, see Ellen Frankfort and Frances Kissling's *Rosie: The Investigation of a Wrongful Death* (New York: Dial Press, 1978). Barbara Smith's essay, "The NEA Is the Least of It," is in the special issue on "Silencing," *American Voice*, Winter 1990, pp. 95–104. Also in this issue, George Ella Lyons' " 'Taking Care': A Response To Censorship" reveals how a story on abortion, developed by adult new readers as part of a literacy program, was cut from their book of stories for rural men and women because of pressure from the National Endowment for the Humanities. The statement written by Chrystos, Audre Lorde, and me was published, among other places, in *Gay Community News*, August 12–18, 1990, p. 5.

24. This performance was "Boys Will Be Men," choreographed by Conrad Alexandrowicz, and performed at Celebration 90, the cultural festival that

ran concurrently with the Gay Games III, in Vancouver, British Columbia, in August 1990.

25. Charles Leroux, "Now, war's most vivid images. . ." in *Chicago Tribune,* February 28, 1991, Section 1, p. 5.

26. "Love Poem," on the posters, is from Audre Lorde's *The New York Head Shop and Museum* (Detroit: The Broadside Press, 1974); her most recent book of poems is *Our Dead Behind Us* (New York: W.W. Norton, 1986). Essex Hemphill's poetry books are *Earth Life* (Washington, D.C.: Be Bop Books, 1985) and *Conditions* (Washington, D.C.: Be Bop Books, 1986). The books of photographs by Joan E. Biren (JEB) are *Eye to Eye: Portraits of Lesbians* (Washington, D.C.: Glad Hag Books, [P.O. Box 2934, Washington, D.C. 20013], 1979) and *Making A Way: Lesbians Out Front* (Washington, D.C.: Glad Hag Books, 1987). "Peach" is from *We Say We Love Each Other* (San Francisco: Spinsters/Aunt Lute, 1985).

27. The National Gay and Lesbian Task Force cites a 1988 Pennsylvania study that documents lesbians and gay men suffer physical and verbal threats and discrimination "seven times more often than the average rate for the adult U.S. population"; see the 1989 NGLTF Fact Sheet. A 1984 national study documented that 94 percent of the lesbians and gay men surveyed had experienced some type of victimization because of their sexual orientation; see Kevin T. Berrill, "Anti-Gay Violence and Victimization in the United States," *Journal of Interpersonal Violence,* vol. 5, no. 3 (September 1990), p. 275.

28. William H. Honan, "Finding Fault With New Arts-Grant Law," *New York Times,* November 10, 1990, p. 13.

Other titles from Firebrand Books include:

Artemis In Echo Park, Poetry by Eloise Klein Healy/$8.95

Beneath My Heart, Poetry by Janice Gould/$8.95

The Big Mama Stories by Shay Youngblood/$8.95

A Burst Of Light, Essays by Audre Lorde/$7.95

Cecile, Stories by Ruthann Robson/$8.95

Crime Against Nature, Poetry by Minnie Bruce Pratt/$8.95

Diamonds Are A Dyke's Best Friend by Yvonne Zipter/$9.95

Dykes To Watch Out For, Cartoons by Alison Bechdel/$6.95

Exile In The Promised Land, A Memoir by Marcia Freedman/$8.95

Eye Of A Hurricane, Stories by Ruthann Robson/$8.95

The Fires Of Bride, A Novel by Ellen Galford/$8.95

Food & Spirits, Stories by Beth Brant (*Degonwadonti*)/$8.95

Free Ride, A Novel by Marilyn Gayle/$9.95

A Gathering Of Spirit, A Collection by North American Indian Women edited by Beth Brant (*Degonwadonti*)/$9.95

Getting Home Alive by Aurora Levins Morales and Rosario Morales/$8.95

The Gilda Stories, A Novel by Jewelle Gomez/$9.95

Good Enough To Eat, A Novel by Lesléa Newman/$8.95

Humid Pitch, Narrative Poetry by Cheryl Clarke/$8.95

Jewish Women's Call For Peace edited by Rita Falbel, Irena Klepfisz, and Donna Nevel/$4.95

Jonestown & Other Madness, Poetry by Pat Parker/$7.95

Just Say Yes, A Novel by Judith McDaniel/$8.95

The Land Of Look Behind, Prose and Poetry by Michelle Cliff /$6.95

A Letter To Harvey Milk, Short Stories by Lesléa Newman/$8.95

Letting In The Night, A Novel by Joan Lindau/$8.95

Living As A Lesbian, Poetry by Cheryl Clarke/$7.95

Making It, A Woman's Guide to Sex in the Age of AIDS by Cindy Patton and Janis Kelly/$4.95

Metamorphosis, Reflections On Recovery by Judith McDaniel/$7.95

Mohawk Trail by Beth Brant (*Degonwadonti*)/$7.95

Moll Cutpurse, A Novel by Ellen Galford/$7.95

More Dykes To Watch Out For, Cartoons by Alison Bechdel/$7.95

(continued)

The Monarchs Are Flying, A Novel by Marion Foster/$8.95

Movement In Black, Poetry by Pat Parker/$8.95

My Mama's Dead Squirrel, Lesbian Essays on Southern Culture by Mab Segrest/$8.95

New, Improved! Dykes To Watch Out For, Cartoons by Alison Bechdel/$7.95

The Other Sappho, A Novel by Ellen Frye/$8.95

Out In The World, International Lesbian Organizing by Shelley Anderson/$4.95

Politics Of The Heart, A Lesbian Parenting Anthology edited by Sandra Pollack and Jeanne Vaughn/$11.95

Presenting. . . Sister NoBlues by Hattie Gossett/$8.95

A Restricted Country by Joan Nestle/$8.95

Sacred Space by Geraldine Hatch Hanon/$9.95

Sanctuary, A Journey by Judith McDaniel/$7.95

Sans Souci, And Other Stories by Dionne Brand/$8.95

Scuttlebutt, A Novel by Jana Williams/$8.95

Shoulders, A Novel by Georgia Cotrell/$8.95

Simple Songs, Stories by Vickie Sears/$8.95

The Sun Is Not Merciful, Short Stories by Anna Lee Walters/$7.95

Tender Warriors, A Novel by Rachel Guido deVries/$8.95

This Is About Incest by Margaret Randall/$8.95

The Threshing Floor, Short Stories by Barbara Burford/$7.95

Trash, Stories by Dorothy Allison/$8.95

The Women Who Hate Me, Poetry by Dorothy Allison/$8.95

Words To The Wise, A Writer's Guide to Feminist and Lesbian Periodicals & Publishers by Andrea Fleck Clardy/$4.95

Yours In Struggle, Three Feminist Perspectives on Anti-Semitism and Racism by Elly Bulkin, Minnie Bruce Pratt, and Barbara Smith/$8.95

You can buy Firebrand titles at your bookstore, or order them directly from the publisher (141 The Commons, Ithaca, New York 14850, 607-272-0000).

Please include $2.00 shipping for the first book and $.50 for each additional book.

A free catalog is available on request.